GLOBETROTT
ISLAND GUIDE

Mauritius

NH
NEW HOLLAND

Globetrotter™
ISLAND GUIDE
Mauritius

Lindsay Bennett

Contents

Mauritius Map	5
Island Escape	6
Portrait of an Island Paradise	8
Island Culture	42
Island Getaways	100
Shopping and Markets	122
Island Cuisine	134
Surf and Turf	150
Travel Directory	174
Index	190

MAURITIUS

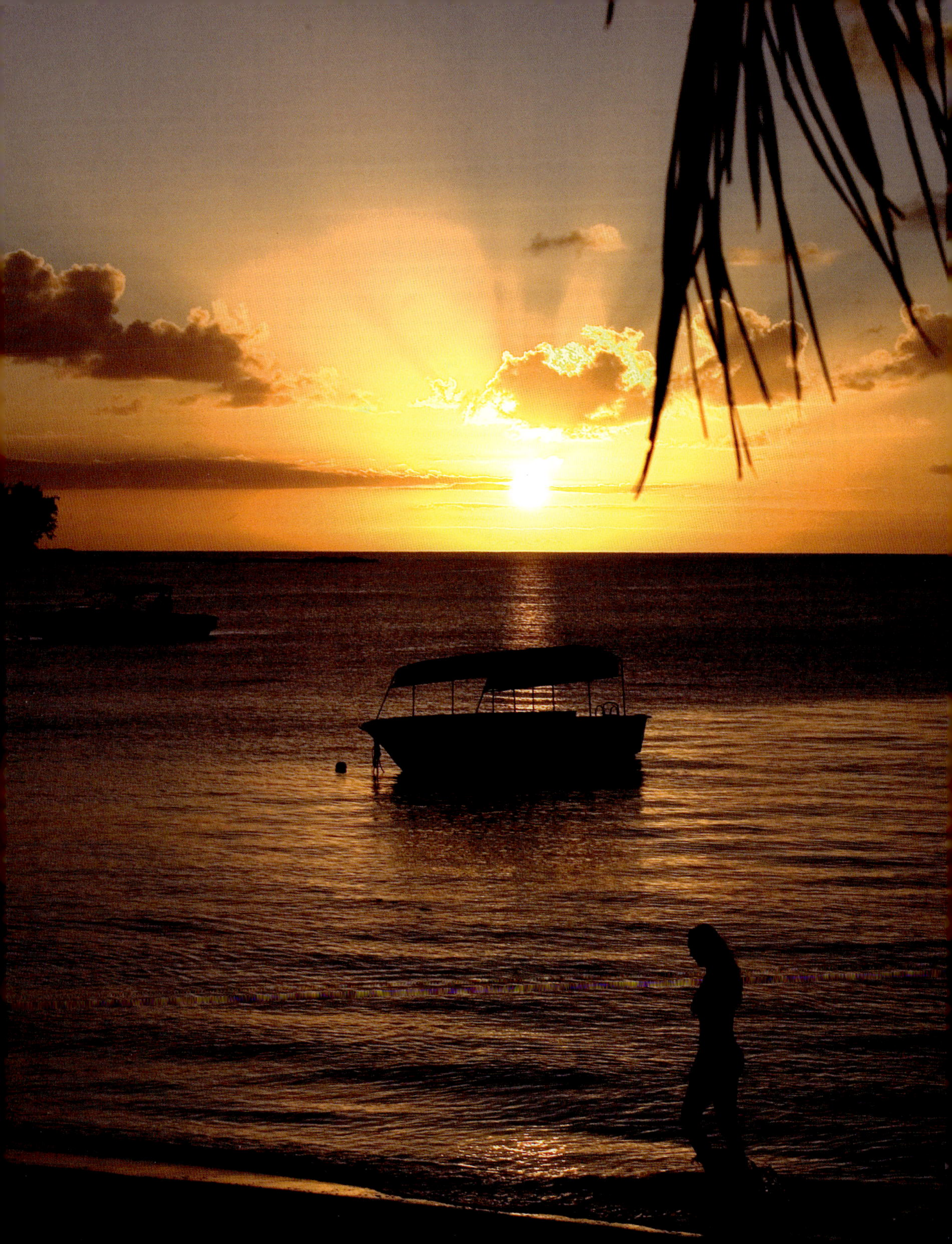

Island Escape

'... you gather the idea that Mauritius was made first and then heaven, and that heaven was copied after Mauritius.'
Mark Twain (1896)

Some destinations conjure a mental image when their name is mentioned, even amongst people who have never travelled there. Mauritius is one of these places. This Indian Ocean island is synonymous with the phrase 'tropical idyll', probably even more so than during Mark Twain's visit just over a century ago.

A tiny green speck strewn into the vastness of the southern Indian Ocean, Mauritius comes supplied with all the basic prerequisites for the perfect holiday. Visually stunning, it offers a plethora of dreamy golden beaches, shimmering azure waters, cerulean skies and gently swaying luscious palms. The sun is an almost constant companion during sizzling days, and balmy nights invite moonlit strolls or romantic alfresco dinners.

The island is the consummate pleasure-dome for modern 'down-time'. Between them Mauritian hotels have accumulated more stars than the Hollywood red carpet on Oscar night, with a host of celebrity admirers from royalty to rock legends, from supermodels to stars of the silver screen. This is one destination that knows the meaning of quality and service, and the island provides all the toys required to keep even the most demanding clients happy.

Left: *Liquid gold sunsets bathe the west coast of the island in wonderful warm light.*

Get active offshore with exceptional diving, sailing and fishing; enjoy a round or two on the magnificent greens; or take to the hills on feet, hooves or wheels. On the other hand, give yourself over to the healing hands of a massage therapist or stretch out on a beach bed with the latest bestseller. Your days can be as dramatically full or deliciously empty as you desire.

Mauritius is a feast for the eyes, but also for the most jaded of palates – the food is mouth-watering, from the humblest of street snacks to the finest gastronomic menus. Savour superb seafood and delight in dainty desserts – it's easy to forget the waistline for while.

Man didn't make it to Mauritius until the end of the 16th century but it's been a busy time since then. Island history is short but sweet – quite literally – intertwined as it is with the world's demand for sugar. By the mid-18th century it supplied more than 10 per cent of the market but was reliant on this singular crop for its economic health.

The population is an incredible melange of Africans and Madagascans, Indians, Chinese and Europeans – some arrived by choice, others were coerced – but where in other parts of the world this recipe has produced ethnic division, Mauritius is proud of its racial mix. There's a relaxed atmosphere everywhere you go and the people have a reputation for friendliness that's well founded; they make fantastic hosts.

What Mark Twain would have made of today's Mauritius is impossible to say, but 21st-century vox pop has declared it one of the world's best up-market destinations, and no-one would argue with that!

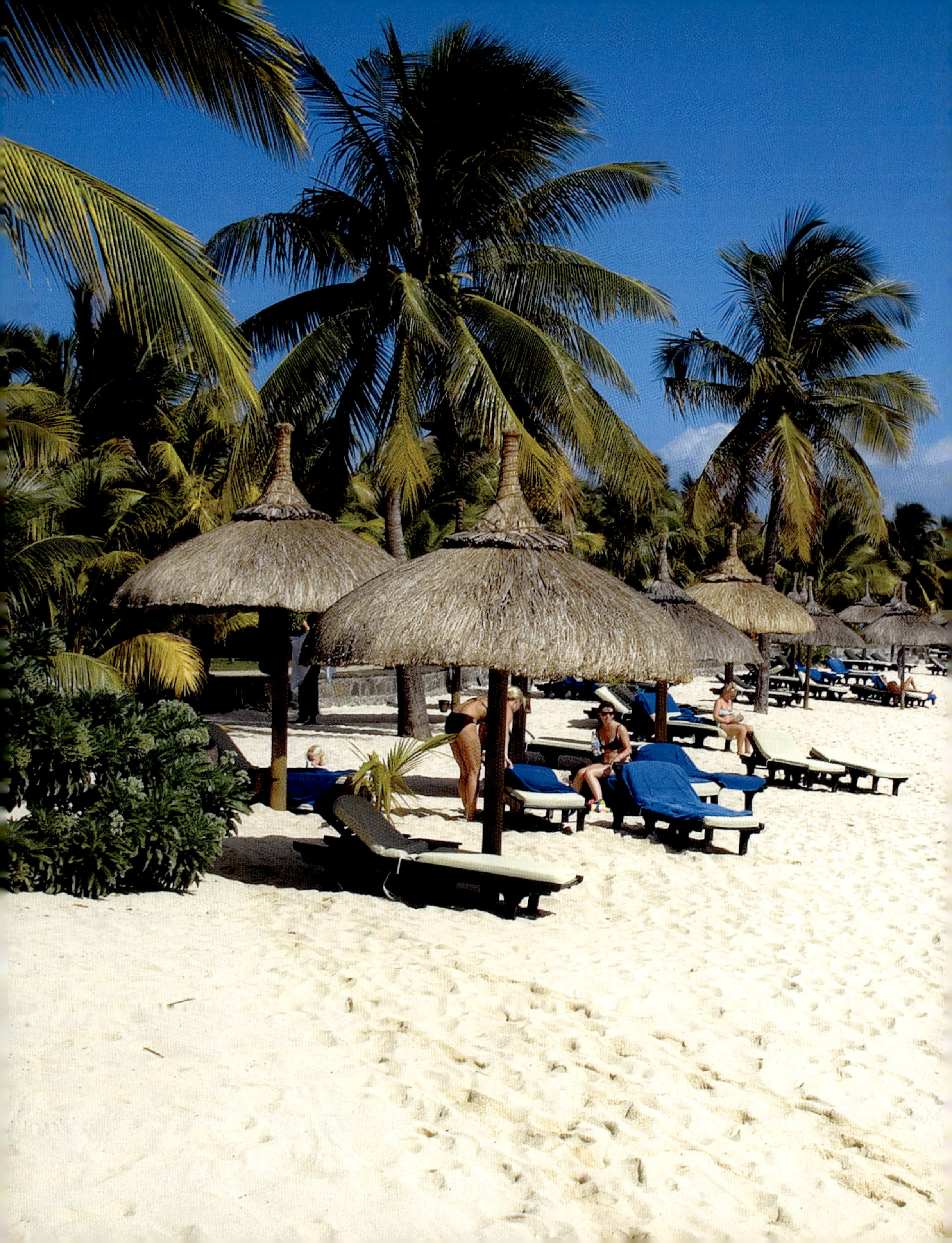

Portrait of an Island Paradise

Left: Glorious beaches, such as this one at the Dinarobin Hotel Golf & Spa on the Morne Peninsula, are one of the main attractions of Mauritius.

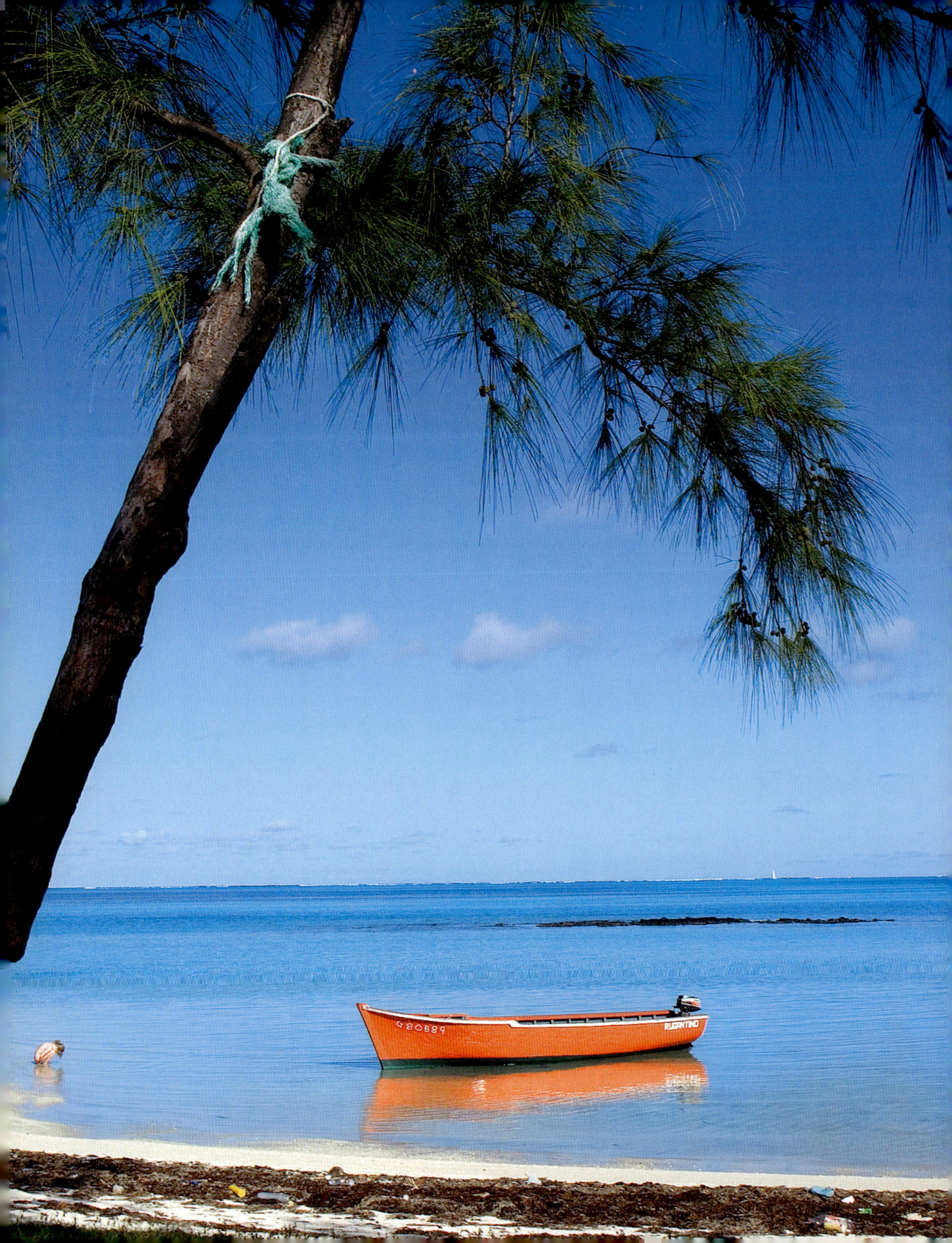
G80889
RUGANTINO

A tiny green island in a huge warm ocean, the allure of Mauritius begins with its natural beauty. Capped by luxuriant volcanic peaks, ringed with golden sand and dotted with swaying palms, it beguiles with its glorious landscapes and exudes an air of enduring tropical splendour fed by abundant sunshine and short, sharp rain showers.

This island spent many millennia out of sight of man and evolved a unique and successful ecosystem incorporating some unusual creatures seen nowhere else on the planet. The extinction of many, including the infamous dodo, shames human history but today Mauritius is home to some of the earth's most rare plant and animal life, and the waters offshore offer yet another realm for exploration.

Left: *Île aux Cerfs is the perfect place to drop anchor.*

Geography and Geology

A tiny, seemingly insignificant speck of land 890km east of Madagascar and 1200km off the African coast, not far from the tropic of Capricorn at latitude 57 degrees east and 20 degrees south, Mauritius is the offspring of volcanic activity that raised a huge hot cone around eight million years ago.

This original volcanic peak constituted 1860km^2 and that's the area of the island today. It collapsed eons ago and the erosion that followed has resulted in the dramatic rock formations and mountain ranges you see around the island. From high above the ground these fragmented lava-rock peaks form an irregular circle, but within the remnants of this older activity lie a series of younger, smaller craters including Grand Bassin and Trou aux Cerfs, indicating that the Mauritius volcano rumbled back to life again after a lull of over 2 million years.

The northern islands – Coin de Mire (Gunners Quoin) and Île aux Serpents – are also the remnants of younger volcanoes that were still active at the time of the last Ice Age. These became separated from the mainland when the sea level rose as the ice shields retreated. It is thought that Flat Island was active as little as 200,000 years ago.

Volcanic activity has ceased on Mauritius but Piton de Fournaise on Réunion regularly signals its wakefulness with plumes of steam, though volcanologists insist that this activity is the benign venting of pressure from tectonic plate movement rather than an explosive build-up of lava.

Below: *This aerial view of the Saint Géran peninsula, on the east coast of Mauritius, shows the hotel's glorious sandy beach and landward lagoon – perfect for water sports – while the island's excellent fringe reef sits just offshore.*

Geography and Geology

MAURITIUS

What About Today?

Mauritius is 61km long at its longest and 46km wide at its widest point. It and two smaller siblings constitute the Mascarene Islands. All three sit on a shallow submarine ridge that arcs northeast from the African coast. Rodrigues, 600km to the northwest, is part of the greater Mauritian state, while Réunion, only 200km to the southwest, is now French sovereign territory. Since independence Mauritius also holds sway over the tiny unpopulated islands of Agalega and the Cargados Shoals and has lodged disputes with France over its territorial claims of Tromelin and with Great Britain over the Chagos Archipelago. Mauritian sea territory is vast in comparison with its landmass, at 1.2 million square kilometres.

Island geography is complicated for such a small landmass. Lowland plains cover over 40 per cent of the island and today much of this is exclusively devoted to sugar-cane cultivation with some vegetables grown for the domestic market. Though fertile, this land was strewn with large fragments of tuff and lava stone forced from the volcano whilst still in a molten state. A constant problem when planting crops, these rocks still inhibit mechanization in all agricultural sectors.

From the lowlands the terrain climbs inland to a central plateau that constitutes around 25 per cent of the total area. The climb south out of Port Louis on the four-lane highway shows the height difference most effectively. This plateau is home to the majority of the 1.2 million Mauritian population.

Below: One of the island's most distinctive mountains, the Pic du Lion, rises majestically above the mangrove beds of the east coast.

GEOGRAPHY AND GEOLOGY

Above: Coin de Mire, the last remnants of an ancient volcanic peak, sits off the north shore beyond the protection of the coral reef.

Mountains make up just under 20 per cent and it's not so much the height – they lie at between 600 and 800m – but the dramatic outline of Mauritian peaks that make them so memorable. The Long Mountain to Anse Courtois ranges wrapping around the capital give Port Louis the most dramatic of settings. The highest and most remarkable peak of this chain is the Pieter Both (823m), because it has a loose rock at the summit sitting like a head on shoulders that from a distance looks as through a sneeze would blow it loose, but closer inspection reveals it's set firmly in place.

The south of Mauritius is dominated by the Rivière Noire Mountains, which include the island's highest peak, Petite Rivière Noire, at 828m, while the central plains have a ridge of peaks called the Trois Mamelles or Three Breasts, probably because of their arresting outline, that rise majestically above the plantation-clad flatlands. Isolated mountains such as the brooding Morne Brabant in the southwest, Lion Mountain in the southeast and the offshore Coin de Mire (Gunner's Quoin) in the north offer unique backdrops to holiday photographs.

There are many watercourses draining from the highlands to the sea and several have steep gradients. Streams turn to torrents during tropical storms when water erosion can be a problem. The country has two natural lakes, Grand Bassin and Bassin Blanc, both volcanic craters, and also several man-made reservoirs.

Equally memorable in the minds of visitors is the narrow strip where the land meets the water. Mauritius has 160km of coastline along with 15 offshore islets and the greatest part of the coast is ringed by coral reef that protects a shallow inland lagoon, stands of mangrove and innumerable exquisite stretches of sand.

Breaks in the reef are where the major towns of Port Louis and Mahébourg were founded because they offered easy access to shipping. The far south has no reef and it's one of the few places where ocean waves lap directly onto the shore.

Once volcanic activity ceased, plant life and fauna arrived predominantly from the landmass now known as

Madagascar to the east, which had pulled away from the African mainland over sixty-five million years ago. Thus the pool of animal and plant life was already limited, because Madagascar itself had long since lost touch with its African roots.

Over eons, a rich tropical forest developed in the Mauritian highlands while the lowland was blanketed in a savannah of tropical palms. The long distance meant only animals that could float or fly could reach Mauritius. There were no large prey species and much of the fauna became specialized and vulnerable to environmental change. Before the coming of man, this island was one of nature's most fascinating ecosystems, with a high percentage of its animals and plants being unique to the Mascarenes.

Riches of the Land
Shoots and Blooms

The passing of the seasons gives Mauritius many faces and your impression of the landscape will most definitely be coloured by what time of year you visit. Though the island is green throughout the year, many plants put on a royal seasonal display that really assaults the eye. Harvest time changes the face of the countryside and this is true particularly of the sugar cane. At its height in late June it blocks many roadside vistas, but the island sports a crop-cut in the months after the harvest, before the sugar sprouts and matures again over the summer. But though the seasons pass as they always have, the flora of Mauritius has been irrevocably transformed in the blink of a geological eye.

Before the arrival of man the lowland flora of Mauritius consisted of a type of palm savannah where giant tortoises grazed and dodos and other seed-eaters foraged amongst the grasses and roots. The higher ground was blanketed in dense hardwood forests of ebony, tambalacoque and makak supplemented by deciduous and evergreen bushes. Around the coast, the sublime beaches were interspersed with vast banks of mangrove swamp adding colour to the brackish inlets.

Today Mauritius is third on the list of most threatened island flora worldwide, coming in after Hawaii and the Canary Islands. Good quality native forest covers 2–4 per cent of the land (depending on official sources) and this is found on a couple of offshore islets, in minute stands in the southeast and in the Black River Gorges National Park in the southwest. Present-day native flora consists of 685 species of which 311 are endemic to the island (and thus found nowhere else), with a further 150 species found only on other Mascarene Islands. Sixty per cent of these species are considered threatened, with 40 species having less than ten individual plants left and another 56 species having less than 50 left.

The dire straits of the flora on Mauritius stems directly from the arrival of human beings at the end of the 16th century. Throughout the four short centuries of habitation homo sapiens has raped the island of its useable native plants and has also replaced vast swathes of countryside with introduced cash crops and decorative species that, once established, ran rampant amongst the native plants.

The Mauritius ebony (*Diospyros tesselaria*) is a prime example. The darkest of any species and a very dense wood, it was prized by the Dutch and became an overnight 'must have' luxury item for the handmade furniture of Europe's elite, being most famously used to form the black keys on pianos.

Unbeknownst to the Dutch it is also extremely slow growing, taking over 150 years to reach full height. They chopped into the forests with enthusiasm and the resource lasted only a few short decades before supplies were all but exhausted. When the British introduced tea in the 18th century it only thrived on the cooler upland slopes then still forested with native trees. These were ripped from the soil, further depleting stocks.

Where the forests were at least of economic value the lowland savannah was simply regarded as dispensable and thousands of acres were cleared to make way for introduced plantation crops. It's difficult to come to terms with the fact that sugar cane is a completely alien species to the island, so ubiquitous is it as one travels around Mauritius. While endemic plants and animals became extinct at its expense, the one species that did thrive was man.

Side by side with cash crops, the European colonists and the Indian and Chinese immigrants brought their own decorative species and these continue to invade native ecosystems. The most important and destructive of these are the Chinese guava (*Psidium cattleianum*), privet (*Ligustrum robustum*) and the ravanale (*Ravanale madagascariensis*).

Introduced animals also destroyed and continue to threaten the few native enclaves of vegetation still left. The deer and hare browse on the finest shoots, monkeys eat the fruits and flowers, and feral pigs destroy root

Opposite: *Mauritius offers languid waters and palm-shaded sand for amazing days on the beach.*
Right: *The island is awash with tropical flowers including cascades of bougainvillea adding a splash of colour to gardens and gable ends.*

systems with their foraging snouts.

The British also cleared thousands of hectares of mangrove swamp in the 19th century in an early attempt to eradicate malaria. Victorian scientists understood that the mosquito carried the disease and this wholesale destruction was a clumsy attempt at eradicating their breeding habitats. Unfortunately there was little understanding of the role played by these vast 'floating' forests in the absorption and dissipation of damaging winds during tropical storms and cyclones, and the loss of the mangrove left many sections of coastline open to more severe damage and destruction.

Since the 1980s, however, Mauritius has woken up to the importance of its remaining native flora, which even with the loss of so many species still constitutes important and unique ecosystems for its many endemic birds and reptiles. The creation of the Black River Gorges (Rivière Noire) National Park (*see* page 27) and continued work by several international and Mauritian conservation groups have had impressive results in conserving the existing forests, regenerating areas by eradicating non-native plant and animal species, and replanting mangroves to encourage the re-emergence of truly traditional landscapes.

RICHES OF THE LAND

The National Flower of Mauritius

The Boucle d'Oreille or earring tree (*Trochetia boutoniana*), chosen as the national flower in 1992, is endemic to the island and is now only found in the wild on the sheer flanks of the Morne Brabant in the southwest. A small bush-type tree, it produces bell-shaped flowers that dangle from the stem looking like an earring, hence the common name. It is one of very few plant species that produces coloured nectar – a bright red – and scientists have discovered that one of the main pollinators of *Trochetia*, the gecko, prefers coloured to clear nectar.

Birds and Beasts

The first settlers who arrived on Mauritius were greeted by a very different zoological array. The island had been isolated for millennia and though the species of fauna were not large in number, many of them were unique to this specific island or only found on the islands of the Mascarene chain. There were very few

Below: The rugged volcanic peaks of the southern hinterland are blanketed by the last remaining stands of the ancient hardwood forest that once covered Mauritius. Today it's protected as the Black River Gorges National Park.

predators and so the major species were grazers; since these were not in fear of the chase they grew large and slow moving – the dodo and the giant tortoise being the prime examples.

A Lost Ecosystem

The Dutch sailors brought back tales of savannah-like plains replete with dodo, a giant flightless bird that had no fear of man. Of course they were easy pickings for the men who were starved of fresh meat. Perhaps the sailors and early settlers didn't think beyond their daily needs and how easy it was to harvest these animals. They probably didn't realize that the dodo was unique to Mauritius. However, they began salting and exporting these birds in vast quantities and within 60 years the dodo was extinct, lost to the world forever. The giant tortoise went the same way. These animals could be carried live onto ships and slaughtered at intervals throughout the long sea voyages to provide fresh meat and delicious fat – a great luxury for the sailors of the East Indies companies. Numbers slaughtered on Mauritius are not known, but at least 280,000 were dispatched on Rodrigues.

However, the main problem was not just that man slaughtered the edible species. Many of the animals and birds that thrived on Mauritius had become highly adapted to their habitat; when the natural flora was transformed very quickly by the introduction of plantation crops, many species couldn't adapt to this sudden change and simply died out.

The Survivors

Only nine species of endemic birds still survive on the island, including Mauritian variants of the flycatcher, the fody and the olive white-eye. The three most rare, the Mauritian kestrel, pink pigeon and the echo parakeet, are now the subject of concerted conservation efforts (*see* page 30). These birds are now restricted to the last vestiges of native habitat in remote corners of the island and are little seen by visitors. Ironically, the very fact that these birds are so few in number makes Mauritius a magnet for bird-watchers who head for the hills in an attempt to add several of the world's rarest to their 'spotted' database.

Your Constant Companions

The common bird species most visitors encounter are all introduced by man. They are intelligent and adaptable, finding the breakfast buffets at hotels across the island a very easy source of food.

The mynah is a cheeky, noisy bird introduced in 1763 to control locusts, while the bulbul (also known as the Persian nightingale) escaped from captivity when a single cage broke open during a cyclone in 1892.

Less vocal species include the delicate striated dove, a dwarf species from Malaysia, and the sparrow, also introduced as a form of pest control around 1856.

Mauritius Mammals

There were never many indigenous mammals on Mauritius even before the arrival of man. The dugong (sea cow) was numerous in the lagoon shallows but its salted meat, lamentin, was highly prized by sailors and by 1799 naturalist Cossigny de Palma reported that it was rarely spotted in coastal waters.

The only other native mammal species on Mauritius were bats. Large frugivorous bats were seen as a game species and hunted by the early colonialists, but *Pteropus niger* (the flying fox) still survives in the forests of the southwest, and there are two smaller species of insectivorous bats that you are sure to see hunting as night falls.

Left: *Java deer were introduced in the 16th century by the Dutch. They thrive on Mauritius and, though majestic, constitute a major pest, grazing on the dwindling native flora and on commercial crops.*

Animal Arrivals

The deliberate introduction of many non-indigenous animal species to the island also accelerated the ride into oblivion for native wildlife. The rat was the sailor's constant companion and it jumped ship, quite literally, from the wreck of a Dutch vessel in 1598. Thriving on snakes and lizards, it then decimated bird populations by eating their eggs. Cats arrived around 1710 to control the rats but also took a liking to the same birds and reptiles. In 1900 it was the turn of the mongoose, introduced after a plague epidemic to counter the rats thought to carry the disease. Unfortunately they found the island's game birds more appealing and numbers soon plummeted.

Even non-predatory animals were not neutral because grazers devastated the plant life that provided both food and shelter for less aggressive native animals and birds. The macaque brought by the first Dutch settlers was singularly responsible for the loss of some indigenous trees because it crushes seeds as it eats rather than letting them pass undamaged through the gut.

Deer introduced from Java in 1638 are now so abundant that Mauritius still has a hunting season and a number of deer have been sent back to the Indonesian island to restock the dwindling native population.

The hare arrived in 1754 from India to munch through the remaining ground vegetation and by around 1900 it was joined by the tenrac or tendrac – a small insectivorous mammal native to Madagascar whose burrows destroy plant root systems.

Today, in addition to the tortoise, three species of reptile are extinct and five are only found on the offshore islands. However, the remaining five species – including the colourful day gecko and the noisy night gecko – can be spotted or heard all around the island, even in resort hotels.

Exploring the Ecosystem

For more information on native Mauritian animals past and present visit the Natural History Museum (*see* page 85) in Port Louis, Île aux Aigrettes (*see* page 41) close to

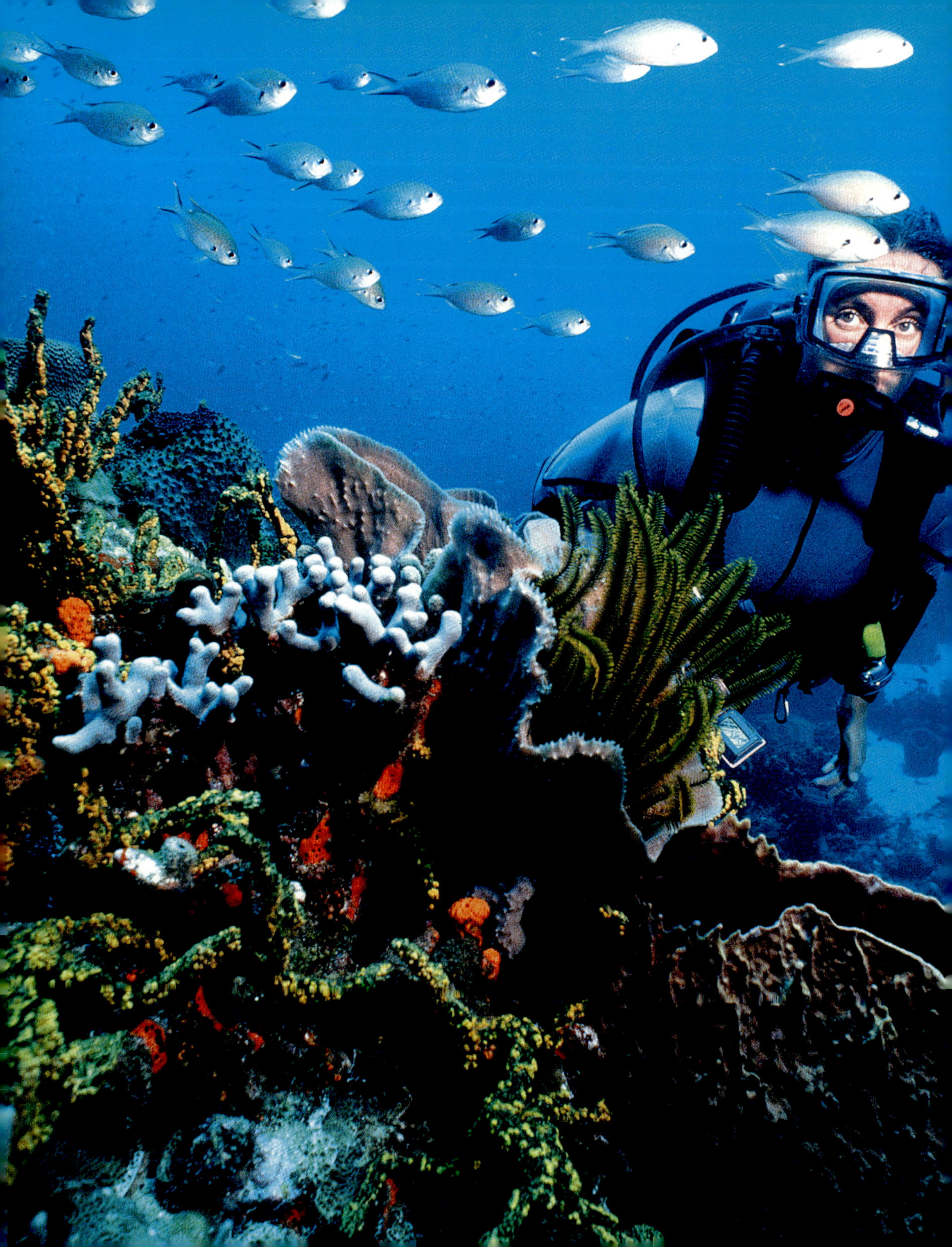

Mahébourg or the Rivière Noire (Black River Gorges) National Park. La Vanille Reserve des Mascareignes (*see page 92*) allows you to explore the Mauritius ecosystem with hands-on experience of giant tortoises in a re-created palm savannah.

Very little is known about the habits and lifestyle of the ill-fated dodo but the discovery of an undisturbed mass dodo grave in the southeast of Mauritius in December 2005 will add greatly to our knowledge over the next few years.

Offshore

Where the landmass of Mauritius shows little biodiversity, it's a different matter in the territory beneath the waves, which seems to be teeming with life. The island is surrounded by 150km of the healthiest coral reef in the Indian Ocean attracting myriad tropical fish, while deeper waters are the domain of much weightier species including some of the world's largest marlin, sharks and sailfish.

The health of the coastal waters is of paramount importance to the Mauritian economy, with many tourists travelling here specifically for sport fishing and diving. The coral reefs are also critical in the preservation of the island's beaches – a major draw for holiday-makers.

Coral Reefs

One of the world's most unusual and delicate animal forms, coral comprises millions of minute, simple, soft-bodied animals called polyps. Hard corals are so called because the polyps extrude an outer skeleton of calcium carbonate which then links with the skeletons of other hard coral polyps and over time these create what we know as a coral reef, comprising many millions of individuals. New polyps grow on top of the skeletons of the dead polyps, so hard corals are responsible for the greater part of reef growth.

Coral polyps get nutrition in two ways. They catch their food by means of stinging tentacles that paralyse any suitable prey – microscopic creatures called zooplankton – and also engage in a symbiotic relationship with zooxanthellae that live within the polyp structure. The fact that zooxanthellae need the sun's energy to produce their own food means that coral can only thrive in clear, shallow waters where the sun's rays can penetrate to their depth. To form an extensive reef, corals need waters of at least 23 degrees but not above 28 degrees Celsius. Growth is slow at between 5cm and 20cm per year and the structure is incredibly fragile, being susceptible to physical damage and changes in water quality.

Coral reproduces asexually, by the division of existing individual polyps, but also sexually – by combining egg and sperm from two different polyps. This results in a free-swimming polyp that will be carried by ocean currents to found a new colony and commence a new reef. Many tropical countries, including Mauritius, are purposely sinking old ships (15 around the island since 1980) to give these polyps something to attach to, thereby kick-starting new reef formations.

Coral reefs account for only 2 per cent of the world's ocean floor but are under pressure everywhere due to global warming and rising sea temperatures. The reefs around Mauritius have almost ideal base conditions but care needs to be taken to stop physical damage by divers and pleasure craft and to decrease the run-off of fertilizers from farmland, and waste discharge from resort developments. Mauritius also has one of the most developed coral sand dredging industries in the region, with 500,000 tons being ripped from its national waters every year.

Protected marine parks at Blue Bay and Balaclava cover just 711 hectares of the island's coastline where over 250 species of marine plant have been noted, as well as 57 species of coral and 120 species of fish. At present the rest of this valuable ecosystem is open to all kinds of abuse.

Left: The waters around Mauritius team with life from acres of coral to magnificent fish, making the island a paradise for divers.

Deep Water

Beyond the boundaries of the reef, the deeper water is a favoured haunt of numerous pelagic species including giant moray eels, marlin, barracuda, sailfish, dolphin and several species of shark. These denizens are particularly attracted to the natural breaks in the reef where the water is churned by the constant inward and outward flow; they come in search of smaller fish species which are in turn attracted here because of the ample nutritious microscopic plankton.

What about the weather?

The weather in Mauritius could be described purely and simply as tropical and it does indeed lie in the tropical climate zone. But for a very small island it has many microclimates that make precise forecasting a bit of an art form.

The temperatures are warm throughout the year but the island has two main seasons – a hot summer (November–April) with temperatures around the coast averaging 30°C and a warm winter (May–October) when average temperatures sit at around 24°C along the coast. The island is on the receiving end of the easterly trade winds that temper even the hottest day, and the highlands will always be 3–5°C lower than the coast – more when they have cloud cover.

Humidity is high throughout the year – over 90 per cent on the inland plateau, a little less on the coast – but the winter months see a slight drop in clamminess.

Rainfall – yes, you can't get lush green forest and succulent palms without rain – varies by region with a yearly total of 1200mm in the north and an impressive 3600mm on the plateau. The saying in Curepipe is that the town has two seasons – the rainy season followed by the season when it rains a lot. However, it's rare to have a whole day of rain and cloud. Most precipitation falls in short, sharp storms interspersed with periods of sunshine, even in the winter, and storms are very localized, leaving the coastal resorts sunny while the mountains get drenched. Local people habitually carry umbrellas but as much to protect against the hot sun as against precipitation.

Mauritius lies in the cyclone zone. Cyclones are the name given to powerful tropical storms of the Indian Ocean (they're called hurricanes in the Atlantic and typhoons in the Pacific). The season lasts from November until April but not every season brings a dangerous storm; the most recent was Dina in 2002.

The Mauritius government operates a sophisticated meteorological service with records dating back to the French era when daily observations were undertaken by Mr Céré, then Director of the Botanical Gardens. Today's state-of-the-art Mauritius Meteorological Service headquarters in Vacoas provides valuable information on approaching cyclones during the season, plus the daily forecasts posted in your hotel throughout your stay.

Getting Around

Mauritius is divided into nine districts that were created during the time of the French in the 18th century – Pamplemousses and Rivière du Remparts in the north, Flacq in the west, Grand Port in the southwest, Savanne in the south, and Black River in the east, with Moka and Plaines Wilhems covering the landlocked centre. The capital, Port Louis, has a separate municipal structure.

One of the best-kept secrets on Mauritius is how to get from one place to another. Many roads were created

MAURITIUS	J	F	M	A	M	J	J	A	S	O	N	D
AVERAGE TEMP. °F	82	82	81	81	77	73	73	73	73	75	79	81
AVERAGE TEMP. °C	28	28	27	27	25	23	23	23	23	24	26	27
Hours of Sun Daily	8	8	8	7	7	7	7	7	8	8	9	9
SEA TEMP. °F	82	80	82	80	78	75	73	73	73	75	79	80
SEA TEMP. °C	28	27	28	27	26	25	24	23	23	24	26	27
RAINFALL in	7	7	4	3	2	1	1	1	1	4	1	4
RAINFALL mm	165	183	91	87	41	24	20	24	31	18	33	91
Days of Rainfall	8	6	8	7	4	4	3	5	4	3	2	6
Humidity	75	78	74	78	68	65	77	62	62	61	68	71

Right: Despite a modernization programme that has seen many roads asphalted, Mauritius is still criss-crossed by many rural dirt roads that see little traffic, such as here at Pointe Lafayette.

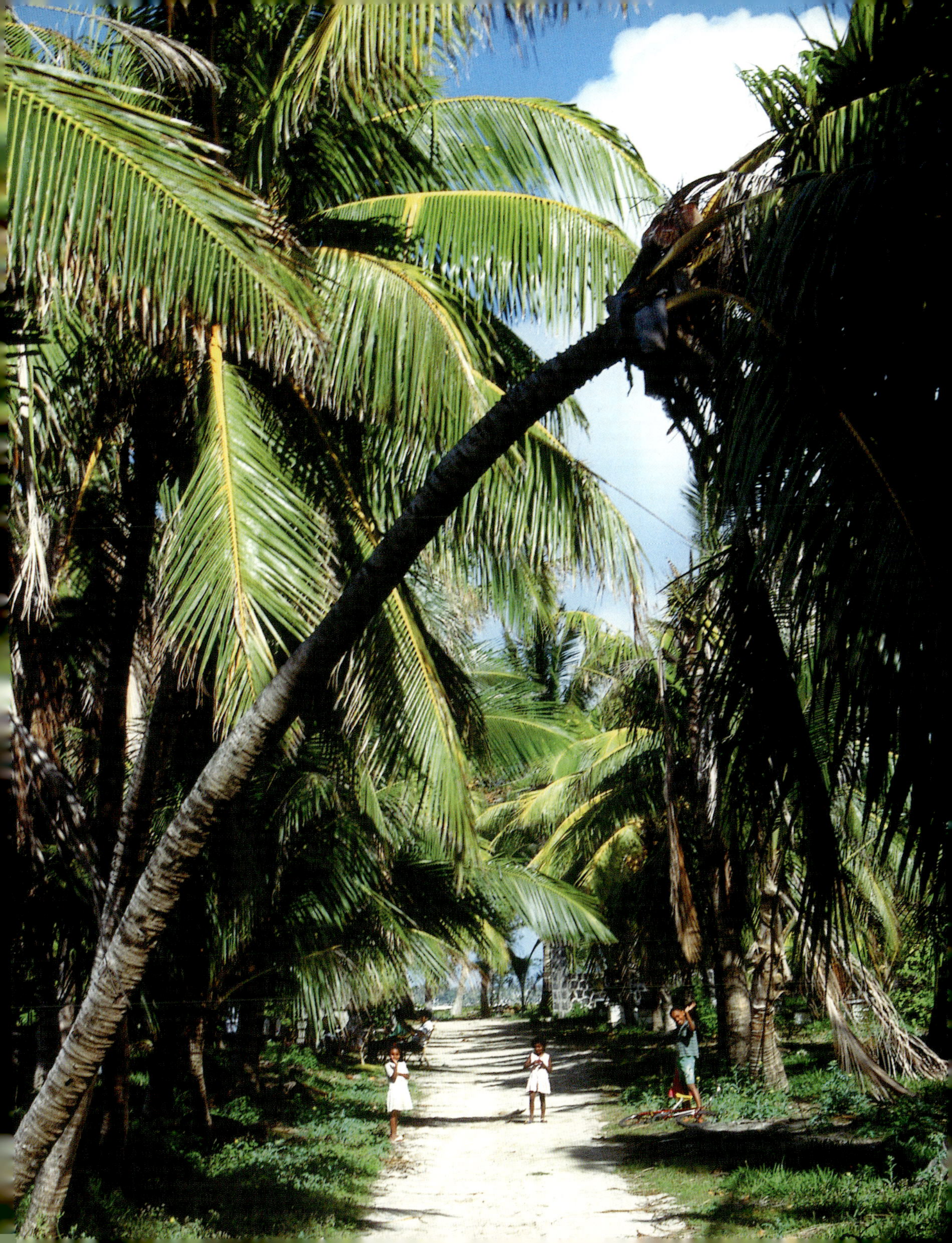

across plantation land to transport workers and crops, not to support the traffic that's grown exponentially over the last couple of decades. Even today some cross-country roads belong to private domains and you'll need permission to use them – not very helpful for independent travel.

The round-island coast road is an easy route to navigate and the few major settlements are well signposted, but inland there's a confusing maze of narrow lanes and frustratingly slow bottlenecks such as at Quatre Bornes where four major roads intersect in one of the most densely populated areas of Plaines Wilhems. The fast cross-country four-lane highway has helped to cut journey time from the airport to Port Louis and the north but it isn't the most picturesque of roads.

Mauritius has few large settlements but the main towns – Port Louis, Mahébourg and the seemingly endless urban sprawl of the plains communities – present their own problems for visiting drivers. A lack of maps, confusing one-way systems and little on-street parking can lead to frustration. In Port Louis the most practical solution is to leave the car in the parking area at the Caudan marina and walk into town – it takes less than five minutes.

If you don't want to drive, taxis are cheap, plentiful and comfortable. You can hire one for the day and your driver will be happy to advise on your itinerary and act as an unofficial guide.

Below: *Île aux Aigrettes is now managed by the Mauritius Wildlife Foundation. A concerted effort is under way to clear the island of non-native species, paving the way for the re-introduction of a self-sustaining natural native ecosystem.*

Protecting Precious Ecosystems
National Parks and Reserves

Little indigenous vegetation remains on Mauritius and since the late 20th century the government has worked hard to implement a plan both to protect the last vestiges of virgin flora and create havens for native fauna.

In June 1994 the government proclaimed the Black River Gorges National Park Project, the island's first land-based park with an area of 6574 hectares encompassing the highest peak on Mauritius and almost 100 per cent of the remaining hardwood upland, boggy heath land and tropical forest (totalling 3.5 per cent of the island's surface). Over 300 species of plants and nine species of birds can only be found on Mauritius so this park is vital to their continued survival.

The park encompasses four field stations to carry out research work and monitor the threatened species – especially birds on the brink of extinction. Ten CMAs (Conservation Management Areas) covering 73 hectares within the national park offer extra protection to specific ecosystems, where non-indigenous plant species have been cleared and grazing animals banned.

Not only ecologically important, the park is one of the most beautiful parts of Mauritius, with dramatic landscapes of seemingly endless volcanic peaks, vertiginous gorges and deep waterfalls, plus long-distance views down to the coast. There is public access on 60km of walking and hiking trails, along with several panoramic viewpoints, two visitor centres, toilet facilities and picnic areas.

Of the 15 islands and over 30 islets off the shoreline of Mauritius, seven have been declared national reserves and eight national parks. Because of their isolated locations these reserves have excellent potential for the preservation of rare flora and fauna and work is currently concentrated on eradicating predators and removing non-indigenous plants.

The North

The northern islands are closely grouped together just off the coast of Grand Gaube outside the coral reef and consist mainly of degraded volcanic cones. Many of the islands are totally misnamed, leading to all sorts of theories about the role of early cartographers in the region. Round Island – which isn't round – is particularly important because it is the only relatively large landmass in the Mascarenes that is still free of introduced mammals and plants. Goats and rabbits were eradicated after a long campaign in the mid-1980s and non-native weeds were systematically removed to let endemic species breathe. The resulting second-growth palm forest now constitutes the only savannah environment on Mauritius. It is home to ten threatened native palm species and eight species of native reptiles including six that are on the endangered list. Five now only occur on Round Island, which is off-limits to visitors to allow numbers to improve.

Flat Island is the largest national reserve at 253 hectares. Vegetation here is still very much degraded but it is home to two rare species of reptile. Used as a quarantine station during the 19th century, the remaining ruins are also of socio-historical interest and could be developed as a museum. Flat Island is accessible on boat trips.

Gabriel Island, the most distinctively shaped island, is home to several important native palm forest species including *Dicliptera falcate*, a genus last noted in 1858 but rediscovered by botanists as recently as 2005.

Other northern island reserves and parks include Serpent or Snake Island, where you'll find no snakes and very little plant life but vast numbers of breeding sea birds (terns and noddies), and Coin de Mire (Gunner's Quoin) and Pigeon Rock National Park at 0.6 hectare, which are both havens for shearwaters and tropicbirds.

Île d'Ambre National Park

Situated 400m or so off the northeast coast, Île d'Ambre or Amber Island sits inside the coral reef. It's a popular day-trip destination, though surprisingly it has little beach area, the best being at Îlot Bernache, a small sub-islet on the main island. Named after the ambergris trees that used to grow here, the 140 hectares has quite

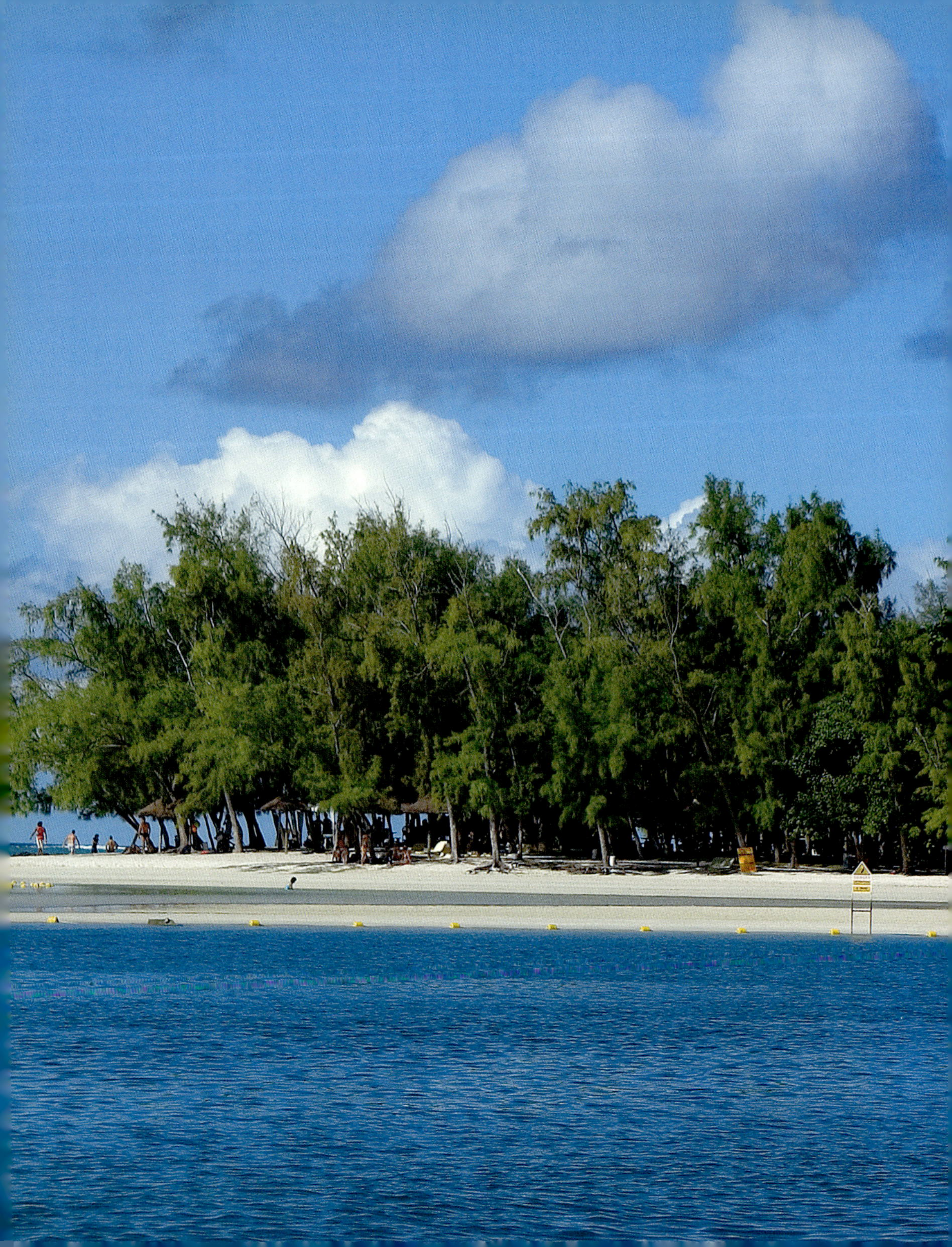

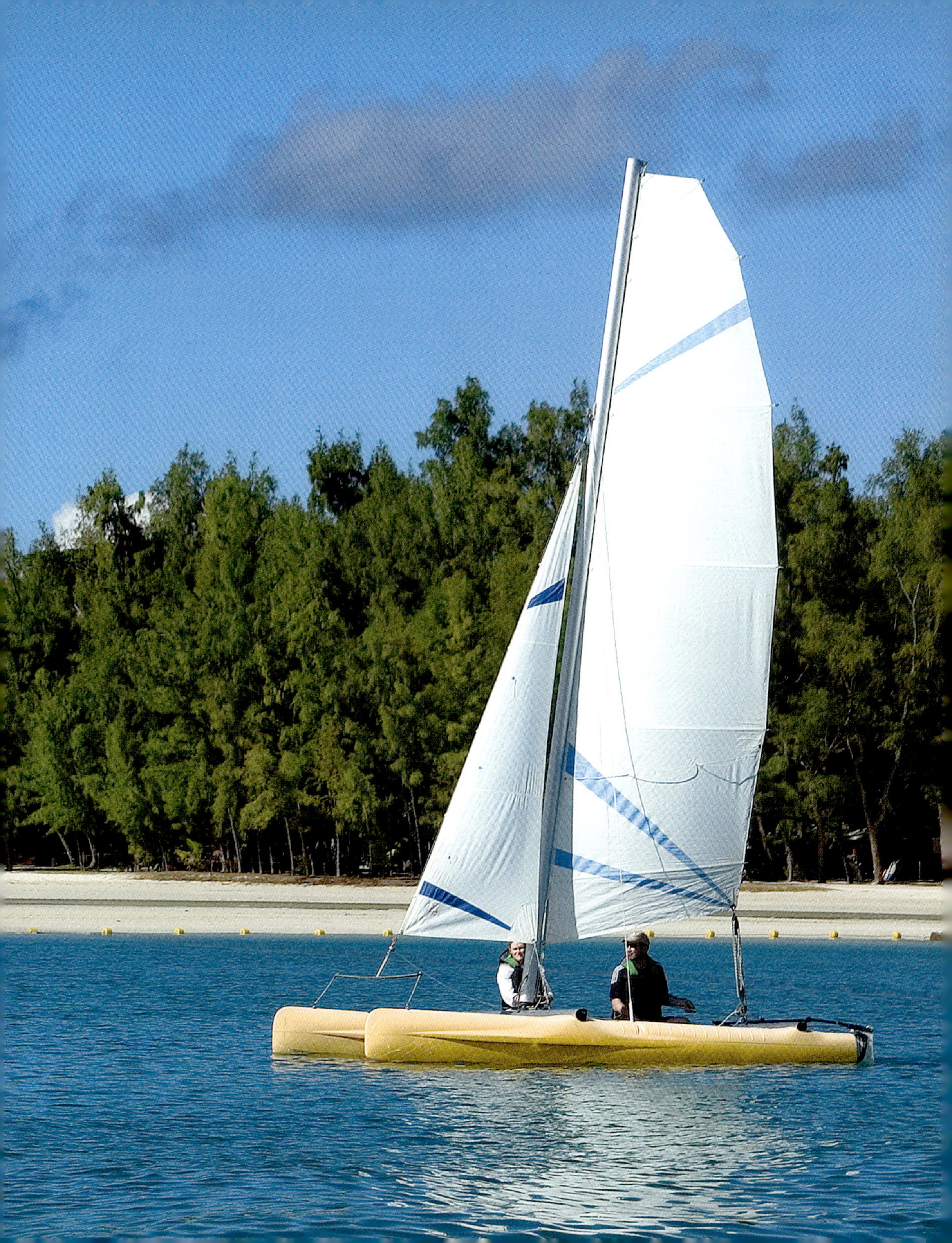

degraded native vegetation but it does have Latanier bleu palms and some of the healthiest tracts of mangrove in Mauritian waters.

The Baie de Mahébourg
Another cluster of islands sits off the coast in the southeast. The Île aux Aigrettes National Reserve west of Mahébourg is a coral island with the best-preserved indigenous lowland forest in the whole of the Mascarene chain, including the last stands of native ebony forest and several rare plants. Declared a nature reserve as early as 1965, the island remained under attack by alien plant species until a restoration programme was implemented in 1985 and this is still ongoing. The island has 20 per cent of the world's population of pink pigeon and a population of endangered Mauritian fody. Run by the MWF, this is the best-managed public access eco-programme on the island.

Three other islands off the coast at Mahébourg have been protected to preserve the old colonial ruins of fortifications that guarded the bay of Mahébourg during Dutch and French rule. Îlot Mariannes National Reserve and Îlot Vacoas National Park currently have minimal management activity, while Île de la Passe Ancient Monument is now under the auspices of the Ministry of Arts and Culture who are integrating the remains into the cultural-historical fabric of the island.

Previous page: Îlot Mangenie is the smaller sandy sibling to Île aux Cerfs and a luxury 'desert island' experience for One&Only hotel clients.
Below: The Curepipe Botanical Gardens has some exceptional specimens of native flora among its attractions, including these beautiful mature tropical hardwoods, as well as a range of recently propagated endangered palm species.

Several other protected islands, including Île aux Oiseaux National Park (0.7 hectares) and Rocher aux Oiseaux National Park (0.1 hectares) are important bird colonies but constitute less than 4 hectares in total.

Protected Wetlands

Although bird-watchers wax lyrical about the possibilities of catching sight of a Mauritius kestrel or echo parakeet in the protected forests of the Black River Gorges National Park, the only specialist bird sanctuary in the Mascarenes protects not native species but overwintering migratory populations. The Rivulet Terre Rouge Estuary Sanctuary is surprisingly close to the centre of Port Louis and is in fact the only Ramsar (International Convention on Wetlands, so called because it was signed in Ramsar, Iran, in 1971) site worldwide that is situated in a capital city. It protects rare humid wetland that attracts species from Europe, the Near East and landlocked Siberia, including curlews, plovers and ruddy turnstones, throughout the European winter. A visitor centre, opened in 2004, has a viewing platform where you can use telescopes to watch these birds feeding and roosting.

Conservation 'Movers and Shakers'

The Native Plant Propagation Centre was established at the Botanical Gardens at Curepipe in 1997 to reproduce native species. By 2005 it was successfully growing 164 out of the 311 endemic flowering plants and 26 of the most endangered species.

The prime mover in the conservation movement on the island is the Mauritian Wildlife Foundation (MWF – see page 189). Founded initially as a fund-raising organization in 1984, it is now responsible for a programme of habitat management and restoration schemes and is expanding into ecotourism development. Today it operates six field stations and two nurseries across the island raising endemic plants to re-vegetate protected land on the main island and offshore islands. It is a non-governmental organization and relies on public donations to continue its work.

Working closely with the MWF from its earliest days is the Durrell Wildlife Conservation Trust (see page 189), founded by author and naturalist Gerald Durrell in the 1960s. It has pioneered on-the-ground conservation worldwide and has an international reputation that has added kudos to the MWF programmes and expertise and training for Mauritian staff. The Durrell Wildlife Conservation Trust began their programme with the Mauritius kestrel. When the Trust first came to the island the birds numbered only a handful of individuals but today, through a programme of captive breeding and release, numbers have improved to over 600. The Trust then turned its attention to the Mauritius pink pigeon, whose numbers in the wild have reached 250, and is now concentrating on the echo parakeet.

Environmental Pressures: Plus Points and Negatives

This island community faces many environmental pressures beyond the worldwide concerns of global warming. With a population density that's one of the highest in the world and an up-market tourist base that places heavy demands on fresh water and domestic food supplies, there are growing concerns about sustainability. As the economy expands so the demands of the general populace rise, increasing the amount of goods that need to be imported. Mauritius is self-sufficient in very little – although salt and venison are two commodities – and even has to import its basic staple foodstuff, rice. With recycling in its infancy, the resultant problem of rubbish disposal is another thorny issue.

It does, however, have one waste item that keeps down the cost of electricity and reduces the need to import other fuels. Bagasse – stems of the sugar cane after they have been crushed and the sweet juices removed – makes an excellent fuel and is incinerated in plants at the sugar mills. The resultant heat is converted into electricity that helps to fuel the cane-crushing machinery and any superfluous power is diverted to add charge to the Mauritius national grid.

Botanical Gardens

Historically always much more a repository for the acclimatization of plantation cash crops and exotic foreign species than the promulgation of native flora, the two contrasting Mauritian botanical gardens now play an important role in protecting and showcasing Mascarene species.

Sir Seewoosagur Ramgoolam Botanical Gardens

Founded by the French and known as the Royal Botanical Gardens throughout British rule, the Sir Seewoosagur Ramgoolam Botanical Gardens are the most important such gardens in the Indian Ocean. Most Mauritians know them simply as Pamplemousses Gardens after the village where they are located.

The land started out as Mahé de Labourdonnais's vegetable patch in 1735 when he built his mansion Mon Plaisir on the site. After Labourdonnais departed, this developed quickly into a small market garden venture supplying nutritious and medicinal plants to Port Louis and the many ships that docked there.

However, in 1767, Pierre Poivre was appointed island administrator and, as an avid horticulturalist, he imported plants from around the known world and designed the formal gardens that form the basis of the modern collection. Pamplemousses was all but abandoned during the initial phase of British rule but was restored in the 1850s by James Duncan who introduced many new and spectacular plants, including the then fashionable gardenia, azalea and camellia, all Southeast Asian flowering shrubs.

Today more than 800 plant species can be found at Pamplemousses and the total number of individual plants tops 8000. Twenty-five indigenous Mascarene species, including beautiful hardwoods such as ebony and mahogany, are now important mature examples and the 80 species of palm, including the royal palm, the queen palm and the talipot palm, which matures for 60 years before bringing forth a giant flower then dying almost immediately, constitute one of the southern hemisphere's finest collections. On Talipot Palm Alley, one of the main thoroughfares through the gardens, over 30 stately mature examples form an impressive and shady avenue.

Today the gardens cover more than 37 hectares with several discreet sections to explore. The large arboretum is criss-crossed with numerous lanes and is also dotted with sculptures and statues, including a bust of Pierre Poivre. There's a spice garden and a medicinal herb garden plus collections of Java deer and Mascarene tortoises.

The original Mon Plaisir cottage was replaced by a grander, younger mansion that now holds the garden offices. The lawns in front of the house also play host to the large stone *samadi* (funerary monument) of Sir Seewoosagur Ramgoolam, the island's first prime minister and father of modern Mauritius.

The highlight of the gardens is the giant Amazon water lily whose monumental fibrous leaves are said to be able to hold the weight of a human adult – though testing the theory isn't recommended. The delicate flowers show an ivory white when they first open but mature to a dusky pink during their two days of life.

Engaging the services one of the inexpensive official park guides is well recommended as they offer a wealth of interesting background information.

Curepipe Botanical Gardens

The Curepipe gardens are much smaller and less spectacular than Pamplemousses but they perform critical practical work on the propagation of endemic flora, including several joint ventures with Kew Gardens in London and the Royal Botanical Gardens in Edinburgh. One of the most successful programmes at Curepipe Botanical Gardens has been the proliferation of the Round Island bottle palm. Once down in number to six individuals, the palm has responded well to emergency propagation procedures. Sadly the same cannot be said for the *Hyophorbe amaricaulis* palm. The plant has been cloned but the resulting seedlings have not survived transplantation into the wild and the sole remaining individual of this genus is on view at Curepipe.

On the Shoreline

It's difficult to find words to do justice to the beauty of Mauritian beaches – sublime, breathtaking and heavenly are at the very least overused and some might even say clichéd, yet so fitting when you are faced with the stunning tropical vistas that are the island's stock-in-trade.

Exceptionally fine sand and translucent turquoise waters fringe over 100km of coastline ranging from diminutive, perfectly formed coves to ribbons stretching for many kilometres. Protected by the offshore reef there's little wave activity and the water laps the shore in almost silent rhythmical rivulets. The reef protects, but it also nourishes the beaches. Parrotfish bite the coral and, as it passes through the digestive tract, it is broken down into the fine particles we know as sand. The far south has fewer sandy stretches than the rest of the island because there is no offshore reef and waves crash directly against the shoreline, but even here you'll be able to sun yourself in certain sheltered bays.

It is fair to say that if you want to find the best beaches on Mauritius you should look at where the best hotels are. Up-market resorts have pinpointed the finest

Below: The famed giant Amazon water lilies of the Sir Seewoosagur Ramgoolam Botanical Gardens are said to be able to support the weight of a man. The undersides are protected by long sharp barbs to deter hungry fish and amphibians.

strands so it's only a few short steps from your patio to the water's edge – you wouldn't want your holiday to be too strenuous!

The main areas to choose from are Flic en Flac in the west – a long strip of golden sand with a compact resort area; a stretch from Trou aux Biches through Mont Choisy to Grand Baie in the north; the Morne Peninsula with several kilometres of fine sand in the shadow of the Morne Brabant mountain, but with little infrastructure outside the big hotels; and Belle Mare, the northerly point of an exceptional sandy stretch on the northeast coast continuing south through Palmar and Trou d'Eau Douce to Île aux Cerfs, whose offshore beaches are arguably the island's highlight. By contrast the Baie du Tamarin – at the mouth of the Tamarin River in the west – is regarded as the best surfing spot.

Public beaches are very well kept and have facilities such as toilets and refreshment stalls plus lots of shade under casuarinas (*filao*) or palm trees. They get particularly busy at weekends when families head out of town with picnics for a day of relaxation. On the west coast and at Le Morne Peninsula you may find groups of young Creole Mauritians getting together to play the sega drums, which add to the buzzing atmosphere.

There are no truly private beaches on Mauritius – anyone can walk below the high-tide line past even the most up-market hotel, and this narrow stretch is where you'll meet the ubiquitous hawkers selling their collection of inexpensive souvenirs. Some visitors dislike being approached while they are relaxing, but hawkers

LAKES AND WATERFALLS

rarely become a nuisance, though some of their wares – including some incredible seashells and coral products – are not environmentally friendly.

Lakes and Waterfalls

Mauritius's ancient volcanic past has left a legacy of deep gorges, rock curtains and collapsed craters that make perfect water features, especially combined with the ample tropical rainfall deposited in the interior. Unlike the island's readily accessible coastline, inland fresh-water features take a little more effort to find but are well worth the time for their lush setting. If setting out on foot, ensure you wear sensible shoes for the rough terrain, carry fresh water and sun cream, plus a warmer outer layer just in case the weather changes.

Grand Bassin

Grand Bassin is by far the most visited lake on Mauritius. A perfectly formed volcanic crater filled with water, it sits high in the interior at just over 700m above sea level. The swirling vestiges of tropical cloud that play across the hillsides offer exciting vistas, and volcanologists will have a field day studying the geology, but Grand Bassin is now most visited for its close ties with Mauritian Hinduism. Hindus call the waters Ganga Talab (Lake of the Ganges)

Below: For lazy afternoons soaking up the sun, it's hard to beat the public beach at Trou aux Biches, but don't expect the place to yourselves at weekends because the beach is a favourite spot for Mauritian families to spend Saturdays and Sundays.

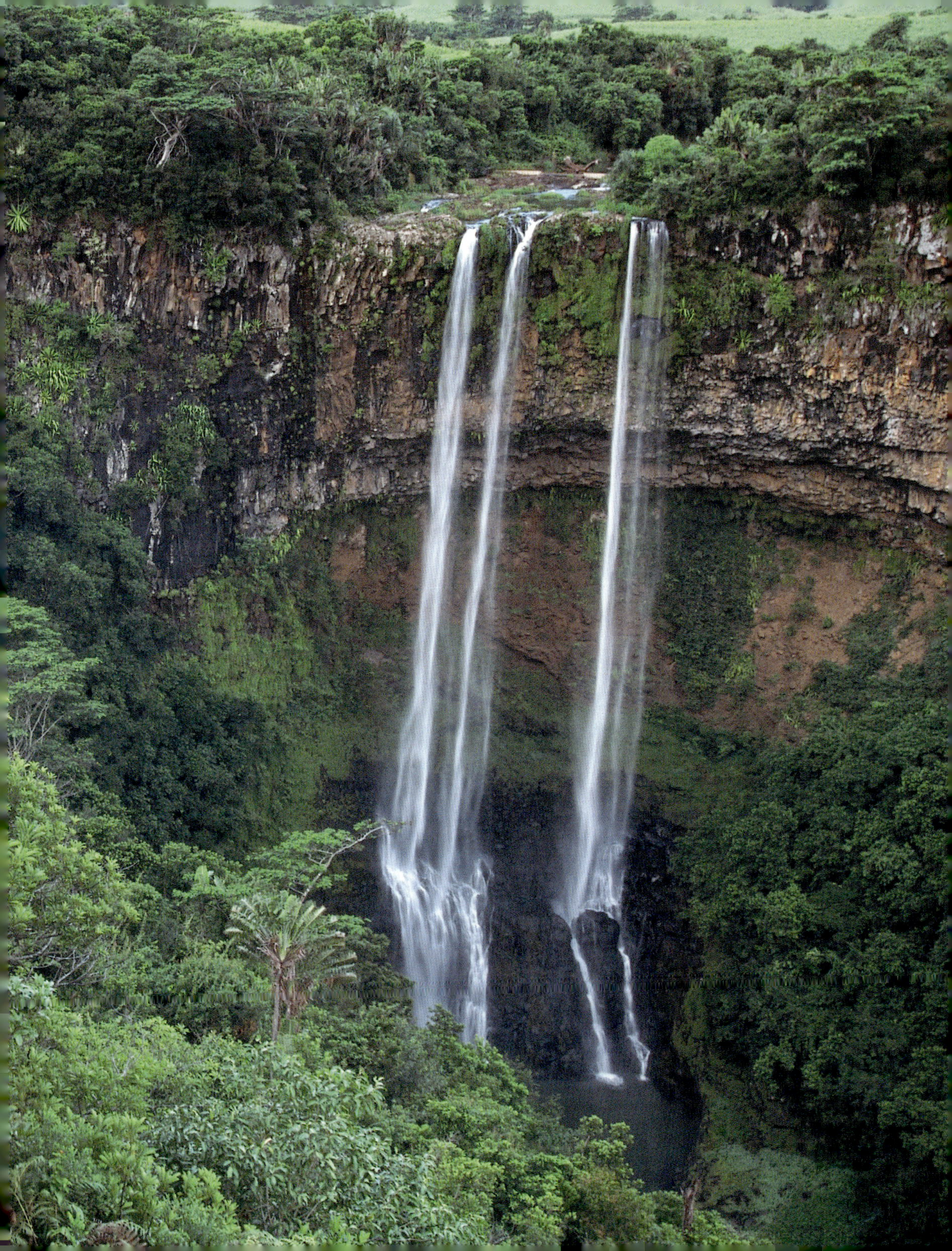

or Ganga Talao (Waters of the Ganges), believing it is linked literally and spiritually with their sacred river in India. There are individual rituals here every day, but many thousands travel from around the island to take part in the major Hindu festivals (*see* page 74).

Bassin Blanc
A more diminutive relative of Grand Bassin, this tiny water-filled crater lies to its southwest off the beaten track in the heart of the national park. This is a great bird-watching spot.

Alexandra Falls
In the heart of the Plaines Champagne plateau, Alexandra Falls sits surrounded by virgin forest. The main platform offers exceptional views not just of the cascade but over the valleys of the national park to the coast beyond. Don't forget your camera.

Eureka Falls
Hidden in the grounds of the old colonial mansion of the same name, Eureka Falls is surrounded by the verdant hills of the Moka coffee district.

Chamarel Falls
The highest falls on Mauritius, Chamarel tumbles 100m over a sheer rock curtain down into a deep gorge surrounded by verdant virgin tropical forest that's remained unchanged even with the coming of man – the perfect place to imagine yourself as one of the first explorers to discover the wonders of the island.

Rochester Falls
Follow a series of hand-painted signs up through a maze of sugar-cane fields from the main south coast road at Souillac. It's not the height of the falls that impresses

Left: *The dramatic cascades of the Chamarel Falls are the highest on Mauritius and drop over the sheer schism in the volcanic rock deep into the vault of a long-collapsed cave, the floor of which is blanketed with rare virgin vegetation.*

here, but the rock over which the water falls and the width of the watercourse.

The water cascades over a collection of volcanic tuff columns; their extremely regular – some say man-made – shape is the result of very slow and regular cooling of the extruded volcanic lava many millions of years ago.

Tamarind Falls
Some way off the main road along trails leading from Henrietta or Tamarin, you find this wide cascade that rushes over several drops resulting in plenty of sound and white water. It's possible to bathe in the deep freshwater pools at the base of the final drop.

Grand River South East Waterfall
This waterfall cascades directly into the sea and is best visited by boat. It can be added to the Île aux Cerfs itinerary and is included in several full-day trips run by the leading tour operators.

Island Domaines
Mauritius has found several unusual ways to introduce you to its verdant hinterland. The Mauritian Wildlife Foundation educates about the very serious business of saving endangered species but the island has a number of less academic attractions with a nature theme – often plantation estates or domaines that have diversified away from traditional farming into eco-style attractions. This policy has to be the way forward as the market for the country's most important crop – sugar – continues to contract and small-scale production becomes less and less economically viable.

Domaine le Val Nature Park
High in the hills in the southeast, Le Val is a small domaine that combines commercial enterprises with eco-activities. The pure, cool springs rising within the domaine are used to rear huge freshwater prawns – a delicacy at hotels and restaurants across the island – and the more mundane watercress. Tropical anthurium flowers, long-lasting blooms with a tough fleshy flower

and white spear-like stamen, are also commercially and packaged for shipping worldwide. Forest trails, a bird park and a collection of deer add to the mix.

Domaine du Chasseur

Covering over a thousand hectares of highland landscape in the southeast of the country, Domaine du Chasseur is one of the pioneers of ecotourism on Mauritius. Opened in 1988, the estate offers a range of activities, all of which promote the natural beauty of the island. Extensive tracts of ebony forest make a perfect backdrop for informative guided nature walks and there are exciting quad-bike and riding trails to enjoy.

Hunting is a major year-round activity with dynamic management of a population of around a thousand wild deer, plus a number of more secretive wild boar, to maintain the current balance between vegetation and grazers. The domaine has been an enthusiastic participant in the fight to save the Mauritius kestrel, with several pairs released and now living happily in the forest canopy.

Essential Oils

The essential oil industry has grown massively in recent years, in line with the rise in interest in holistic medicine and natural remedies. Essential oils can be a powerful tool but must be handled responsibly as they can be harmful and should never be taken internally or applied to the skin in their concentrated form. Rather a few drops should be dispersed in a lighter, skin-friendly, 'diluting' oil. Popular diluting base oils include those produced from sweet almond kernels, grape seeds or sunflower seeds.

There are over 70 different essential oils and each has a particular use. The three main oils produced on Mauritius are eucalyptus, lemon grass and ylang ylang. Eucalyptus has a strong and pungent aroma and is said to be particularly effective against catarrh, sinusitis and the common cold; lemon grass can benefit muscle aches but is better known as an insect repellent, while ylang ylang is used to reduce stress and anxiety.

The Paramour restaurant, serving traditional dishes made with meat from the estate, is reputedly the highest on the island. From the terrace there are exceptional views west into the hills or east across Lion Mountain to the coast north of Vieux Grand Port.

If you want to immerse yourself totally in the forest experience, the domaine has several thatched bungalows where you can stay the night and enjoy the deer and birds during the day, then follow the hours to sunset when creatures such as flying foxes take to the air, all well away from the lights and noise of the tourist resorts and towns.

Domaine de l'Ylang Ylang

In the lowlands between the national park and the east coast, close to Domaine du Chasseur, this new estate has invested in the production of natural essential oils, a new enterprise for Mauritius. The small factory takes vast amounts of raw materials such as scented ylang ylang blooms, aromatic lemon grass, or pungent eucalyptus leaves to produce even one small bottle of essential oil. These oils are used in the massage and aromatherapy wellness industries and they are viewed as being benefi-

Below: The fruits and leaves of ylang ylang, lemon grass and eucalyptus form the raw material for essential oil production at the Domaine de l'Ylang Ylang.

cial and mood enhancing. They can be mixed with a base oil to create a fragrant massage oil, or heated to release their aromas into the air. It's a fascinating process watching the raw materials being transformed, as is a stroll or jeep tour around the fragrant crops.

Chamarel

One of the most visited natural attractions on Mauritius is found in this tiny enclave just outside the Black River Gorges National Park. Terre de Sept Couleurs or the 'Seven Coloured Earth' of Chamarel is exactly that, a rare geological occurrence that brings several strata of the natural substrate to the surface, each with a different colour or tint. Seen at their best the colours meld and swirl in a kind of neutral-toned kaleidoscope that captures the imagination. Towards sunset the show gets even better as the whole area almost seems to glow, absorbing the light to give off a vaguely golden hue.

The Chamarel souvenir shop sells bottles of the soil with differing colours arranged in pretty freeform patterns or kitsch desert-island scenes.

The 'Seven Coloured Earth' isn't the best place to visit on a dull or rainy day when it resembles a recently ploughed field; it needs sunshine to bring out the subtle contrasts. However, the Chamarel waterfall (*see* page 37), the island's highest, sits close by and shouldn't be missed whatever the weather.

Close to these natural attractions is the Parc Aventure Chamarel, an adventure playground set in 4.8 hectares of forest where you can explore the natural flora and fauna of the forest canopy on rope bridges or try the

Below: *The 'coloured earth' of Chamarel is one of the most unusual natural attractions on the island – an area of multicoloured mineral-rich volcanic rock thrust to the surface and surrounded by contrasting verdant forest.*

Above: The tiny Île aux Aigrettes leads the way in island conservation, protecting small populations of several species of critically endangered and rare flora and fauna, including the only area of Mascarene lowland forest left on earth.

more difficult *via ferrata* preset climbing course. The canopy walk is said to be suitable for all ages but isn't advised for sufferers of vertigo or those with mobility problems. It offers a wonderful and eye-opening perspective on life in the trees. The structured climbing course is well supervised and offers a great introduction for budding conquerors of Everest. Each trail takes around an hour to complete.

Île aux Aigrettes

This tiny 26-hectare island just a stone's throw off the southeastern shores close to Mahébourg mimics the fate of Mauritius on a miniature scale, having been stripped of many of its natural and native assets by the Dutch, French and British. Declared a reserve in 1965, it constitutes the most important eco-programme in the Indian Ocean and offers an ideal opportunity to explore the cutting edge conservation measures taking place on Mauritius today. Run by the Mauritius Wildlife Foundation since 1987, the guided tours take you to all corners of the conservation area.

Île aux Aigrettes is now free of human beings and most introduced predators and acts as an incubator for species such as the day gecko, pink pigeon and Telfair's skink. In the skies you may be lucky enough to see a Mauritius kestrel, the eco-success story of recent years. The island is also dotted with historical remains including military batteries used in the Anglo-French skirmishes during the 17th and early 18th centuries, and an old lime kiln.

A marked trail leads to the aviaries and nurseries that contain future generations of what are hoped to be wild plants and animals. Over 40,000 plants a year are transplanted to enhance the vegetation, and there's a tortoise pen and a reptile pen housing two Telfair's skinks waiting to be reintroduced into the wild.

The dry coastal forest at the heart of the island is the last of its kind in the whole Mascarene chain, with wonderful stands of dense ebony forest and Bois de Chandelle that can be enjoyed from a viewing platform at canopy height.

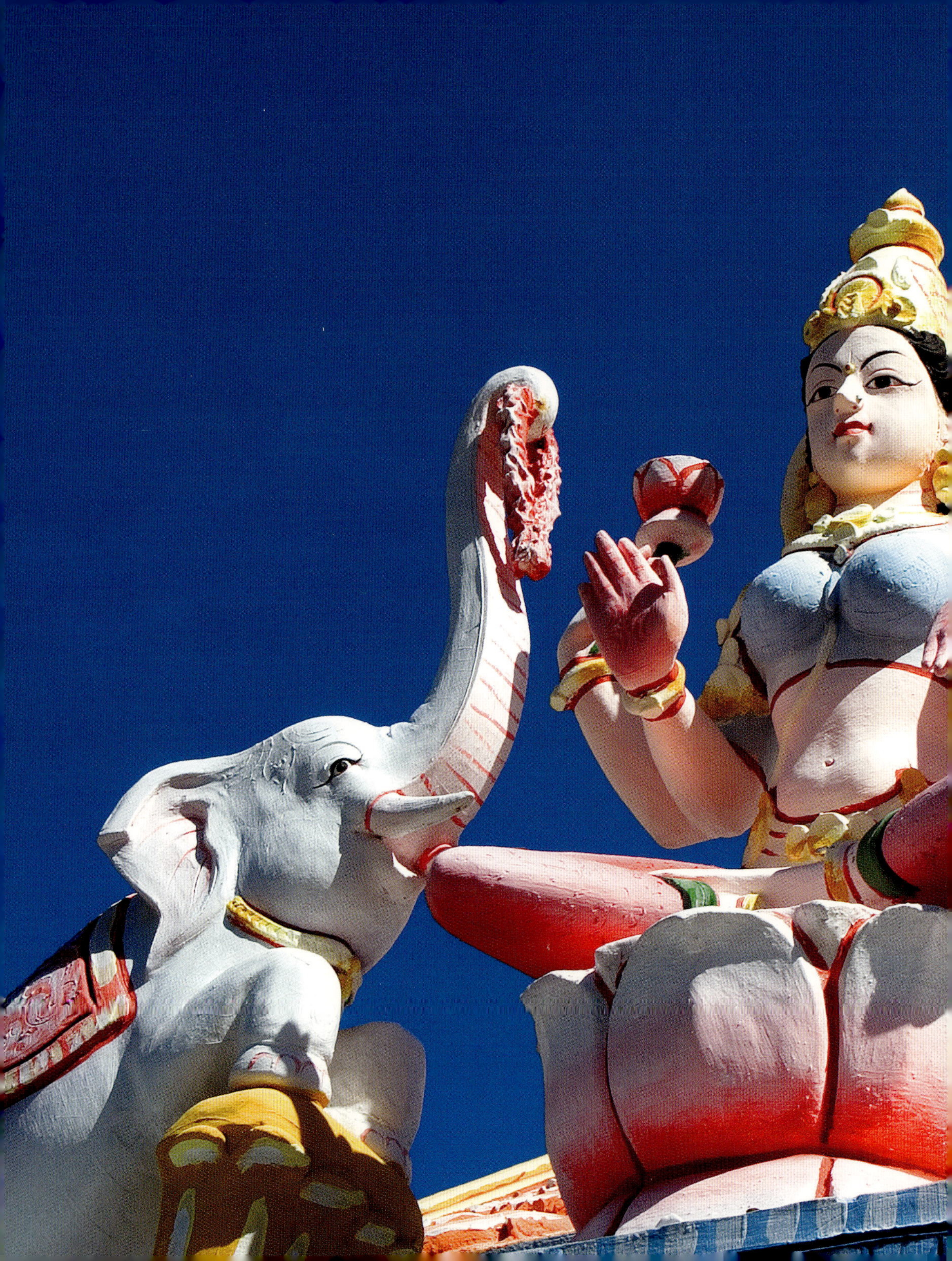

Island Culture

Left: *Graphic depictions of gods and deities make Hindu temples colourful and fascinating places to explore, as here at Belle Mare.*

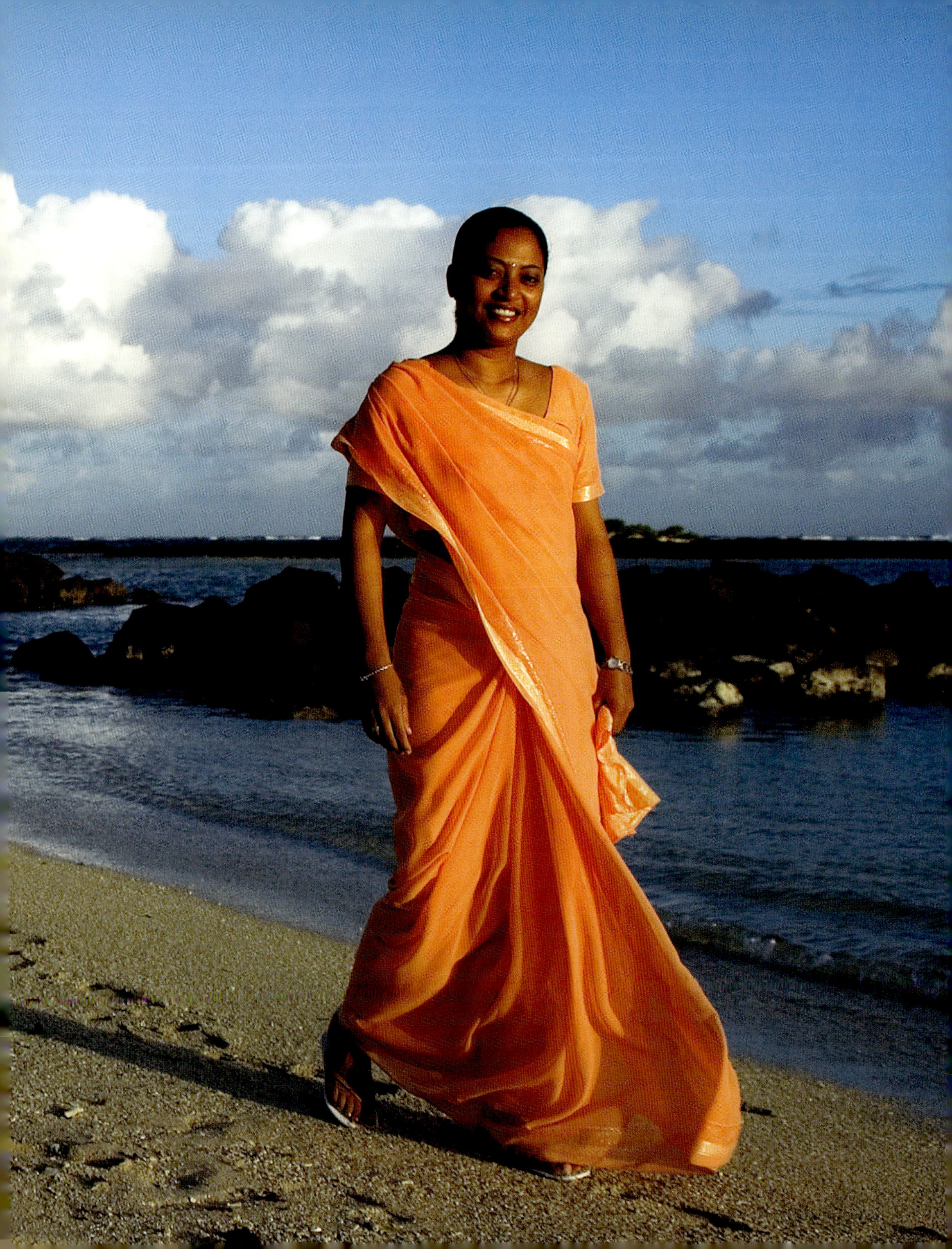

One of the world's youngest countries, Mauritius cut loose from its colonial past in 1992.

The phrase 'the sum of its parts' could well have been invented to describe the culture here. Diverse, energetic and evolving, it's a living, breathing multi-ethnic society that's unashamedly carrying its traditions into the 21st century.

The ancestors of today's Mauritians sailed for many days to reach these shores, some under physical duress, others through economic necessity. Life was hard for most and still is for many, but the *joie de vivre* that exudes from young and old here is genuine and heartfelt. The racial and religious melange is a fascinating element of the Mauritius story – a story that's worth exploring.

Left: *The voluminous saris worn by Hindu women on Mauritius are both elegant and cool.*

History
What's in a Name?

Being so far from any populated landmass, Mauritius didn't register on the human radar until the end of the first millennium CE. In around 975 Arab seamen put it on their maps as Dinarobin or 'Silver Island' but they didn't settle. It was a further five hundred years before Europeans found the place. Portuguese explorer Domingo Fernandez chose the name Ilha do Cerne or 'Island of the Swan' during his brief stop in 1507, naming the island after his boat. He dropped off some livestock to replenish other passing ships but strangely didn't claim the island as Portuguese soil. Less than a decade later in 1513 Portuguese Captain Pedro de Mascarenhas toured the area and named the island chain, including Ilha do Cerne (and modern Réunion, Rodrigues and the Seychelles), the Mascarene Islands.

The Dutch found Mauritius almost by accident when a fleet led by Admiral van Warwyck was shipwrecked during a storm in 1598. He named the island after Prince Maurits (Maurice) of Nassau, who was Stadhouder (appointed monarch) of Holland at the time, and laid claim to the island for the Dutch Crown.

Right: The plethora of gorgeous sandy beaches were of little interest to the colonial settlers when they arrived on the island. Formed by the natural breakdown of coral into minute particles, the beaches of Mauritius are now regarded as some of the best in the world.

c975CE	1507	1513	1598	1638
Arab seamen make landfall on Mauritius, giving it the name Dinarobin (Silver Island), but they don't settle.	Portuguese explorer Domingo Fernandez renames Mauritius Ilha do Cerne (Island of the Swan). Livestock is landed to replenish ships, but the island isn't claimed by Portugal.	Portuguese Captain Pedro de Mascarenhas names the island chain (including Mauritius, Réunion, Rodrigues and the Seychelles) the Mascarene Islands.	Dutch Admiral van Warwyck makes landfall after a storm and renames it yet again, after Prince Maurits (Maurice) of Nassau. He claims the islands for Holland.	A small number of colonists arrive. The first slaves arrive from Madagascar as the Dutch begin exploiting the ebony forests. Prisoners arrive from Dutch colonies in the East Indies to supplement the workforce, along with deer from Java, sheep, geese, ducks, pigeons and other livestock.

1639	1658	1664	1710	1715	1721
Sugar cane is introduced.	The first Dutch colony is abandoned and runaway slaves establish themselves in and around the dense forests of the southwestern part of the island.	The Dutch try again creating a settlement just north of Vieux Grand Port on the southeast coast.	The Dutch abandon the island for good.	The French arrive under the command of Jean-Baptiste Garnier de Fougeray. He renames the island Île de France.	The first French colonists arrive and eke out an existence but find the Dutch settlement not conducive to their plans – poor sea access, etc. – so they found Port Louis.

Island Culture

Let's Found a Colony

This was the era of the great sea trading routes that supplied spices, tea and silk from the east to the markets in Amsterdam, London and Paris. Mauritius was initially a sort of pit stop along the route where ships could stock up on meat (dodo and giant tortoise), fruits and fresh water.

Then, in 1638 a small band of intrepid Dutch colonists founded a settlement called Fort Frederik Hendrik on the southeast coast at what is now Vieux Grand Port, and their arrival set in motion an irrevocable chain of events that have shaped the country we see today.

The Europeans were not farmers but hardened adventurers who came to exploit the island's valuable

1735	1767	1779	1789	1796
Bertrand François Mahé de Labourdonnais is appointed governor (father of the island). Labourdonnais transforms the island by energizing the settlers, putting forward concrete plans for development. The capital and main port is moved to Port Louis. Wheat and cotton crops are introduced and sugar cane is planted on a large scale.	Pierre Poivre is appointed as administrator and introduces new strains of plants and agricultural practices to the island.	François Vicomte de Souillac is appointed governor.	The French Revolution.	Revolution on Mauritius – primarily against the abolition of slavery – is followed by a period of self-rule. Piracy is encouraged against the English ships in the area and the island becomes a favourite pirates' hideaway.

History

> **Statistics**
>
> **Area:** 1865km
> **Coastline:** 330km
> **Highest point:** 828m
> **Population:** 1.2 million (official 2003)
> **Religions:** 51 per cent Hindu, 30 per cent Christian (23 per cent Catholic), 17 per cent Muslim, with Taoist and Buddhist adherents
> **Official language:** English is the official language, with French and Creole being the languages of everyday commerce. Bhojpuri (a dialect of Hindi) and several Oriental languages are also spoken.
> **Government:** A democratic state on the UK model but elections are modified first past the post with numbers of seats being reserved for the various minority groups to ensure balance within the decision-making process.
> **President:** Sir Anerood Jugnauth
> **Prime minister:** Navin Chandra Ramgoolam
> **Currency:** The national currency is the Mauritius Rupee (MUR or Rs). Each rupee is divided into 100 cents. Notes are issued in denominations of 25, 50, 100, 200, 500, 1000 and 2000. Coins have values of 5, 10, 20, 25 and 50 cents, and 1, 5 and 10 rupees.
> **Time:** Mauritius is four hours ahead of Greenwich Mean Time.
> **Literacy rates:** 83 per cent
> **Life expectancy:** 72 (68 for men and 76 for women)

ebony forests. For that they needed labour, or, for labour, read slaves. Hundreds were forcibly removed from their homes in Madagascar who, along with a contingent of convicts from Java, outnumbered the Europeans many fold.

Despite reaching a population of almost 500 people at its height the colony didn't thrive. When a new Dutch dependency was founded in South Africa in 1652 the colonists on Mauritius jumped ship and in 1658 left the slaves and livestock to their own devices.

In 1664 a more concerted attempt was made and commercial plantations were founded. The Dutch tried a range of crops on Mauritius but they discovered that sugar cane was best suited to the varying climatic and topographical conditions. However, the colonists were not well supported by the their backers, the Dutch East India Company, and when they finally abandoned Mauritius for good in 1510, Holland let its interest in the island lapse.

Left: *Much of the arable land is given over to sugar-cane production but small family-owned farms grow a whole range of fruits and vegetables for the local market. Workers keep themselves covered up against the hot sun.*

1803	1810	1814	1833	1835
Napoleon Bonaparte dispatches Charles Mattieu Isodore Comte Decaen to restore the island to French rule.	The Battle of Grand Port sees Napoleon's only naval success, but by the end of the year the British have taken Mauritius (and Réunion). Governor Robert Farquhar is appointed.	British rule of the island, along with Rodrigues and the Seychelles, is ratified in the Treaty of Paris (though Réunion is returned to the French). The island reverts to its Dutch name – Mauritius. The colonists are allowed to keep their property, French law, religion, language and customs.	The British Parliament abolishes slavery but Mauritius plantation owners defy the ruling.	Slavery is finally abolished. Many ex-slaves choose to settle away from their old plantation homes, eking out an independent existence at the margins of the island, and the economy suffers a massive labour shortage.

Island Culture

Allez La France

It wasn't too long before word got out on the international grapevine and the French laid claim almost before the last Dutch camp fires had died out. They immediately stamped their mark by renaming the island Île de France.

The first French settlers arrived in 1716 but found life as difficult as the Dutch did. Fort Frederick Hendrik didn't suit them – it had always been a tricky entry through a narrow break in the reef – so they looked for a suitable location for a new capital. They found it in a natural harbour on the northwest coast and called the town Port Louis.

The French East Indies Company who ran the island 'recruited' a motley assortment of mercenaries, pirates and press-ganged women from the homeland – in the hope of attracting more male settlers – but there was little community spirit and attacks by the escaped slaves of the Dutch colonists made life even more difficult. But just as the fledgling colony seemed on the verge of collapse the company made an inspired and pivotal decision in appointing Bertrand François Mahé de Labourdonnais, a sailor from St Malo, as governor.

Labourdonnais's personal magnetism and natural leadership skills honed the colonists into a working unit but

Left: Bertrand François Mahé de Labourdonnais turned a failing and disorganized distant colony into the most successful French East Indies enterprise in the world. His influence in the Mascarene Islands is undisputable.

1841	1847	1860s	1864	1885	1901
Père Laval lands on Mauritius to begin his missionary work.	Mauritius begins to print its own stamps.	Outbreak of cholera kills over 40,000 islanders. There is mass movement from Port Louis to the central plateau.	The Mauritius railway system is opened. Death of Père Laval.	First elections, with suffrage extended to 2 per cent of the population.	Mahatma Ghandi visits Mauritius, then sends a representative – Manilall Doctor – to help organize Indo-Mauritian workers.

History

he was also canny enough to use their somewhat questionable skills as privateers to harry rival British shipping in the region and it wasn't long before Mauritius became well known as a pirate hangout. While the enemy was harassed at sea, a well-oiled and profitable plantation system was organized on land, with sugar cane, spices and indigo the main crops.

Within a couple of decades Île de France became the French East Indies Company's most profitable colony and Port Louis was transformed into a suitably formal capital with jurisdiction over neighbouring Bourbon Island (now Réunion).

The success of Labourdonnais prompted a contingent of ranking families to arrive on the island, adding a touch of blue blood, and when the French Crown took control after the bankruptcy of the French East Indies Company in 1767, the colony recorded a population of over eighteen thousand – but of these fifteen thousand were slaves of African or Madagascan origin. The Crown sent Pierre Poivre to administer the island, but his main interest lay in horticulture and he imported numerous new and exotic plants and reorganized the plantation system to vastly improve output.

In 1779 Vicomte de Souillac, the last royally appointed governor, arrived and he brought the excesses of the Bourbon court to Port Louis. Business was forgotten for the hedonistic life of leisure. This gravy train was to come to a sudden halt in 1790 when news of the French Revolution arrived in Mauritius. The repercussions were initially minor – mass name changes and a confiscation of church property – but in 1796 some startling news hit the streets: slavery had been abolished throughout the Republic. Not surprisingly the colonists were up in arms and sent the delegates of the revolutionary council packing. A chaotic period of self-rule ensued during which Port Louis once again became a privateers' paradise. British ships were raided with impunity and Surcouf, one of the most successful buccaneers of this era, became a national hero.

Below: *During Pierre Poivre's custodianship Mauritius expanded its agrarian economy. He is remembered most for the care and attention lavished on the Sir Seewoosagur Ramgoolam Botanical Gardens.*

1926	1936	1956	1959	1964	1968
First Indo-Mauritian representation in parliament.	The Mauritius Labour Party is formed.	Last passenger train service.	Universal suffrage is granted to Mauritians, though the island remains under British rule. In the first election Hindu Sir Seewoosagur Ramgoolam is made Leader of the House.	Last public freight train service.	Mauritius becomes an independent island within the British Commonwealth, with Queen Elizabeth II as head of state.

Napoleon Bonaparte sent General Charles Decaen to bring the errant colony back into the fold in 1803, but any yoke would have chafed after a decade or so of independence. Decaen re-imposed French law, including the new Code Napoleonique, but continued to encourage piracy and the British decided they really needed to do something about this thorn in their side.

The Coming of the British

Things came to a head in 1810 when the two sides clashed in Mauritian waters and the French Navy won a battle just off Vieux Grand Port, the only naval battle won by Napoleon during his rule. However, Decaen realized that he had little support from the colony and offered only token resistance when the British invaded the island later that year. The victors allowed French forces and any French plantation owners to leave, but very few colonists did.

The enmity between the British and the French might have been expected to prompt a wholesale spring-clean of all things Gallo-Mauritian – indeed the British quickly reverted back to the old Dutch name, calling the island Mauritius – but the Treaty of Paris in 1814, which ceded Mauritius to Britain permanently, guaranteed the French colonialists the right to their language, laws and customs; plus, the islanders got another 'man of the moment' in governor Robert Farquhar.

Farquhar worked tirelessly on behalf of the colony and he had to cope with some tough times. Fire ravaged the wooden buildings of Port Louis in 1816, the island was devastated by two strong cyclones in quick succession, and the population was plagued by a cholera epidemic. In the aftermath of the cyclones Farquhar pushed plantation owners to abandon other crops in favour of sugar cane because it stood up to the high winds much better than more delicate plants. He also declared Port Louis a tax-free port, thus encouraging the trade that ensured it remained prosperous.

Emancipation and Indentureship

However, slavery was becoming a hot subject in Britain too. Trade in slaves had been banned in 1807, before the British takeover, and in 1833 the death knell of the whole system rang in London when owning slaves became illegal. Although Mauritius held out until 1835 it couldn't hope to continue independently and the colonialists accepted the situation, mustering as much good grace as possible.

The Creole slaves threw off the shackles of oppression with relish and refused to play any part in the economy of the colony, preferring to eke out an existence in the last remaining uncultivated areas of the island than work willingly with their former masters.

Landowners faced economic ruin but for an ingenious solution. Indian labourers or 'coolies' would take the place of the slaves. Indentured to a plantation owner for

Right: Hectares of sugar cane swaying in the breeze in the lee of precipitous volcanic peaks – the landscapes found in the Mauritian interior match the beaches for beauty.

1970	1979	1981	1982	1985	12 March 1992
The Export Processing Zone (EPZ) is launched to diversify the economy.	Beatification of Pero Laval by Pope John Paul II.	Last private sugar-cane train service signals the death of the rail system.	Aneerood Jugnauth, another Hindu, becomes prime minister.	Death of Sir Seewoosagur Ramgoolam, then governor general of the island.	Mauritius is declared a Republic and Veerasamy Ringadoo, the then governor general, is declared president before Cassam Uteem is voted into the role. Government is based on the British system with first past the post elections modified to allow the many minorities of society to have a say.

History

1998	2001	2003	2005	2005
Tourist numbers reach 570,000.	The Mauritian sugar-cane industry introduces experimental precision farming to improve profitability.	Sir Aneerood Jugnauth becomes president – his son Pravind Jugnauth now leads his father's political party, the Militant Socialist Movement.	Navin Chandra Ramgoolam, son of Sir Seewoosagur, now leads the Alliance Socials incorporating the Mauritius Labour Party. He is currently prime minister of the island.	The abolition of the global quota system threatens the textile sector. Visitor numbers reach 760,000.

Above: *Sir Seewoosagur Ramgoolam was the father of modern Mauritius. Architect of independence in the 1960s, he was instrumental in creating the modern economy.*

ten years in exchange for free passage from all around the subcontinent to Mauritius, they worked in conditions very similar to the slavery that had gone before, but their arrival changed every facet of island life. The first contingent arrived in 1835 but there was soon a steady stream of families setting sail from India, with a small percentage of Chinese immigrants arriving from British colonies further east. The vast majority of Indians were Hindus, with around 20 per cent being Muslim and smaller numbers of Telagu. Within only a few years, people of Indian origin were in the majority on the island.

Père Laval

The packet boat from Europe brought Jacques Desiré Laval, a recently ordained priest and qualified doctor, to Mauritius in 1841 and he went to help the freed Creole. He lived as one of them, working as a community doctor and teacher, improving living conditions for all the poor and oppressed. Many thousands were converted to Christianity by this pious man Mauritians called Père Laval.

King Cane

The mid-1800s was the great era of sugar. From 11,000 tons in 1825, production leapt to 100,000 tons in 1854 when Mauritius was the British Empire's largest sugar producer and accounted for almost 10 per cent of the world's supply. But the resultant wealth lay in the hands of a tiny number of old colonial families.

In 1864 the Mauritius railroad opened for the movement of crops and passengers. A small network developed and continued to run for over 100 years, but with the advent of cars the passenger network became unprofitable, and the last couple of decades services were on private lines run by the sugar-cane barons. Eighteen sixty-four also saw the death of Père Laval and an estimated 40,000 gathered to wish him a final farewell.

A serious outbreak of cholera during the 1860s killed 40,000 people and forced the inhabitants of Port Louis to move onto the central plateau, the until then sparsely populated Plaines Wilhems region of central Mauritius. They never moved back, finding the climate more suitable, and today several small towns have melded together into one vast conurbation that's home to 30 per cent of Mauritians.

Before recruitment stopped around the turn of the 20th century, over 200,000 people had arrived from India to make a new life on Mauritius. Some Indian and Chinese families played a big role in the mercantile life of the island and held an increasing amount of wealth, but the indentured labourers and their Mauritian-born offspring had few rights and very little political influence. However, the wheels of social change began to grind slowly, starting with a new constitution in 1885. This heralded the first of the island elections, though suffrage was granted to less than 2 per cent of the population and excluded the Creole and Indo-Mauritian majority. The moneyed Creole population, led by Dr Eugene Laurant, formed Action Libérale to gain representation, while a visit by Mahatma Ghandi in 1901 planted the seeds of Indian political consciousness when he sent lawyer Manilall Doctor to help organize the indentured labourers.

History

The 1926 elections saw the first representation for Indo-Mauritians and resulted in some improvement in workers' pay and conditions, but the volatile nature of the sugar market left them vulnerable to total loss of income in difficult years. The Mauritius Labour Party (MLP) was founded in 1936 by Creole Dr Maurice Curé to champion the workers' cause. At the same time the Indian Cultural Association was being led by a Hindu Indo-Mauritian doctor and political activist, Seewoosagur Ramgoolam. Universal franchise wasn't introduced until 1959 but the first truly representative election brought victory for the MLP and a ministerial position for Ramgoolam. He was to remain in parliament until 1982, becoming prime minister in 1968.

Independence

In 1968 Mauritius became independent but remained in the Commonwealth of Nations, with Queen Elizabeth II as head of state (represented by a governor general). The parliamentary system was based on the Westminster model but included a unique 'best loser' system, which allows even the smallest minority to have some form of representation. In 1971 the new constitution faced its first serious challenge when the recently formed Mouvement Militant Mauricien (MMM), led by Franco-Mauritian Paul Berenger, incited civil action across the island, in response to concerns about the Mauritian economy and workers' rights. Ramgoolam declared a state of emergency and Berenger spent a year in prison.

However, the main thrust of Ramgoolam's custodial era was to widen the island's single-industry economic base. In the same year as the riots, the Export Processing Zone (EPZ) was created. Businesses could set up manufacturing bases and benefit from tax-free trading, and Mauritius used beneficial trading terms with the EEC (now the EU) to draw in foreign companies. The textile industry was the big winner, bolstered by protected trading agreements with several countries. Today, the companies of the EPZ provide over 120,000 jobs on the island. The 70s also saw the birth of the tourist industry with the opening of the Hotel Saint Géran. From the outset the island marketed itself as an up-market jet-set destination, an image it continues to promulgate.

On a more personal note, at the end of the decade in 1979, local hero Père Laval was beatified by Pope John Paul II for his unswerving dedication to the poor of the island.

The 1982 general election brought about a sea change in parliament when the MMM won all 62 seats. Berenger took a ministerial role, with party chairman Hindu Aneerood Jugnauth becoming prime minister, but the victory brought immediate divisions that split the party. Jugnauth went on to found a new party, the Mouvement Socialiste Militant (MSM), and ruled in coalition with the MLP. In the same year Ramgoolam was appointed governor general of the island, leaving Jugnauth to dominate party politics into the 1990s. In 1985 there came an end to two eras on the island. Sir Seewoosagur Ramgoolam, 'father' of modern Mauritius, died and for the first time in 300 years sugar cane lost its place as primary foreign income earner to manufacturing. The winds of change had begun to blow!

Below: *The Mauritian flag comprises stripes of the colours red (for freedom), blue (for the ocean), yellow (the shining light of independence) and green (for the verdant vegetation).*

Island Culture

The Mauritian Republic

On 12 March 1992 Mauritius was declared a republic and began to look to the future. The diversification of the Mauritian economy seemed to be on track. Visitor numbers in 1992 were 150,000 but by 1998 this had ballooned to 570,000, with several up-market resort properties in the planning stage. The figures from 2005 show a rise to 760,000, with the vast majority of visitors arriving on high-value packages. The Mauritian government has consistently refused to allow charter airlines to set up routes and this, along with the high quality of the accommodation, has helped keep the island firmly in the luxury sector of the market.

In the same year that Mauritius became independent, the Mauritius Offshore Business Activities Authority was set up to manage an expanding tax and banking sector, and to date 9000 companies and other organizations have taken advantage of the regime.

Textiles have been the big economic success story of the late 20th century but the abolition of the global quota system in 2005 opened markets to mass producers such as China, threatening Mauritian jobs. The industry is currently targeting the 'high-quality short-run' niche sector of the market, capitalizing on their reputation for quality.

However, sugar cane still dominates the countryside and in the first decade of the new millennium sugar still accounts for 19 per cent of exports and 5 per cent of GDP. Longstanding sugar quotas are currently being renegotiated but Mauritius is unlikely to receive the same preferential treatment it has enjoyed in recent decades, so change is inevitable.

In 2001 the Mauritian sugar-cane industry introduced experimental precision farming to improve profitability. What is certain is that increased mechanization and the closure of several smaller sugar mills will mean fewer jobs than the current 37,000.

Right: *The historic Government House in downtown Port Louis was built during the French era and expanded when the British took the island in the early 1800s.*

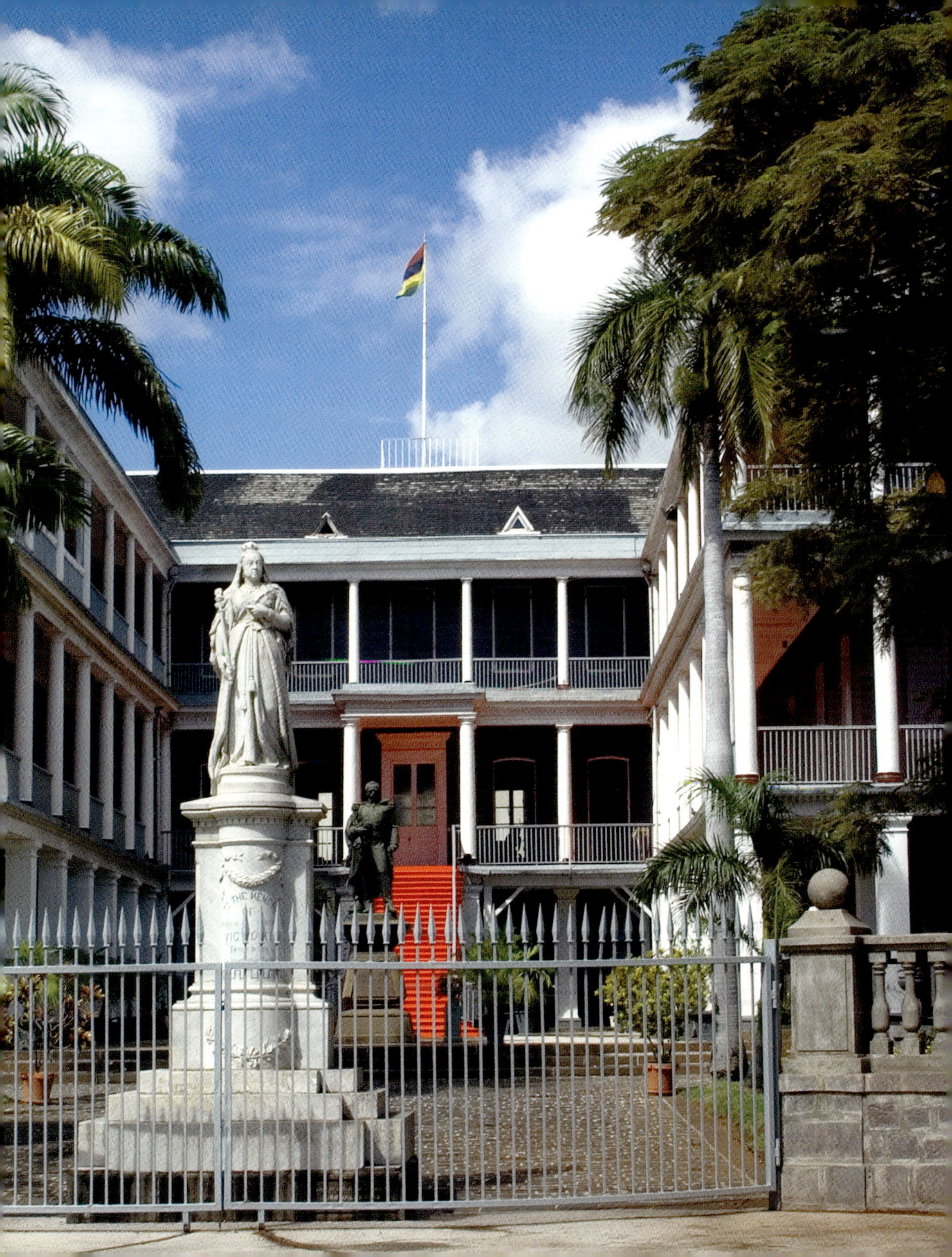

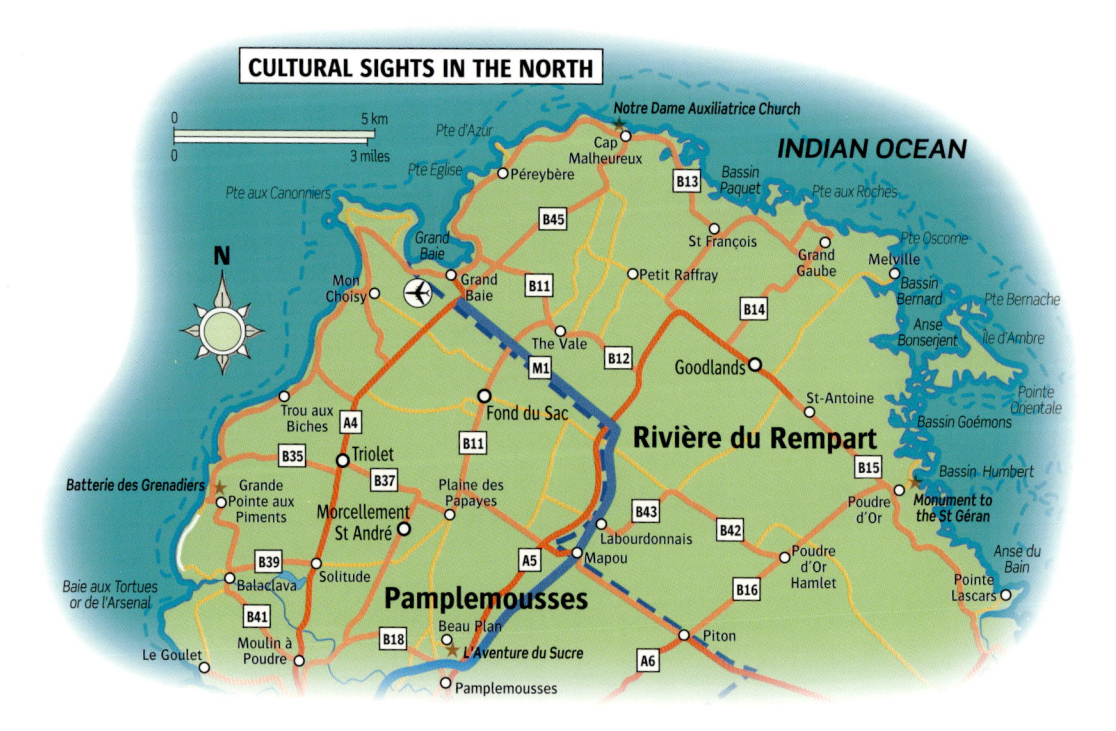

Politics has been a little like a swinging pendulum between the opposing factions straddling the centre right and centre left. Times have moved on and the Ramgoolam and Jugnauth mantles have passed to a new generation.

In 2003 Sir Aneerood Jugnauth became president and his son Pravind Jugnauth now leads his father's political party, the Militant Socialist Movement. The MSM currently sits in opposition to an MLP-led coalition government – the Alliance Socials – headed by Navin Chandra Ramgoolam. These two families look set to dominate politics well into the 21st century.

Culture

The first permanent human settlement on Mauritius was founded some 400 years ago and sustainable growth was so agonizingly slow for the first few decades that the island had to be abandoned twice, but since the initial problems were ironed out it has been a short but fascinating journey to the truly unique culture of the modern Mauritian state.

This rich cultural mix is inextricably linked to a colonial plantation production system that dominated commerce well into the 20th century and centred on one crop in particular – sugar cane – whose efficient production depended on a vast labour force. Ironically, Mauritius is one of the few places on earth where human beings were not an indigenous species but that didn't stop the onward march of production. In fact it resulted in the mass movement of very different peoples under completely disparate circumstances, from two contrasting continents, to feed the seemingly insatiable demands of the people of a third, far-away Europe.

Today the country is one of the most densely populated on earth with a cultural diversity that belies its small size and a seemingly harmonious society that owns, embraces and celebrates its complicated ethnic make-up.

The Dutch Legacy

A simple monument north of Vieux Grand Port marks the point of landfall made by the Dutch in a shallow mangrove-shrouded bay on the east coast in 1598. The remains of Fort Frederik Hendrik, the first Dutch settlement just north of Vieux Grand Port, constitute the oldest buildings on the island. Scant remains of volcanic stone walls sit by the water's edge close to the break in the reef that allowed the ships to enter the inner lagoon. There's not very much of substance to add atmosphere to the skeletal buildings, and lush lawns now surround the old bakery and the church, diminishing the sense of place, al though there are a number of artefacts – found in a recent comprehensive archaeological study – on show at the Frederik Hendrik Museum on site.

Little other architectural evidence reminds us of the Dutch era but when they abandoned the island, they had already altered the ecological balance. They stripped away much of the valuable hardwood forests, the basic natural habitat for many native animals birds and reptiles, and caused the quick extinction of the dodo and the giant tortoise, by far the most common species on the islands when man arrived there just over a century before.

The French Influence

Though they were here for less than a century, the French left an indelible mark on Mauritius, or Île de France – Island of France – as they named the landmass. The French language is widely used in everyday business in preference to the official language of the country, English. Place names, too, are the province of the Gallic imagination – from Trou aux Cerfs (Hole of the Male Deer) to Trou aux Biches (Hole of the Female Deer) and Curepipe, so named because it sits on an important crossroads where in the past the carriages would stop for passengers to take a stroll and drivers to clean out or 'cure' their pipes. The oldest church on the island is the Catholic Church of St François at Pamplemousses, built in 1759.

Thanks in great part to the business ethos instilled by Mahé de Labourdonnais, Île de France was the French East Indies Company's most profitable colony, and Port Louis a wealthy and sophisticated town. Although many changes have taken place in the intervening years, Labourdonnais would certainly recognize many aspects of the town were he to take a stroll today. Modern Port Louis still sits on the same regular grid pattern as his original with some of the buildings still extant. In the 1730s he oversaw the erection of Government House and Line Barracks – which was expanded under British rule and still houses the Police Headquarters – to bring

Below: *The French-built fortresses found at regular intervals around the Mauritian coastline formed a protective cordon against the British. Today very few are as well preserved as this example at Belle Mare.*

Above: Women prepare platters of beautifully arranged offerings for the gods at Grand Bassin, the holiest Hindu site on the island.

The towns of Mahébourg (founded in 1805 by Decaen, the last French governor of the island, just before the British took Mauritius) and the capital of the Seychelles Islands, Mahé, are both named after Labourdonnais who is credited with being the father of Mauritius.

Later during the French era, the marshy stream running through Port Louis was channelled and the surrounding land drained to create Company Gardens, now a wonderful place to relax during your sightseeing visit. The rows of immense mature ficus trees form a shady canopy enjoyed by numerous subsequent generations of Mauritians.

In 1748, just after Labourdonnais departed from the island (he was to meet an sad end, being thrown into the Bastille in Paris after a false charge of accepting a bribe was laid against him), a small fort or redoubt, known in French as Le Réduit, was built in the hills above Port Louis. By 1778 a mansion built on the site had became the official residence of the governor. Greatly renovated and expanded throughout the British era, today it's the official residence of the Mauritian President but, disappointingly, only open to the public on the last Sunday in August.

There are scant remains of defensive batteries built by the French dotted around the Mauritian coast, giving rise to names such as Pointe aux Canonniers. Most are little more than outer walls but they are best seen at Batterie des Grenadiers along the coast north of Port Louis, around Balaclava at Belle Mare, or north of Mahébourg. A well-preserved Martello tower at La Preneuse near Tamarin is the only complete French defensive structure open to the public and houses a small museum. Château Gheude in Mahébourg is probably the finest French-era mansion remaining – a beautifully proportioned building of three storeys with a magnificent stone twin-winged entrance staircase – though its rooms now house the collections of the National History Museum (*see* page 88).

Where the château offers a glimpse of the lifestyle of the colonial landowners, it's difficult to imagine the hardship suffered by the slaves except perhaps by watching today's workers during the sugar harvest when

both law and order to the island. The parade area – Place des Armes – on the waterfront in the heart of the town is little changed in dimension, though it now has a formal garden in place of an open drill arena, but the 20th-century high-rise Bank of Mauritius building might cause the old governor to raise an eyebrow.

long hard days are spent cutting, stacking and transporting the crop. There are few physical reminders of the era but the volcanic stone pond at Pamplemousses village is called Bassin des Esclaves because legend says that this is where the slaves were washed after their sea journeys before they were auctioned.

For the slaves the main form of escape was the sega (*see* page 78), an erotic and mesmerizing dance set to the simple music produced by home-made instruments and the chanting of mournful lyrics bemoaning a slave's lot, which would escalate into a rum-induced sexually charged frenzy as the evening went on. The contrast with the sedate courtly music of the plantation masters could not be more startling. But the main contribution of the early African and Malagasy slaves came from a rejection of the complicated conjunctions and tenses of the French language spoken by their owners. They melded a much more simplified French with African or Malagasy words to create Creole, a language that was used in the fields and now constitutes the lingua franca of Mauritius.

One can't examine the French influence on Mauritius without taking into account the effect of the French Revolution in 1789 – a pivotal moment for France metropolitaine, as the French call the mainland, but a total surprise to the colonies, and not a pleasant one. Until that time the colonists had been loyal to the motherland, but when news of the overthrow of the monarchy reached the island, the plantation owners were dismayed to discover that the rallying cry of the new regime, *Liberté, Égalité, Fraternité* (Liberty, Equality, Fraternity), also applied to the thousands of slave labourers that formed the backbone of the Île de France success story. This was anathema to the colonists and the major reason that the British didn't meet more resistance when they took the island in 1810. Even when peace was declared between the two nations after the fall of Napoleon and Mauritius was granted to the British, almost all of the French colonists chose to stay, setting the scene for an almost unique social structure where the colonial overlords were not the same nationality as, nor spoke the same language as,

the leading economic class. The fact that the French preferred to work under the British and that the British allowed them to keep their language, religion and customs – including Napoleonic Law – meant that all things French didn't slip into the realms of history but continued to enrich Mauritian society throughout the British era and into modern times. A prime example of this is the strength of Catholicism on the island. Two important churches built late in the British era are Catholic, not Anglican – the Cathedral of Port Louis (1932) and the pretty church of Notre Dame Auxiliatrice built in 1938 at Cap Malheureux; ther latter's coastal setting and distinctive red tiled roof make it one of the most photographed on the island.

The British Era

The British era would usher in the last great cultural and religious changes that contribute to Mauritian culture. These had little to do with British-ness per se, but lots to do with the lifestyle and beliefs of the natives of other British colonies in India and Asia.

The Impact of Hinduism

The enormous influx of peoples from the Indian subcontinent – half a million are said to have arrived with over 200,000 staying permanently – couldn't help but change every facet of life on Mauritius. The vast majority of the indentured arrivals were Hindus, and this colourful and energetic religion was in total contrast to the sober Catholicism of the French colonists and the starchy Anglican British. The first rainbow-hued Hindu temple was built at Triolet on the northwest of the island in the 1850s, and it's still the largest complex on Mauritius, but across the countryside images of the god Ganesha, complete with his elephant trunk, and voluptuous goddesses began to rise up between the palms and sugar cane. Every Hindu garden has a shrine to protect the family home and tiny shrines overlook island beaches.

During French rule Grand Bassin in the heart of the island was a simple freshwater crater-lake but Hindu

An Introduction to the Hindu Gods

All Hindus are trying to reach moksha, to be pure enough to lift oneself above earthly existence. Hindus believe in reincarnation, that each lifecycle offers the opportunity to work towards this state through self improvement. The Hindu gods exist in a different realm to the earthly, and rituals and devotions create a communion to entreat positive outcomes for self, family and mankind.

Major deities within the panoply include Vishnu, lord of preservation and sustenance who is accompanied on his journey by Lakshmi his wife, goddess of wealth and of courage; of offspring and success. Their partnership offers benevolence to every facet needed for a happy life.

Brahma, the lord of creation, was born from the navel of Vishnu. He is the provider of knowledge and wisdom while his wife, Saraswati, is the possessor of the ultimate knowledge. Together, they rule the search for moksha.

Ganesha, the elephant-headed god, is the most widely worshipped in his role as the remover of obstacles, while Hanuman, the monkey-god, is considered a wise sage with powers including the giving of courage and wisdom.

In contrast to the above positive deities, Shiva is the lord of destruction who works in cooperation with his consort Parvathi, goddess of disintegration.

---

worshippers transformed it by dint of a spiritual link with the sacred waters of the Ganges into a holy site – and today it is the location of one of the largest Hindu gatherings outside India. Worshippers take lake water for their religious rituals and offerings float on the surface. The hills around Grand Bassin, or Ganga Talao as its known to the faithful, now sport several temple complexes and a magnificent monumental statue of Shiva. Up to 300,000 Hindus crowd the area during major festivals.

Rituals and festivals are a major feature of Hindu worship. Small daily blessings can be as simple as sprinkling holy water on the feet of a statue of a god, leaving an offering of aromatic incense, flowers or a small oil-burning candle at the garden shrine. Weeks of cleansing mark the build-up to an important celebration when elaborate, colourful costumes are further enhanced with fragrant garlands. The Hindus brought with them the cult of body chastisement, undertaken during the festival of Thaipoosam Cavadee (see page 74), and the more frivolous shouting and throwing of coloured powder during Holi (see page 76), acts that must surely have shocked the staid Europeans.

The conservative structured frocks of the Victorian Christian colonialists were suddenly displaced by the vivid saris of the Hindu women – a flowing garment gracefully draped around the body – that created a kaleidoscope of colour on every Mauritian byway.

Even in relation to death the Hindu religion differed greatly from the Christian. Cremation of the body releases the spirit and is a compulsory ritual for all but the most lowly of castes, in contrast to the earthly interment of the colonialists and Creoles whose burial places are marked by ornate monuments or simple stones depending on personal circumstances.

There are some exceptional Hindu and Tamil temples across the island. The oldest and largest is at Triolet; it was begun in 1857 but expanded in the following decades. Other large temples can be found on Royal Road in Grand Baie and on Île aux Goyaviers at Poste du Flacq in the east, with smaller but equally exquisite examples being the Raimbel Drawbadhee Ammen Kovil at Raimbel in the south and Lord Dakshinamurti Temple between Belle Mare and Poste du Flacq.

Followers of Mohammed

Small *masjids* (mosques) can be found in all Muslim villages calling the faithful to prayer five times per day, but the finest mosque on the island is the Jummah or Friday Mosque built in the heart of Chinatown in Port Louis in 1895 – a proverbial confection of ornate white stucco whose interior is a peaceful haven from the hubbub of the capital's hot and busy streets, sheltered by the canopy of a huge Badamia or tropical almond tree.

Food for Thought

Dietary habits changed too. Rice became the staple carbohydrate and strong spices a compulsory element in island cuisine, gradually melding with the French dishes of the earlier colonial era to create a new range of dishes now known as Creole. Both Hindus and Muslims have strict religious rules relating to meat. Hindus don't eat beef or pork and Muslims are forbidden pork, so this encouraged the raising of sheep and goats at the expense of pigs and cows but also encouraged the degradation of the remaining tracts of natural vegetation by the indiscriminate nibbling of vast numbers of these voracious grazers. Tea was the national drink of India and much in demand from the new arrivals, so the British planted tea here too on a limited area of upland slopes. The island is self-sufficient in tea today and the Route du Thé (*see* page 90) tells the fascinating story of 'tea – when and how'.

Indian languages have contributed several interesting new words to the Creole lexicon but even today over 200,000 Mauritians speak pure Hindi, Urdu, Telugu, Tamil or Bhojuri at home, only engaging in Creole out on the street.

From the Far East

The Chinese were far fewer in number than the Indians but have certainly made their mark. A bustling mercantile Chinatown was founded in the heart of Port Louis that still thrives today. The Chinese community fanned out to set up village stores across Mauritius, their names proudly painted above the doors. Initially Taoist, many Chinese have adopted Catholicism since they settled on Mauritius, though there are a few oriental temples to be found and Chinese New Year is celebrated with relish.

Below: This Hindu shrine at Riambel in the south is typical of the smaller rural temples found at villages across the island where families will visit daily to make offerings. A guardian is responsible for keeping the temple clean and the gardens tidy.

RUE
Emmanuel ANQUETIL

P
Zone 1
Limit 2 hrs
Mon - Fri
Saturday

WAH L

The Freed Slaves

After the abolition of slavery, the freed descendants of the original Africans and Madagascans took refuge in the last remaining unpopulated parts of Mauritius, in the southwest and the deep south, to eke out an independent living. Today this area is still the most Creole part of the island, characterized by small rustic fishing communities with tiny shacks sitting at the heart of well-tended vegetable plots. The former animist Creoles embraced Père Laval's Christian teachings because he devoted his life to their welfare and spiritual development. Laval promoted a much more personal relationship with God that can still be seen in the southwest, with numerous Maisons de Dieu, or Houses of God, wooden shacks and sometimes even open spaces with simple altars, where people gather to pray. Sunday morning is a great time to be touring the south, when Christian families head to church dressed in their finest clothes, the older ladies sporting flamboyant hats.

The British Legacy

Aside from the official language, the education system and banking, the era of British rule has left behind a few sturdy tuff-stone reminders, but didn't 'stamp' its mark, preferring to work with rather than rule over the French colonists. Island society seemed to transcend the tensions of the greater colonial squabbles centred in Europe. The British even allowed the erection of a statue of Labourdonnais in 1859 in one of the most prominent locations in the capital directly across from the packet ship landing docks, the first sight new arrivals to the island would see.

The devastating fire in Port Louis in 1816 destroyed the majority of the wooden-built French-era buildings and left Governor Farquhar with an almost clean slate on which to

Previous page: Chinatown in Port Louis is one of the most colourful and atmospheric quarters of the capital, with its old colonial balconied buildings and street stalls. The shops here sell everything from feng shui tokens to Chinese herbs and medicines.

create the new stone-built city. Whole blocks to the north of the Place des Armes still have the colonial buildings erected in the wake of the fire. Many are difficult to see because they are festooned in cloth or clothes sold by bustling shops on the ground floor and street stalls block the view, but the first-floor balconies embellished with wrought iron are the big giveaway. In the same rebuild the British added a theatre, the first such palace of entertainment south of the equator. Fort Adelaide, the rather ugly castle above the town, was erected in the 1830s in the tense days just after the abolition of slavery, but the island held its nerve and there was little civil unrest. The British added a storey to Government House to create a fine administrative mansion, built a very handsome Post Office and erected the Mauritius Institute building in the 1880s as a fitting home for the study of natural sciences on the island. This is now the home of the Natural History Museum (*see* page 85).

At the northern corner of the Caudan Waterfront you'll find the old Customs House, the first port of call for all new arrivals before the opening of the international airport and now welcoming the merchant seamen or independent yachtsmen who reach the island by sea. The small run-down fortress and mill just behind now wait for a government-approved plan of renovation.

Further afield there are fewer British-era public buildings, though the court at Centre du Flacq is a listed Victorian building. There are, however, a number of private mansions including Eureka (*see* page 185) and St Aubin (*see* page 91) that reveal the relatively comfortable living conditions of the plantation owners. The château at Bel Ombre, the family home of Charles Telfair (plantation owner and amateur botanist) in the early 1800s, is now incorporated into the new Le Telfair Golf and Spa Resort.

An Industrial Inheritance

Of the over 250 sugar mills that sprang up when sugar was at its zenith, there are few comprehensive remains, though blackened mill chimneys stand sentinel above the sugar cane all across the island. The concept that this technology might be an important element in social history or architectural heritage is only very recent, so much has been lost. If a mill closed completely the stone would often be recouped and many old machines were simply discarded when new technology was introduced, so long-standing mills like Savannah or Britannia in the south look remarkably modern even though they were founded almost 200 years ago. The skeleton of the old mill at Belle Mare is reasonably well preserved, and the Café des Arts (*see* page 147) at Trou d'Eau Douce is housed in a wonderful and well-renovated mill building dating from 1840. Domaine Les Pailles (*see* page 95) does still have the last remaining traditional mill machinery so it is possible to see how sugar cane was processed in the early British era.

Of the once thriving rail network first opened in the Victorian era not a line remains. There's a train ride at Domaine Les Pailles, and a sole engine sits in lonely homage at La Vanille Reserve des Mascareignes, but at its peak the system had over 100 miles of standard track and carried thousands of commuters daily from the plateau to jobs in Port Louis, and tons of sugar and molasses from the plantations to the docks. What an asset it would have been to the tourism industry had the tracks not been pulled up and recycled.

One of the most absorbing glimpses of Mauritius throughout the late Victorian era and into the 20th century can be found at the Photography Museum in Port Louis.

Stamping a Mark on Philately

Philatelists have a special regard for Mauritius because the island has given them one of the rarest and most collectible of stamps. Being only the fifth country in the world to issue its own stamps, the very age of the earliest

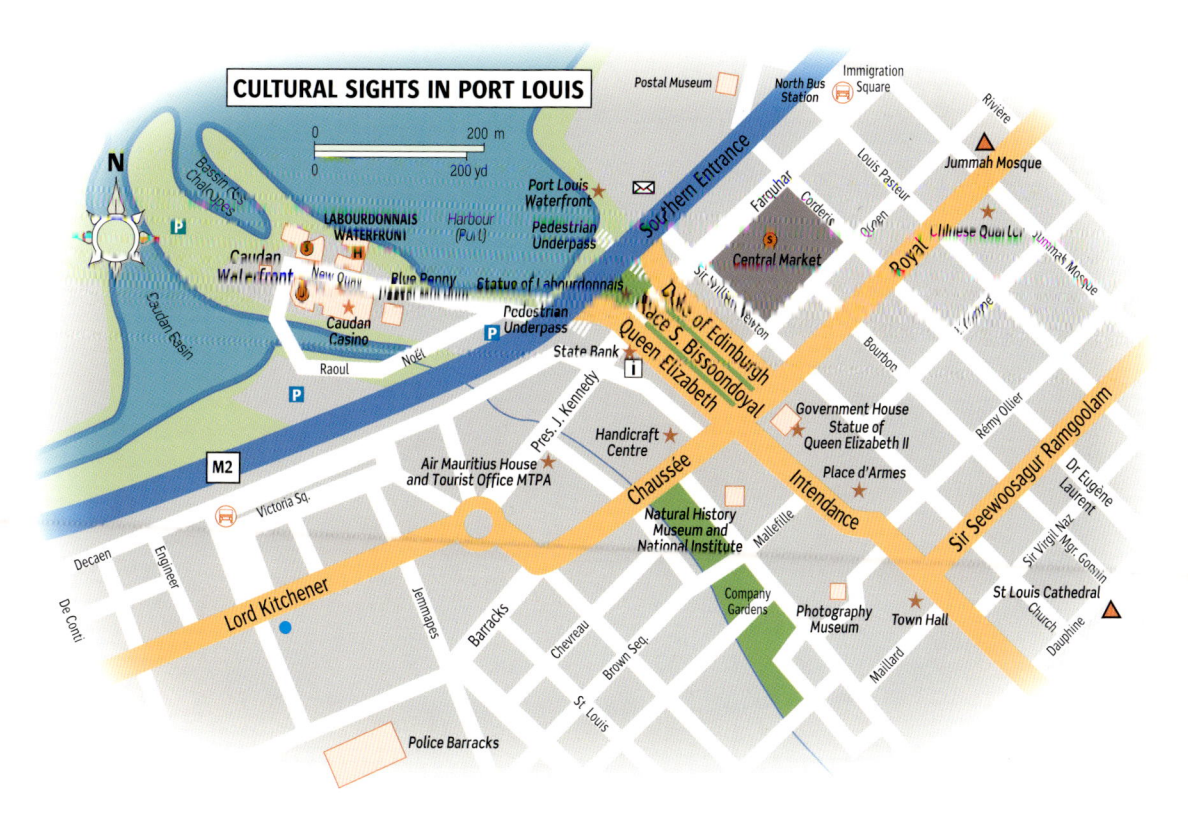

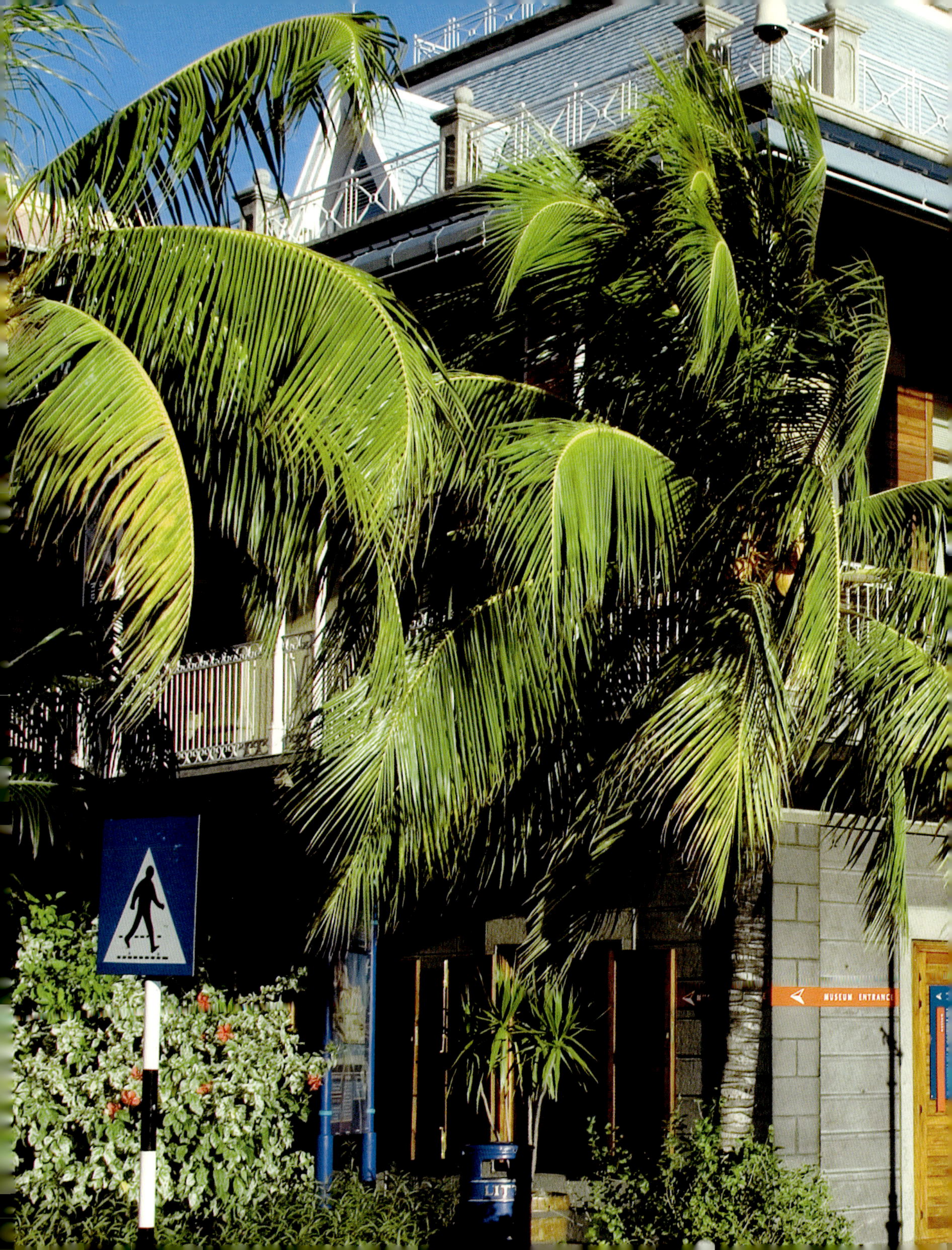
MUSEUM ENTRANC

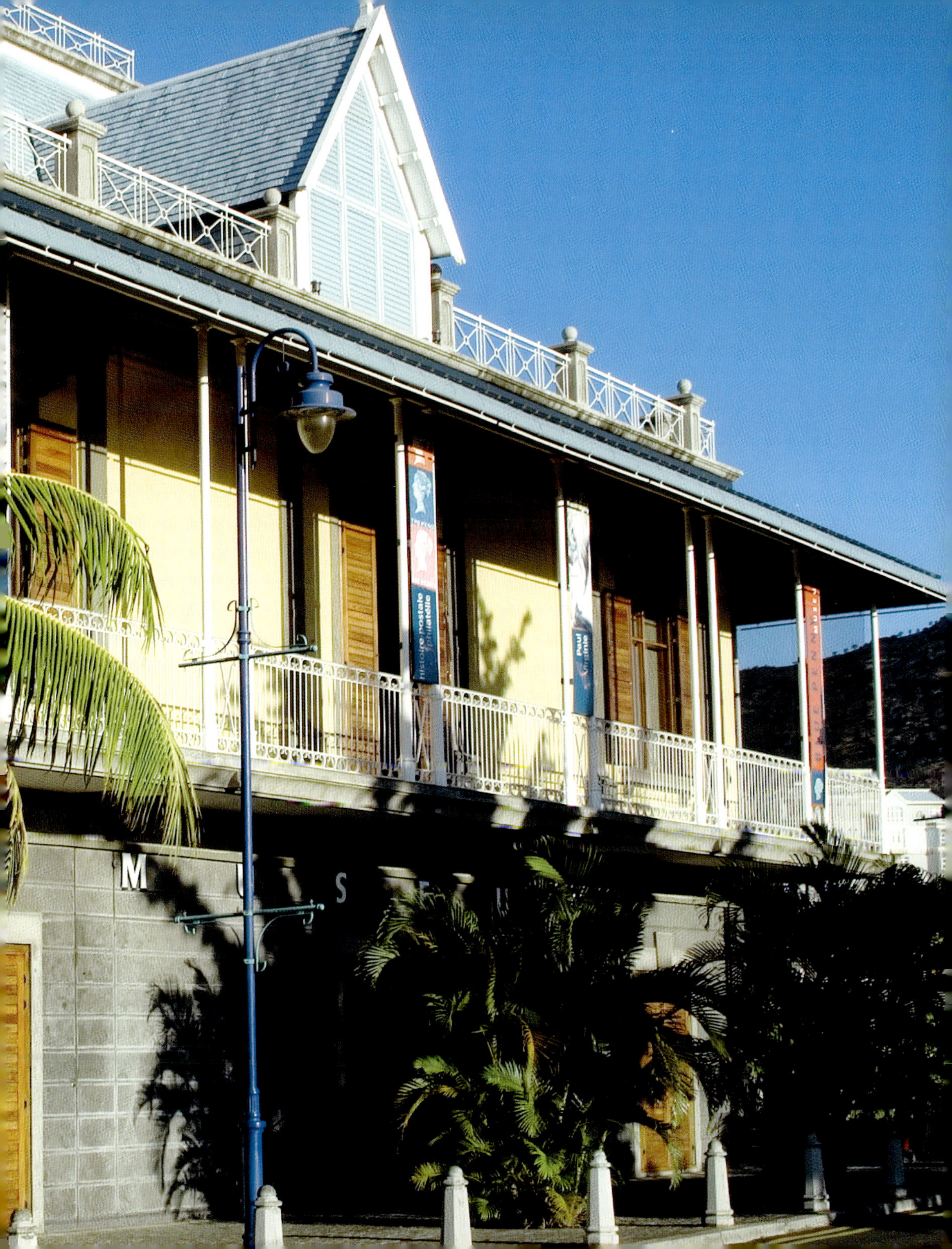
histoire postale
philatélie
Paul
Virginie

Previous page: The Blue Penny Museum at the Caudan Waterfront in Port Louis holds examples of two of the world's rarest and most valuable stamps – printed on Mauritius in 1847.
Above: The beautiful church of Notre Dame Auxiliatrice at Cap Malheureux is one of the most photographed buildings on the island.
Right: Downtown Port Louis is a mixture of modern high-rise buildings and older colonial-era architecture. The open-air cafés of the Caudan Waterfront offer a shady place for a cooling drink.

examples makes them valuable but the first print run of 1500 red one-penny and blue two-penny stamps in 1847 also contained a crucial mistake, having the words Post Office rather than the conventional Post Paid printed on them. Many of these stamps were bought immediately by the governor's wife and used on invitations to a ball she was organizing. Only two one-penny stamps are still known to exist while there are four unused two-penny blues. The Blue Penny Museum in Port Louis explains the background to the whole debacle and has originals of both stamps on display. Many other first-day covers and Mauritian stamps are on view at the Post Office Museum, next door to the main Post Office.

Late British-era buildings tended to be of the utilitarian variety – the first air terminal at what is now Sir Seewoosagur Ramgoolam International Airport at Plaisance or additions to the extensive docks and warehouses around Port Louis for example – though many of them have been swept away by further modernization in the later 20th century.

Mauritius Today

Mauritius is a young nation working hard to embrace its cultural history and diversity and carry it on into the modern era. At an official level this can be seen in the fifteen sanctioned holidays enjoyed by the people that include festivals of all the major religions, but it is more apparent in everyday life on the streets where there's a palpably relaxed atmosphere and Creole, Indo-Mauritian and Franco-Mauritian live side by side and respect their neighbours' beliefs and lifestyles.

The confidence that the country has developed since the transition to independence can be seen in the architectural monstrosity that is the new Parliament building in Port Louis, or the rather more appealing Central Bank building on the Place des Armes. The redevelopment of the Caudan Waterfront has breathed new life into the city, while up on the plateau the emerging glass towers of Cyber City will put Mauritius at the forefront of Africa's push into the high-tech age.

Of course the modern era brings its problems, not least the growing divide between the richest and poorest that has accompanied the economic growth of the last two decades. 'Old money' still talks, even in an age of universal suffrage, though the small number of landed colonial families who for many years held all the power find their influence waning. 'New money' is more likely to be Indo-Mauritian, with a generation of educated and energetic entrepreneurs exploiting the opportunities of the EPZ and two powerful Indo-Mauritian families also dominating island politics. The poorest areas are still the Creole south and southeast of the country but with adult literacy running at a worthy well over 80 per cent, the children of this coming generation may have more to say than their parents about this disparity.

All this is happening at a time when the island's economic mainstays – tourism, sugar and textiles – are going through major changes. The tourism industry, once considered a milch cow, must now be more carefully managed than ever. The island has been very successful in positioning itself at the luxury end of the market, but will need to be mindful of the environmental effects of future plans to avoid criticism from an ever more eco-concerned travelling public. Long-standing quota agreements in both the sugar and textile industries are due to lapse, with markets experiencing an increase in competition and price volatility. As recently as 1990 over 90 per cent of the cultivated land was given over to sugar cane, but mills continue to close. One has been saved for posterity and now offers one of the most absorbing socio-historical explorations of the island. L'Aventure du Sucre (*see* page 87) at Beau Plan tells the story of Mauritius and its sugar and intertwines the fate of the industry with island history, from the first sightings of the island by Arab sailors through the Dutch, French and British rule to the arrival of the modern era.

Celebrating the many and varied roots of its family tree has allowed Mauritius to break free from the last psychological vestiges of colonialism and stand tall as a fully fledged and inclusive nation.

Statues and Monuments

Grand statues and humble plaques tell some fascinating stories. The great and the good have their place but islanders also remember some lesser-known incidents and characters from Mauritian history. A stroll around downtown Port Louis brings you face to face with many of the historical 'big-hitters' of Mauritius. A majestic statue of Mahé de Labourdonnais dressed in his finest breeches presides over the Place des Armes looking out over the port he worked so tirelessly to create, and facing Labourdonnais across the main highway on the Caudan Waterfront is Sir Seewoosagur Ramgoolam with arms outstretched to embrace the island he spent a lifetime serving.

Outside Government House Queen Victoria appears less than amused as she looks out over her far-flung dominion. She never visited the island but her son, the future George V, unveiled the plinth for the statue during a short sojourn in 1901. The darker stone statue behind Her Majesty in the Parliament courtyard is that of Sir William Stevenson, governor of Mauritius from 1857 to 1863. A man ahead of his time, when he took office he arranged that native Mauritian civil servants should get the same pay and fringe benefits as ex-pat staff. The grateful employees paid for this statue from their own funds.

The Place des Armes and Company Gardens offer a plethora of smaller and less ornate tributes to the Hindu,

Taoist or Muslim lawyers, activists or doctors who contributed to the development of modern Mauritian society, including Manilall Doctor and Jean Alphonse Ravaton, better known as Ti Frère – the 'King of Sega' (*see* page 79).

The suburb of Ste-Croix is famed as the burial place of Père Laval where a gaudy statue marks the spot of his interment. The tomb is usually bedecked with flowers left by his followers.

Once you move out around the rest of the island the monuments become a little poignant, often commemorating lives lost. Poudre d'Or on the northeast coast has a simple monument to the passengers of the *St Géran*, the island's most famous shipwreck. Lost during a cyclone when it was dashed on rocks off Île d'Abre just offshore in 1744, the incident inspired the French writer Bernardin de Saint-Pierre to write his story *Paul et Virginie* (*see* page 84). Close by at Poste Lafayette on a treacherous rocky stretch of coastline you'll find a plaque to members of the Mauritian Special Mobile Force who drowned whilst undertaking an exercise in 1964.

Below: *Monuments dot the Mauritius coastline commemorating human stories and historical events, including this Monument to the Dutch, the site of the first landing on the southeast coast.*

Above: Hindus believe that the spirits of their gods and goddesses reside within their statues. Depicted here is the Goddess Kali who is the 'mother of time' and is often shown as a fierce, loathsome creature because no mortal can ultimately escape her power – as time passes we all age and die.

A South African Airways plane, the *Helderberg*, came down on the Cargados Carajos Shoals, a low-lying reef northeast of the island, with the loss of 160 lives. The cause of the crash was never identified but a large monument on the beach at Belle Mare remembers those lost.

On a brighter note, an Art-Deco monument at Mont Choisy commemorates the take-off point of the first flight from Mauritius to Réunion in September 1933 that set the scene for the founding of Air Mauritius.

In the far south at Baie du Cap there's a wonderful bronze relief depicting Matthew Flinders, an explorer who landed on the island in 1803 to make repairs to his ship without realizing that France and Britain were at war. The French thought he was a British spy and he was interned on the island for the following six years. Flinders, a fascinating character, was on his way back from Australia where he had been charting the coastline. His influence in the mapping of the southern continent is unrivalled save perhaps by Captain Cook. He proved that Tasmania was an island, and has several natural features such as mountain ranges named after him. He was also instrumental in promoting the name Australia above the then official name Terra Australis and is second only to Queen Victoria in the number of statues erected in his honour in the subcontinent. The sketches he drew while in low security detention on Mauritius during the latter part of his confinement make valuable historical documents.

Look out for the 18m high Millennium Monument on the plateau at Curepipe (close to the four-lane highway), an obelisk built of volcanic rocks erected to mark the island's transition into the 2000s.

Festivals

The pantheon of gods and prophets celebrated by the multitude of religions and sects across Mauritius means the island calendar is crammed with colourful and fascinating festivals. Mauritians will be more than happy to explain what's going on, but do ask permission before taking photographs and respect dress rules when entering places of worship.

Thaipoosam Cavadee: Hindu Tamil (January or February)

Probably one of the world's most dramatic religious festivals, for Tamils the Cavadee procession is the opportunity to suffer as proof of their faith and commemorates the suffering of Idumban who, while carrying a *cavadee* (yoke), was stabbed unjustly by Lord Muraga, son of Shiva, but resurrected by God.

Participants must undertake ten days of fasting and prayer before the festival to rid the body of negativity and evil, and on the day must complete many rituals, the most important of which is to work themselves into a trance which will help them through the coming trial, then to pierce themselves, just as Idumban was pierced at the time of his death, with *vels* (small needles) and metal spikes on the chest, back and around the face. Tongues are pierced to ensure that the adherents bear their pain in silence.

The *cavadee* is then carried through the streets towards the temple in the heat of the day, with the bleeding participants following behind. During the procession the faithful dress in bright fuchsia with the men being stripped to the waist. Their bodies are smeared with ashes from sacred fires. Women do not carry the *cavadee* but carry a pitcher of sacred milk on their heads that should reach the temple before it curdles. When the procession finally reaches the temple oil lamps are lit as a sign of good overcoming evil, offerings are made, and the *vels* are removed as prayers are performed.

Taking part in Cavadee is seen as something of a right of passage for Tamils. Children as young as six are allowed to join the procession but the whole process is voluntary and no-one is ever forced to take part.

Teemeedee: Hindu Tamil (late afternoons between October and March)

Less a festival and more a ritual activity, Teemeedee centres on fire-walking, an act which believers hope will grant them grace. They prepare for the ordeal by fasting, bathing, working themselves into a trance through meditation and affirmations, and undertaking a ritual blessing before they walk on the coals, which represent the flowing sari of Draupadee, a character in the *Mahabharat* (the epic Tamil historical text).

Diwali: Hindu Festival of Lights

Celebrated to honour Rama's victory over evil Ravana, this is the most joyous of the Hindu festivals. Lights welcomed Rama and his wife Sita back to his kingdom (Ayodhya) after 14 years in exile, so today every Hindu house is brightly lit with terracotta votive lamps. The same lamps are floated on the lake at Grand Bassin in their thousands to celebrate the strength of righteous-

Below: During the Teemeedee festival the faithful practise ritual cleansing before working themselves into a trance and walking effortlessly across hot coals. They show no sign of injury after undertaking this seemingly dangerous activity.

ness over evil and of enlightenment over ignorance. The flames represent the soul while the oil represents spiritual knowledge. Keeping the flame alight means an acceptance of enlightenment.

Diwali also celebrates Krishna's destruction of the demon Narakasuran and honours the birthday of Lakshmi, the wife of Vishnu and patron of prosperity. It's a time for new starts both spiritual and physical; houses are cleaned and debts settled, the kitchen gets new utensils and everyone buys new clothes. After the ritual prayers it is traditional that Hindu families visit their non-Hindu neighbours to share special sweets to celebrate the day.

Maha Shivaratree: or Shiva night

The god Shiva saved the world from Kaliyug, a period of intense darkness. Maha Shivaratree takes place at night and is a sombre vigil rather than a celebration; an appeal to Shiva help humanity turn back from darkness and negativity. Shiva has no bodily form so his spirit is celebrated in fire and smoke – two elements that can never be contained.

Thousands make the pilgrimage to bathe at Grand Bassin, which is connected spiritually to the great River Ganges in India. They carry holy water from the lake home to their local temples.

Holi

The destruction of evil Holika, Kasma and Putana means a triumph over the forces of evil, and the Holi celebration expresses a human 'love of life' – one day free from the shackles of everyday responsibilities.

On the night before Holi a bonfire is lit and an effigy of Holika is burned, along with household rubbish, as part of the cleansing ritual. Then everyone goes crazy, throwing handfuls of *gulal* (a red or yellow coloured powder) and water at each other, along with lots of loud music and jokes. All castes and classes enter into the spirit of Holi on an equal footing.

Chinese New Year

New year for the Chinese is all about spring-cleaning in preparation for a new start. Debts are paid, houses are painted and everyone buys new clothes. Chinese legend says that the spirits of the old year might appear to attack communities, so firecrackers are lit to frighten them away. Houses are decorated with images of the zodiac animal that represents the coming year, along with the auspicious colours: gold (wealth) and red (health and happiness). A prancing dragon, a symbol of strength and goodness, draws in the New Year.

No scissors or knives are used on the day and tradi-

***Left**: Chinese temples are now becoming rare on Mauritius, as many Taoists have converted to Catholicism; however, those remaining show exquisite detail. Their design echoes the natural landscape, allowing space for reflection and contemplation.*

tional foods include 'wax cakes' – rice, flour and honey. Although the major celebrations last for four days, life doesn't really return to normal for the Chinese until after the Festival of Lights, 15 days later.

Ougadi

This is the festival of Telegu New Year. The Telegu people originated from the southeast of India, principally from Andhra Pradesh.

Père Laval

Thousands of Mauritians of all religious faiths visit the tomb of Père Laval, patron saint of Mauritius, on the anniversary of his death, the 9th of September, to lay flowers and say prayers.

All Souls' Day (All Saints' Day)

A Catholic Christian celebration where families visit the graves of their ancestors to give thanks, clean the grave and lay fresh flowers.

Eid ul Fitr

The celebrations of Eid-ul-Fitr end the lunar month of Ramadan during which Muslims have undertaken a daytime fast and spiritual purification. Fitr means 'to break' in Arabic and indicates the breaking of the fast period but also the breaking with all bad habits of the past. The day begins with special prayers followed by family meals.

Ghoons

This dramatic Shiite Muslim festival commemorates the martyrdom of Hussein, the grandson of the prophet Mohammed, at the battle for the sacred city of Kerbala in Iraq in 680. Large papier mâché figures called 'ghoons' are carried through the streets and Shiites beat their chests and practise body chastisement to endure some of the pain felt during Hussein's death. For ten days before the procession the sound of drums fills the streets, building the atmosphere for the big day.

Above: *Sega music developed from the rhythmical drumbeats brought to the island by slaves from Africa. The ravanne – goatskin drum – keeps the beat and can often be heard on public beaches at weekends when musicians have impromptu jamming sessions.*

Music and Dance

The traditional music of Mauritius takes its heartbeat from the cadences of the homeland of the original slaves. Called sega, the music was a lament for their lost African homelands in an existence when they had nothing beyond their memories, their voices and their bodies. It had strong and pounding rhythms that raised the blood and was one of the few expressions of humanity that could not be controlled by the slave masters.

The high-energy dance eased the stresses of a life of slavery and, post slavery, a life of hard drudgery, and contrasted sharply with the formal courtly music of the masters and colonialists in their elegant mansions. The Creoles would gather at the beach in the evenings, enjoy a few rums around a camp fire and dance themselves into oblivion. Some sega had a ritualistic purpose in the animist beliefs of the Africans and Madagascans, with certain refrains and songs being particular to birth, marriage or death, but as Christianity replaced paganism, it lost this role and became purely identified with pleasure and the need to escape from a seemingly endless lifetime of pain.

The music of sega provides rhythm, not melody, and in that sense almost any musical instruments – improvised or otherwise – could perform the job. The dance could be performed any time, anywhere, with spontaneity being the name of the game. Initially the twang of the *bobre* – a bowed slat of wood that was slapped with a rod – was a regular part of the ensemble, but over time a trio of instruments became inextricably linked with the music and these were fashioned from readily available materials. The strong background beat that fuels the sega is provided by the *ravanne*, a taut goatskin stretched over a hollow drum. High tones are supplied by the triangle – three sides of metal easily fabricated from waste found around the plantations. The element that completes the band is the *maravanne*, originally a dried *calabasse* (calabash) filled with stones but now a thin wooden box filled with dried peas, that provides a rhythmical rasping accompaniment.

The tempo is measured as the sega starts but gradually builds towards a climax over time. In the early days the vocal performances were totally impromptu though today there are many sega 'standards'. The refrain begins by lamenting the lot of the labourer (the singers and musicians are still always men), a phrase repeated by the whole ensemble, but the sentiment soon changes as the working day is forgotten. The female dancers wear brightly coloured full-length skirts edged with ruffles which they swirl provocatively in front of their male counterparts, their bare midriffs gyrating with the musical beat. They then fall into the sand, bending over backwards to make flirtatious eye contact with the men while they thrust their pelvis skyward in a move called *en bas en bas*. There's no touching, but tantalizing close passes raise the psychological heat while the crowd shouts words of encouragement in rhythm with the drum beats.

Traditionally, eventually sated by their exertions, both dancers and musicians would slow the beat once again and dances would last many hours with different singers and dancers joining in a kind of Terpsichorean round, with the bystanders singing and clapping in encouragement and appreciation of the progression, but in public performances today they build to a high-energy finale for maximum 'showbiz' effect.

It's interesting to note that until the arrival of mainstream tourism, sega was in decline as standard forms of mass-market popular music – including rock and roll – looked set to push it aside. The demand for cultural performances in the major hotels raised its profile, though older Mauritians are quick to point out that the sega

Jean Alphonse Ravaton

The most influential exponent of 20th-century sega is universally acknowledged to be Jean Alphonse Ravaton, also known as Ti Frère, born in Quartier Militaire in 1900 into a musical family who played at colonial soirées across the island. He built his reputation at 'pariages sega', evening contests put on at villages throughout the island where the audiences and dancers would judge the winner. The rebirth of the art form can be said to be traced back to the 'Night of the Sega' held on 30th October 1964 at Le Morne, when Ti Frère was voted the 'King of Sega'. Ravaton died in 1990 but a commemorative bust of the singer can be found in Company Gardens in Port Louis. He is recognized as one of the modern cultural heroes who have shaped the island.

One of Ravaton's compatriots, Jacques Cantin, was the first artist to get sega out to a radio audience, while Serge Labrasse, a protégé of Ravaton, is a more recent exponent. Today, Cassiya is a popular island sega group with several albums to their credit, while Z'Enfants Ti Rivière are moving the music forward with the 'urban' sega which includes the use of electric guitars and other modern instruments.

danced in the 21st century is a rather sanitized version of what really should be a hot and steamy, sexually charged art form.

The heartland of sega today is still found in the traditional Creole region in the southwest of the island around Grand Rivière Noire. Sega enjoyed on sultry evenings on beaches in the shadow of the Morne are now part of Mauritian history, but you'll find impromptu *ravanne* parties on many beaches in the area, especially on Saturdays and Sundays when young guys hang out for the afternoon.

For those who want to know more about sega, the book *Sega: the Mauritian Folk Dance* by Jacques K Lee

Following page: *The traditional sega dance is at its most beautiful and energetic when the female dancers twist and twirl their colourful skirts. The most authentic performances take place on the beach at sunset around a flaming campfire.*

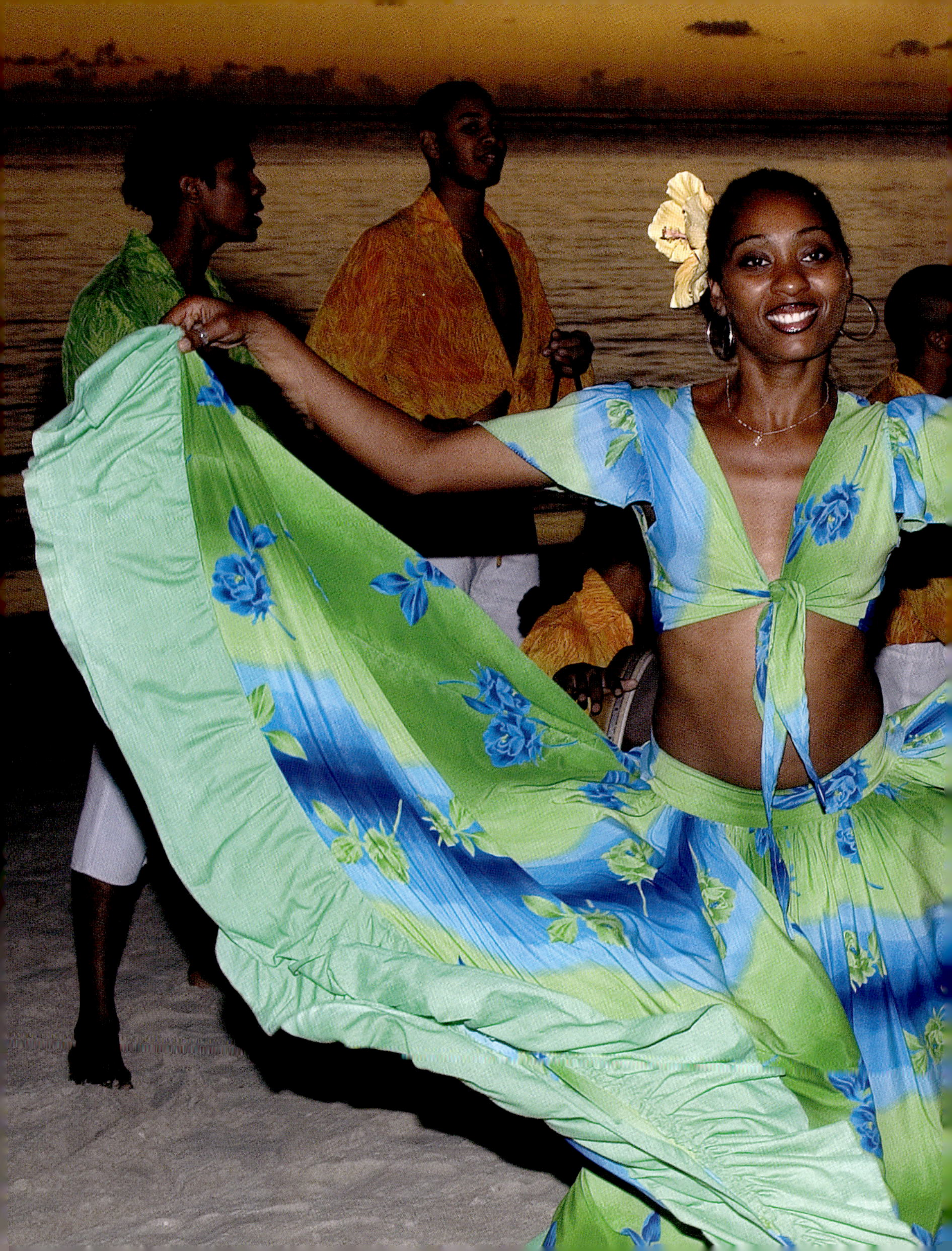

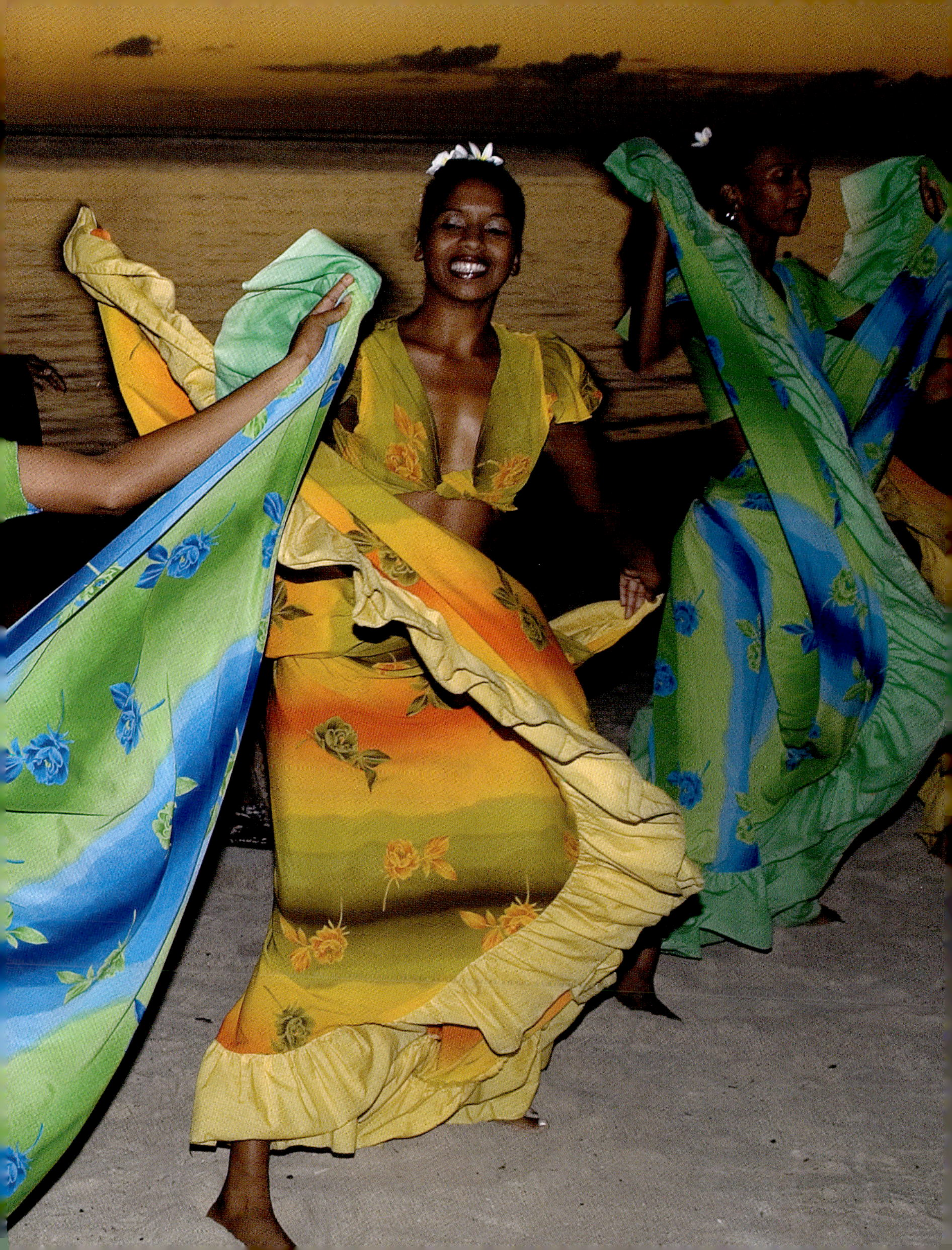

(Nautilus Publishing, ISBN: 0951129619) is available in bookshops and describes the historical antecedents and development of the art form along with information on the best sega performers.

Arts and Crafts

Throughout the colonial era the classic arts were the domain of the upper echelon families, both British and French. Well-connected and wealthy individuals could head to Europe for further study and hone their skills under the wing of talented mentors.

However, throughout the 20th century Indo-Mauritians and Creole Mauritians have increasingly been finding a voice and, since independence, the arts have become a little more mainstream.

Theatre

Despite its diminutive size, Mauritius has historically played, and continues to play in the present, an important role in theatre productions within the region.

The neo-Classical theatre in Port Louis was opened in the 1820s and is thought to be the oldest theatre in the southern hemisphere. Soirées here were the backbone of the colonial social season throughout the Victorian and Edwardian eras but the theatre began to show its age as the 20th century progressed. Restored to its former glory in the 1980s, it doesn't have a regular programme and the heartbeat of modern performance has moved up to the plateau along with the bulk of the Mauritian population.

Surprisingly, the interior of the rather gloomy-looking Fort Adelaide is also used for concerts and plays.

The Plaza Theatre at Rose Hill is the largest in the Indian Ocean. Opened in 1933, it was totally revamped and updated in the 1980s and is used for public performances of all kinds. It is home to a vibrant theatre company and invites local amateur companies to put on performances. There's also a regular programme of visiting ballet, opera and theatre in both English and French and more modern popular concerts.

Dev Virahsawmy, once a student leader and co-founder of the MMM political party with Paul Berenger (see page 55), is the leading light of the contemporary theatre scene. Born in 1942, he graduated from the University of Edinburgh with a good grounding in the three major languages of the island. During his career he has brought classical theatre to a Creole audience, translating Shakespeare's drama *The Tempest* and Molière's comedy *Tartuffe* into Creole, or *Maurisien*, as he prefers the language to be known. On a lighter note he also introduced Andrew Lloyd Webber and Tim Rice's musical *Joseph and the Amazing Technicolor Dreamcoat* to generations of Mauritian schoolchildren. Little known outside Mauritius, his own material is designed to disseminate the current Creole socio-political dynamic and includes the play *Li*, winner of the Concours de Radio-France International in 1981, but banned by the authorities in his homeland.

Left: *Port Louis's theatre is said to be the oldest in the southern hemisphere and was the heart of the colonial social scene during the Victorian and Edwardian eras. It was refurbished during the 1980s.*

Artists

Throughout the 20th century a handful of artists broke into the international arena. Hervé Masson (1919–90) is by far the most prominent, though he is remembered on his native isle much more as a social philosopher and political activist.

His family had a long history on the island, arriving in 1753 just after the era of Labourdonnais, but Masson was not a conservative by nature and was one of the earliest white Franco-Mauritians to join the left-wing Mauritian Workers' Party in the 1940s. He was a fierce advocate of independence and pro a Mascarene federation between Mauritius and Réunion.

Masson left the island for Paris in 1949 to devote himself to art, and his early work shows a definite Cubist influence, but he also wrote several important and influential treatises relating to the future of Mauritius during the 1960s. He returned to the island in 1970 to take up the political cause as a founder member of the socialist MMM along with Berenger and Virahsawmy. He was viewed as a possible member of the Ramgoolam coalition government but spent nine months in prison on the island in 1972. On his release he became estranged from his political allies and left once again for France to concentrate on painting. His later style softened the hard lines of Cubism, though he remained devoted to the abstract and to the tropical colours of his homeland. His work is on display in collections in the Musée d'Art Moderne de Paris in France and also in galleries in Germany, the Netherlands and North America.

A contemporary of Masson, Gaëtan de Rosnay, went to France to study art but returned to Mauritius to work on the family plantation before taking up painting full time. He was one of the founders of the Salon de la Biennale de Paris. He also died in 1990.

Andrée Poilly (b1905) started out as a teacher but she later formed an association with Masson, though her style was much more abstract than that of Masson. She emigrated to Britain but died in Canada, again in 1990.

Current artists include abstract painters, brothers Ismet and Firoz Ganti, and landscape specialist Yves David.

The Mahatma Ghandi Institute

The Mahatma Ghandi Institute in Moka is an Indo-Mauritian-funded institute that has a school of Mauritian, Asian and African Studies and a School of Indian Music and Fine Arts. It is one of the most active organizations in the promotion and development of the arts across the island and holds regular exhibitions and lectures.

Writers

Bernardin de Saint-Pierre is probably the writer most associated with Mauritius, though he was not a native of the island. His love story *Paul et Virginie* (1787) – the heartbreaking tale of star-crossed lovers, an allegory for nature corrupted by disingenuous sentimentality – wove narrative around a real-life event, the shipwreck of the *Saint Géran* off Île d'Ambre in 1744. The book was the toast of the French metropole (mainland France) and many French people still believe that the main characters actually existed.

The poet Robert Edward Hart is the island's most famous native writer. Born in Port Louis in 1891, he was the son of an academic and took over as librarian of the Mauritius Institute from his father, publishing works on the back of his stipend. He was honoured by both the British and French governments for his artistic achievements. He retired to Souillac in the deep south in 1941 and after his death in 1954 the government purchased his small coral cottage as a museum. Reopened in 2003 after a comprehensive renovation programme, the collection contains many of Hart's manuscripts and works plus personal possessions including his much-loved violin.

As the 20th century unfolded, the seeds of a growing social consciousness brought forth another generation of writers. Malcolm de Chazal (1902–1981) was a prolific author famed for his unique essays on philosophical thought – *Pensées* and *Sens-Plastique* – but like Masson he crossed the boundaries into different artistic genres and was also a successful contemporary naïve artist.

Eduard Maunick (b1931) is a mulatto (of mixed white and Creole blood) who laments the lot of his people, discriminated against by whites and blacks, in his poetry. He wrote much of his best work in Paris.

Left: *The ill-fated lovers* Paul et Virginie *are eponymous fictional characters whose story is woven around a real-life event. This statue at the Royal Palm Hotel attests to their enduring popularity.*
Below: *Built in the 1880s, this fine neo-Classical building became headquarters for the Mauritius Institute. Today the ground floor houses the Natural History Museum with displays about the island's fascinating topography, flora and fauna.*

Other leading contemporary writers include René Asgarally, whose works include *Tension gagne corne* (1979), and Ramesh Ramdoyal, whose collected short stories *Tales of Mauritius* published in 1979 and 1981 have captured the essence of life in post-independence Mauritius.

The Natural History Museum

Founded in 1880, The Mauritius Institute was the leading academic body of its day – the product of the insatiable interest in earth sciences that pervaded society during the Victorian era – and collected a vast wealth of physical and intellectual research about the island.

Today the original grand neoclassical building that was built to house the Institute is home to the Natural History Museum, where an eclectic range of artefacts helps to explain the natural history of the island from its volcanic origin to the 20th century.

The collection of flora and fauna constitutes the most comprehensive on the Mascarene Islands and the present day museum also acts as a centre for research and information dissemination about the nature of the Mascarene region, past and present.

The museum has three permanent galleries. The first gallery concentrates on mammals, birds and reptiles

Left: The plant and machinery of the Beau Plan sugar refinery were in perfect working order when the refinery closed in 1999. They now form the backdrop for the L'Aventure du Sucre, a socio-historical exploration of the development of Mauritius.

where the star attraction, the genuine skeleton of a dodo excavated in 1900, is on show. Other specimens include a now extinct Rodrigues solitaire (a large bird) and a giant Mauritian lizard.

The second gallery displays preserved marine life, including an example of *Acanthocidaris curvastipina*, one of the rarest sea urchins still in existence (only three have been verified), a giant clam shell that weighs over 70kg, plus a mollusc, *Conus aulicus*, that is 7 inches long – that's a world record for this species.

The final gallery has displays on geology (including a model of a volcano), meteorology, corals and native woodland. Of several turtles' and tortoises' remains, the Sumaire's tortoise on show was brought to Mauritius by French Governor Dufresne in 1776. When it died in 1918 it was thought to be over 200 years old.

L'Aventure du Sucre

L'Aventure du Sucre tells the story of Mauritius and of the cane that transformed it, but more than this the attraction acts as an ethnological and historical museum in a way that the national collections don't – telling the story through the lives of real people, be they colonial overseers or the humblest workers.

Sugar has long been the economic lifeblood of Mauritius, the wellbeing of the people tied up in the ebb and flow of its fortunes. In its heyday there were almost 300 cane factories and world demand was soaring, but this was an industry built on slavery and crisis loomed for the colonial plantation owners when the system was abolished in 1835. It was sugar that brought more than 200,000 Indian indentured labourers to the island in the 1800s, transforming the cultural and physical landscape. Throughout the 20th century the sugar-cane market became increasingly volatile and prices dropped steadily, squeezing profits and family fortunes, but even today production accounts for 19 per cent of Mauritian exports.

The museum is housed in the vast cane factory of Beau Plan, a plant that was still producing sugar in 1999. Finally beaten by a contraction of the industry, it closed its doors as a commercial entity, but the machinery wasn't scrapped and now forms the physical backbone of your social journey. Every step in the process, from the crushing of the cane stalk to the boiling and reducing of the liquid into molasses and hard cake, is explained and the machines, bearing the names of illustrious engineering companies in the heartlands of northern England and Scotland, look as though they could have been turning only yesterday.

Woven amongst the impressive physical remnants of the factory, a fascinating human story unfolds. Firstly the important question: 'Why sugar?' is comprehensively answered by explaining the convoluted workings of the trade routes of the early colonial era and the major players including Labourdonnais and even Surcouf, the brigand, make an appearance in reproduced paintings and prints.

Slavery is not swept under the carpet here and the heart-wrenching results of the violent capture and removal of humans from their African and Madagascan homelands to a life of perpetual servitude is told with candour and realism.

Only a few decades later when slavery was abolished, the reality of what freedom meant to a generation of men and women without choices is also explored.

As time moves on impressions on canvas give way to sepia-tone as Victorian-era Mauritian families of all classes and castes flocked to be photographed and the first socio-ethnologists sought to capture the reality of life in the mansion house and in the fields. Photographs show the stations of the Mauritian railways crowded with commuters, and horse-drawn taxis plying their trade in downtown Port Louis, where the clattering of hooves on the volcanic stone cobbles was a distinctive and unforgettable sound for visitors. Gradually the images become more modern, leading on into the 20th century. Fashions change, motorized vehicles and ocean liners replace steam packets – finally it dawns on the visitor that 'king sugar' is the only constant through all the technological and social changes.

The final gallery of images is displayed in the last remaining flat-bottomed barge that was used to ferry processed sugar from the quayside to the ships anchored offshore. This system of shuttling cargo from the Port Louis wharfs was only abandoned in the latter half of the 20th century when a modern container and bulk port was completed.

L'Aventure du Sucre is the most complete and successful recent attraction on the island and is a must for anyone interested in the flesh and bones of island history. The attraction is certainly worth taking a couple of hours over – especially to read the personal stories told by the indentured arrivals in the late 19th century of how they journeyed from India and China and how they coped with the first few years on the island.

The National History Museum

One of the finest and oldest remaining French colonial mansions makes a fitting home for the Mauritius National History Museum. Chateau Gheude, built around 1722, was in private hands until 1947, when it was acquired by the government who loaned it to the Mauritius Institute with the express purpose of creating a museum. After renovation work in the late 1990s, it was reopened as a national museum in 2002.

Now a listed building, the house alone would be worthy of a visit. The renovation process has not been too drastic and it still has wonderfully worn woodwork and creaky floorboards as befits its age.

The National History Museum explores the social and cultural history of Mauritius throughout the colonial era to the beginning of the 19th century. The dry and rather old-fashioned presentation of the artefacts is a disappointment but this doesn't negate their historical importance. Coupling a visit here with a visit to L'Aventure du Sucre (*see* page 87) is a good idea as the

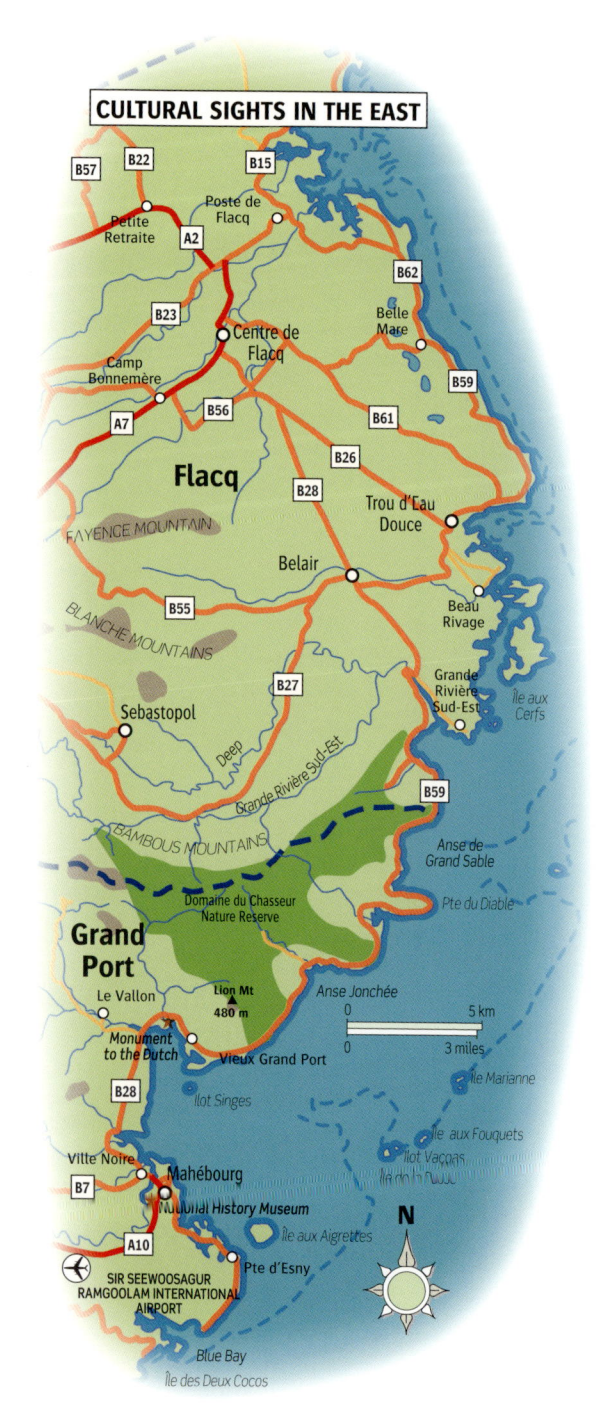

The National History Museum

Above: Built by the French in around 1722, Chateau Gheude now houses the National History Museum with an interesting collection of maps, documents and other artefacts plus items found during recent marine archaeological excavations. The house became a field station for sailors wounded during the Battle of Grand Port off Mahébourg in 1810.

two differing presentations are complementary.

The ground floor concentrates on the early colonial eras, ending with the Anglo-French Wars. The 1568 astrolabe, salvaged from the wreck of the *Banda* which went down just offshore in 1615, is a rare example of this navigational instrument and the third oldest to be found anywhere in the world. Chinese porcelain dating from the Ming dynasty (1575–1620) indicates the range of the Dutch trading links at the time.

One of the highlights of the French period rooms is the simple wooden bed used by Mahé de Labourdonnais during his custodianship of the island. Several mid-18th-century maps show Mauritius as Île de France and there's a collection of portraits of bullish French officials. A bronze bell is the finest artefact recovered from the *St Géran*, sunk off the northeast coast in 1744 during a fierce storm. Lithographs of the fictitious star-crossed lovers Paul and Virginie reinforce ties with the ill-fated ship.

The beautifully preserved palanquin, an early 19th-century form of transport, makes one of the few direct references to slavery. This wooden conveyance had to be carried on the shoulders of four slaves. They would then have to march over the rough terrain of the interior at a time when men were cheaper than horses.

There's a whole room devoted to the Battle of Grand Port – the 1810 naval encounter between the British and French that resulted in Napoleon's only success at sea – with military artefacts salvaged from ships and oil paintings depicting the action. The sabre of French Captain Drieux and the sword of British Captain Rivington are on show. The commanders of the two fighting forces were both treated for their injuries at the mansion after the skirmish and were said to have become goods friends.

The second floor concentrates on the period of British rule, the development of the sugar-cane industry and the arrival of indentured labour. Furniture and artefacts from the Victorian era are supplemented by some interesting photographs and paintings of Victorian and Edwardian Mauritius.

One fascinating and personal exhibit is a small cache of Indian coins, thought to be the life savings of an anonymous indentured labourer which had been hidden and lain undiscovered for almost 100 years.

Above: Tea-pickers in the Mauritian highlands have a daily quota to fulfil. Only the youngest and freshest leaves are used to create the infusion, so the bushes are cut regularly to encourage new growth at about waist height. Picking starts as early as sunrise when the air is cool, hence the heavy jacket and scarf worn by the picker. Most workers have their quota at the tallyman weigh station by 10:30 when they receive money according to how many kilograms of leaves they have picked.

The Route du Thé

Tea oiled the colonial wheels of the British Empire and, though the bulk of it was grown in India and Ceylon (now Sri Lanka), the highlands of Mauritius were also deemed suitable. Today the island produces enough tea for its own domestic market and Mauritian tea is also used to 'bulk' out more expensive or aromatic crops. The Route du Thé (Tea Route) combines three historical attractions – each with a tea connection.

The tea plantation at Bois Cheri is the most important producer on the island and opens its factory to visitors throughout the year. You'll need to arrive early to watch the tea-pickers in action in the surrounding fields as they have usually fulfilled their quota by 10:30. The plucked leaves (only the youngest shoots of the tea bush) are transported to the factory where they are left to dry overnight before being cut, fermented, dried, graded and bagged.

The factory processes 40 tonnes of leaves per day during the summer but less than 15 tonnes in winter (May–October) when the lower temperature means the plants grow more slowly. However, the previous day's crop is always processed each morning, so you'll be able to watch the whole process.

The fascinating museum on site charts the development of the plantation from its founding in 1892. Photographs show the various incarnations of the factory over time and explain the well-established tea routes and how the trade was organized and prices set by the tea auction house in London.

The mansion at Domaine des Aubineaux in Curepipe was built in 1872 for the family that owned Bois Cheri. Much of the furniture on display is younger than the building but it all belonged to the family.

St Aubin in the south of the island forms the final part of the triangular route. Once a leading sugar-cane estate, the owners have diversified into various other fields. There are several interesting attractions in the grounds of the family mansion, built for Pierre St Aubin when he founded the domaine in 1819. The ground-floor rooms are still decorated with a range of furniture belonging to the St Aubins, while upstairs a comprehensive range of photographs chart the history of the family and the development of the estate.

Behind the mansion is the St Aubin distillery, a small and very successful brand producing 300 bottles of rum a day. You can see the whole process, from the crushing of the sugar to the diluting and flavouring of the 40 per cent proof rum that's the standard commercial strength. White rum agricole, the kind they put in your rum cocktails, sits for 10 days, while the aged rum matures in oak casks for five years.

Across the garden is the Vanilla House where you'll be able to see these aromatic pods drying during the season (or a video explaining the process out of season), then take a tour of the anthurium sheds where these popular tropical blooms are grown under protective nets.

Le Saint Aubin mansion also offers delicious table d'hôte lunches. Tables are set out on the old veranda with views out across the formal lawns.

La Vanille Reserve des Mascareignes

The most versatile attraction on Mauritius, La Vanille Reserve des Mascareignes is difficult to sum up, being part farm, part zoo, part conservation project and part botanical gardens.

Children will be awe-struck at the gargantuan Nile crocodiles on view here. Up to four metres in length, they lie motionless in their pens, jaws parted to show rows of gleaming teeth. The open jaws may look threatening but in fact it's not that they are about to strike; crocodiles lose heat through the skin of the mouth so in effect they are just keeping cool. The crocodiles are not native to Mauritius – there's not sufficient mature river environment on the island to support a population and the water is too cold – and the 100 here were imported when the park opened in 1985. They seem to thrive here in captive conditions, and La Vanille farms them to produce an income from the skin and meat.

La Vanille gets the epithet Reserve des Mascareignes because of its giant tortoise conservation project. This is the largest reserve for Aldabra and radiata tortoises

Above: *Crocodile species from all around the world are on display at La Vanille Reserve des Mascareignes. Some of the species are farmed, but the attraction offers several other eco-animal displays and is an important centre for the breeding of giant tortoises that are being used to repopulate nature parks and protected areas across the Mascarene chain. The tortoise savannah is home to hundreds of adult animals, and the tiny hatchling tortoises in the nursery are incredibly cute.*

in the world. Over 300 of these magnificent reptiles live in an open savannah ecosystem that has been designed to mimic the habitat of Mauritius before man arrived on the island. Of course the dodo is no longer around, so the park has substituted flocks of guinea fowl instead and they grub for food in the undergrowth. You can walk through the compound and even touch the tortoises, then take a look at the tortoise nursery where the diminutive one-year-olds totally belie their final adult size.

La Vanille is playing an important part in improving populations of tortoises and is breeding Aldabra tortoises for a new reserve on Rodrigues.

It's a fascinating fact that although adult tortoises need to eat 2kg of food per day, crocodiles only need 3–5kg of food per week. Both animals can store fat for when food is scarce and can live off these reserves for many months.

There are other native animals on show, including a friendly flying fox, the largest Mauritian bat species, and a rare Round Island skink. Examples of introduced species are a family of ravenous wild boars and a tribe of cheeky monkeys. There's a small museum with background information on the animals that were lost after man arrived. Another fascinating exhibit consists of over 20,000 species of butterfly, insect and spider collected and catalogued by Jacques Siedlecki, his labour of love over the last 30 years. Many of the beautiful iridescent butterflies and fearsome beetles come from Madagascar to the west of Mauritius, but others are from further afield in Southeast Asia.

The reserve is set on sloping land cleared for the introduction of tea but the crop failed and the plantation was abandoned in the 1840s, allowing native second-growth vegetation to return along with introduced tropical plants. There's a nature trail through the forest (take mosquito spray) where a freshwater spring feeds several ponds rippling with hungry koi carp.

Casela Nature and Leisure Park

Known to everyone on Mauritius as the 'bird park', Casela has expanded and reinvented itself over the last few years to offer many more mainly animal-based attractions. It has recently undertaken a restoration programme and hopes in the future to be approved to run conservation programmes and work with the Mauritian species threatened with extinction.

The collection started out with a few individual birds kept as family pets but has expanded over the years and now comprises an impressive 140 species – many thousands of beaks and bills whose constant quacking, squawking and tweeting coalesce to produce a wall of sound. The rarest species at Casela is the endangered Mauritius pink pigeon, but this decidedly understated bird, with its sober dusky and grey plumage and timid personality, doesn't attract half as much attention as the more colourful, cute and downright cheeky types that colonize the other aviaries.

Below The pink pigeon is one of Mauritius's most rare birds, though a concerted effort to build numbers is paying dividends. Casela Nature and Leisure Park has an example amongst its 140 more common species, plus Bengal tigers, macaques and giant tortoises.

Above: Giant tortoises were the major grazers on the lowlands of Mauritius before being made extinct by man (along with the dodo). Today a Mascarene species is being bred and introduced – and what characters they are!

Right: The cheeky macaws are some of the most popular residents among the 140 bird species found at Casela Nature and Leisure Park.

Most visitors are immediately attracted to the macaw aviary. These largest members of the parrot family sit one metre high from tip to tail and are as curious about their human audience as we are of them, climbing down the grille of the enclosure for a closer look. The spooning lovebirds are also a great favourite. Another species of parrot, scientific name *Agapornis*, they are known as lovebirds because when they began to be kept as pets, owners noticed that they kissed and snuggled each other, especially when getting ready to sleep. Elegant pink ibis, spoonbills and flamingos are amongst the water-loving species. They take their colour from their diet, which is rich in carotenoids – the same pigment that makes salmon pink. The birds filter this from the water when

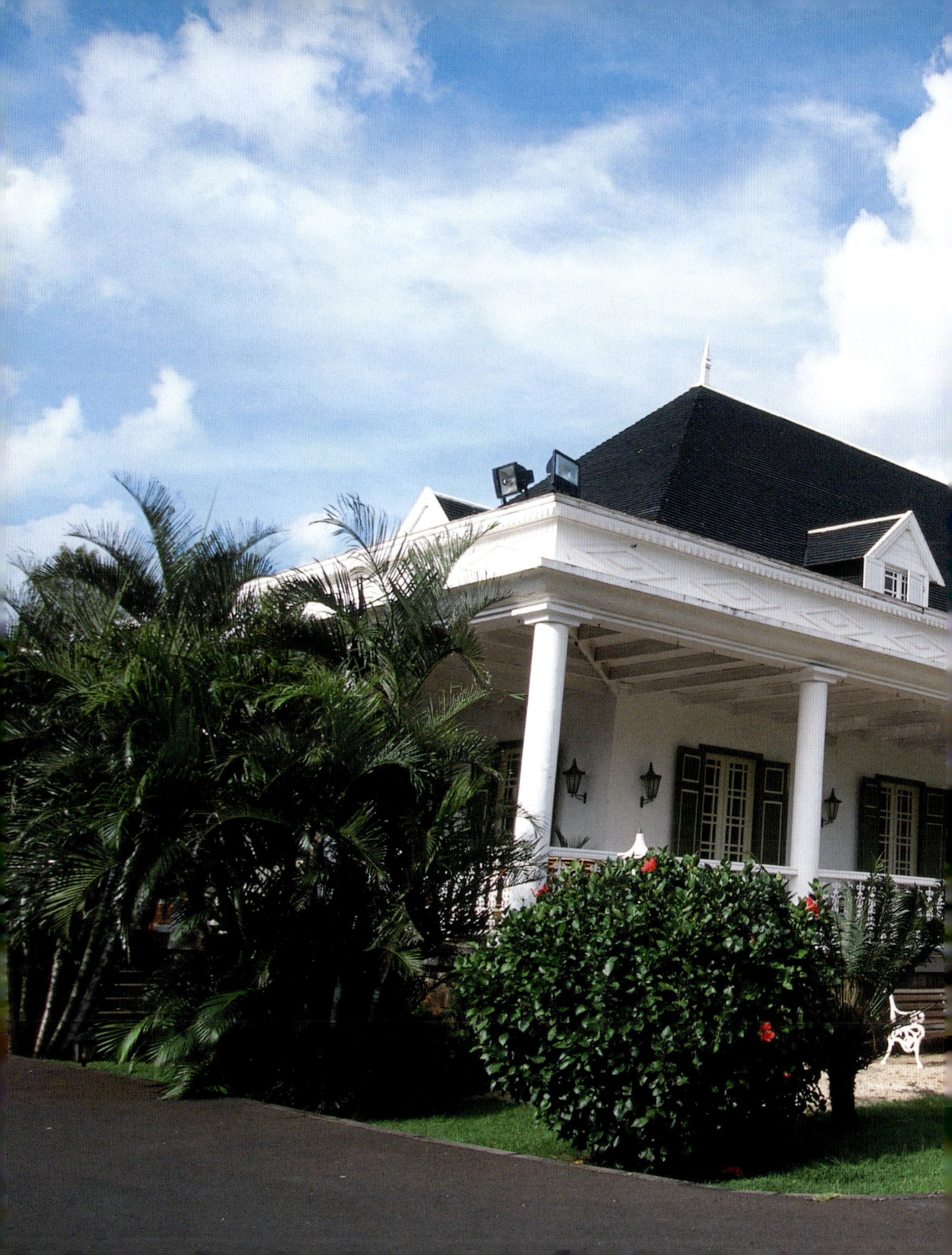

they feed; the strength of their body colour directly relates to the amount of carotenoids they eat because any excess is pushed through into their feathers.

Or you can enjoy a rainbow collection of budgerigars and some beautifully plumed exotic finches. One thing that's very noticeable, aside from the brilliant colours and patterns on the individual birds, is how differently they behave when in groups. Parrots, budgerigars and finches are all naturally gregarious birds, used to living in colonies. The constant interaction, either squabbling or mutual grooming, is fascinating to watch.

Aside from the birds, Casela has a rather eclectic collection of animals including a couple of impressive Bengal tigers who gaze haughtily out through the grille of their compound, seemingly oblivious to crowds of young visitors eagerly urging them to growl. The tigers look well fed, which is probably why they don't seem too interested in the noisy macaque family in the adjoining pen. Visit the giant tortoises in their walled enclosure. One of them is purported to be 150 years old. The petting zoo gives kids of all ages the chance to feed and stroke young fawns, goats, sheep and Cecile, the wild boar, or you can cast a rod onto the tilapia pool but you'll have to release any fish you catch.

Casela recently opened a sister attraction in 4500 hectares of adjoining reclaimed lowland savannah. Casela Yemen adds to the animal theme with a safari ride through the grassland where populations of Java deer and introduced African animals such as ostrich, zebra and antelope roam. The attraction also offers outdoor action sports such as *via ferrata* (climbing on a preset course with fixed hand and rope holds), quad-bike riding and mountain biking, or Creole evenings by the fire in an open-air encampment.

Domaine Les Pailles

Nestled in the lee of the Moka Mountains just south of Port Louis, Domaine Les Pailles was never the site of a plantation, but the clever idea of a savvy Mauritian businessman in the 1980s. He brought together a series of historical attractions and fun activities across just over 1200 hectares (3000 acres). It's probably the nearest thing to a theme park that Mauritius has and there's a little bit of something for the whole family.

On the beautifully lawned plateau you can take a tour of several recreated and historically important buildings. The ox-driven sugar mill was a standard feature of every cane plantation during mid-18th century when it was built, but animal power was superseded by steam, and now it is unique on the island. The juice produced at the mill passes directly to the Queen Distillery, built in 1757, where Domaine Les Pailles rum is distilled. Production is small scale but the results are excellent. You can tour the distillery and watch the process before tasting a range of young and aged examples. In the Coffee Hut you can watch beans harvested from the surrounding hills being grilled and milled, and the Aloe Vera Hut showcases traditional basket-making crafts using the dried and prepared leaves of this tropical succulent. An International Museum of Masks is one of the more unusual and perhaps least strictly Mauritian attractions at the domaine – with ceremonial and decorative examples from around the world.

The old steam train *Lady Alice* takes a stately tour of the grounds. This is the only working engine on an island that once had a thriving railway system. Or you can choose to take to an old-fashioned landau drawn by a handsome steed. Both are favourites with children. The domaine caters specifically to youngsters with a Children's Corner (for the over-fives) featuring a playground and pony rides.

All these activities take place on compact and neatly manicured grounds, but the domaine has many hectares of forest, especially around the northern foothills of the Moka mountains and stretching northeast towards Port Louis, that offer a different kind of experience. For sedate exploration, take a horse ride through the countryside; there are several trails and the domaine runs a full-day trek with a delicious picnic lunch included.

If all things equine aren't for you then try something a little more technical. Get off the beaten track on a Land

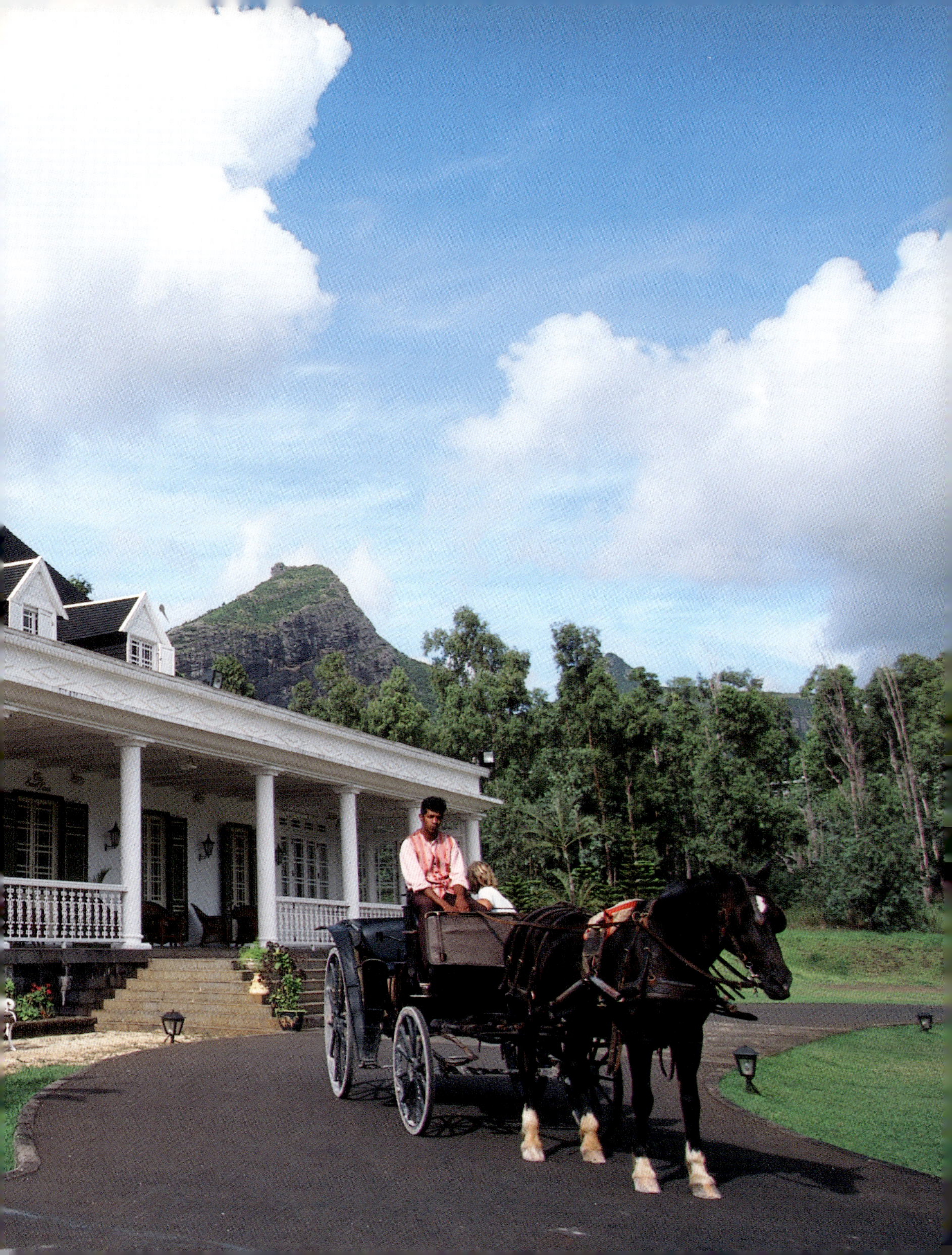

Rover Safari where your driver heads into the hills through dense forest over some rough terrain to spot deer or wild boar, stopping for refreshment at The Lodge with its high-rise panoramic views. Or try a rip-roaring quad-bike ride where you are in control – hopefully – of one of these powerful little fun machines as you tear across the terrain. You can combine activities at Domaine Les Pailles and spend the whole day here.

Food is pretty important at Domaine Les Pailles. There are four formal restaurants on site, each with a different type of cuisine. Clos Saint Louis is the most up-market, with a colonial mansion setting and a formal French and Mauritian menu (Monday–Saturday for lunch, Friday and Saturday evenings); La Dolce Vita (see page 145) is an authentic Italian trattoria (daily for lunch, Wednesday, Friday and Saturday for dinner); while Indra serves refined Indian cuisine (Monday–Saturday lunch and dinner) and Fu Xiao offers excellent regional Chinese dishes (Sunday–Friday lunch and dinner, Saturday lunch).

If you only want a snack try the Spicy Hut where you can find out about the spices traditional to Mauritian cuisine – all grown on site – and where fresh samosas are made every day, or head to The Lodge up in the hills where you can accompany your meal with panoramic views out across the countryside.

As night falls the emphasis of the domaine changes. In addition to the restaurants there are regular sega shows, and the Casino de Domaine opens nightly, giving you the chance to 'break the bank' or 'lose your shirt' at the roulette wheel or blackjack table.

Island Itineraries

Mauritius tour operators offer many well-organized pre-set tours that take in the major natural and cultural attractions on the island; however, it's easy to explore independently. Even if you don't want the hassle of renting a car and driving yourself, hiring a taxi by the day is an inexpensive option and you can do as little or as much as you desire. Here are a few suggestions to help you plan your days.

Delights of the North

Start the day at the Sir Seewoosagur Ramgoolam Botanical Gardens at Pamplemousses before the sun gets too high and hot. Engage the services of a guide to get the inside story. Just opposite the main car park of the gardens is the Comptoir des Mascareignes shopping mall for a spot of retail therapy. It also has a café.

Less than a kilometre from the gardens is L'Aventure du Sucre, the most interesting socio-historical attraction on the island. Le Fangourin, the café-restaurant here, offers a range of dishes for lunch.

Travel north along the main road, not the four-lane highway, to Triolet, said to be the longest village on the island; the Hindu temple here is the oldest and the largest. The guardian is a mine of information in return for a small donation. Finally, go to Grand Baie, the biggest and most bustling resort on Mauritius.

Fun in the Southeast

The birthplace of modern Mauritius, Fort Frederik Hendrik at Vieux Grand Port makes a suitable start to the tour. The small museum contains an interesting collection of artefacts found on the site.

From here, drive south to Mahébourg, the island's second city, to stroll the late French-era streets, enjoy the river views and visit the National History Museum charting development during colonial times.

Return north for a typical Creole lunch amidst magnificent scenery at Domaine du Chasseur, then take a stroll into the hills to spot a rare kestrel or more numerous deer, before heading back down the hill to explore the fragrant delights of Domaine de L'Ylang Ylang.

Central Highlands

You'll need to start early to watch the tea-picking at Bois Cheri. Visit the factory for a fascinating back-room tour and a tea-tasting session. Head further into the hills to Grand Bassin, the most holy Hindu site on Mauritius, with a collection of temples set around the volcanic lake and a monumental statue of Shiva dominating the skyline.

Island Itineraries

From here it's only a ten-minute drive to the Pétrin Visitor Centre in the Black River Gorges National Park where you can take a walk in the forest. Carry on west and stop for a late, and well-deserved, lunch at Varangue du Morne before finishing the day at Chamarel, to view the 'seven-coloured earth' and the forest canopy at Parc Aventure.

The Far South

Visit the cottage owned by poet Robert Edward Hart (1891–1954) in the final years of his life, now a museum to his memory. North is St Aubin, a historic plantation with a mansion, distillery and vanilla house. Have lunch here on the veranda before spending the afternoon at La Vanille Réserve des Mascareignes, with its animal collections and tropical trails.

Previous page: The Mauritius of yesteryear is brought to life at Domaine Les Pailles.
Below: Single-storey rustic stores with colourful shuttered façades are the mercantile heart of every village in Mauritius, carrying an array of items from biscuits to fishing tackle.

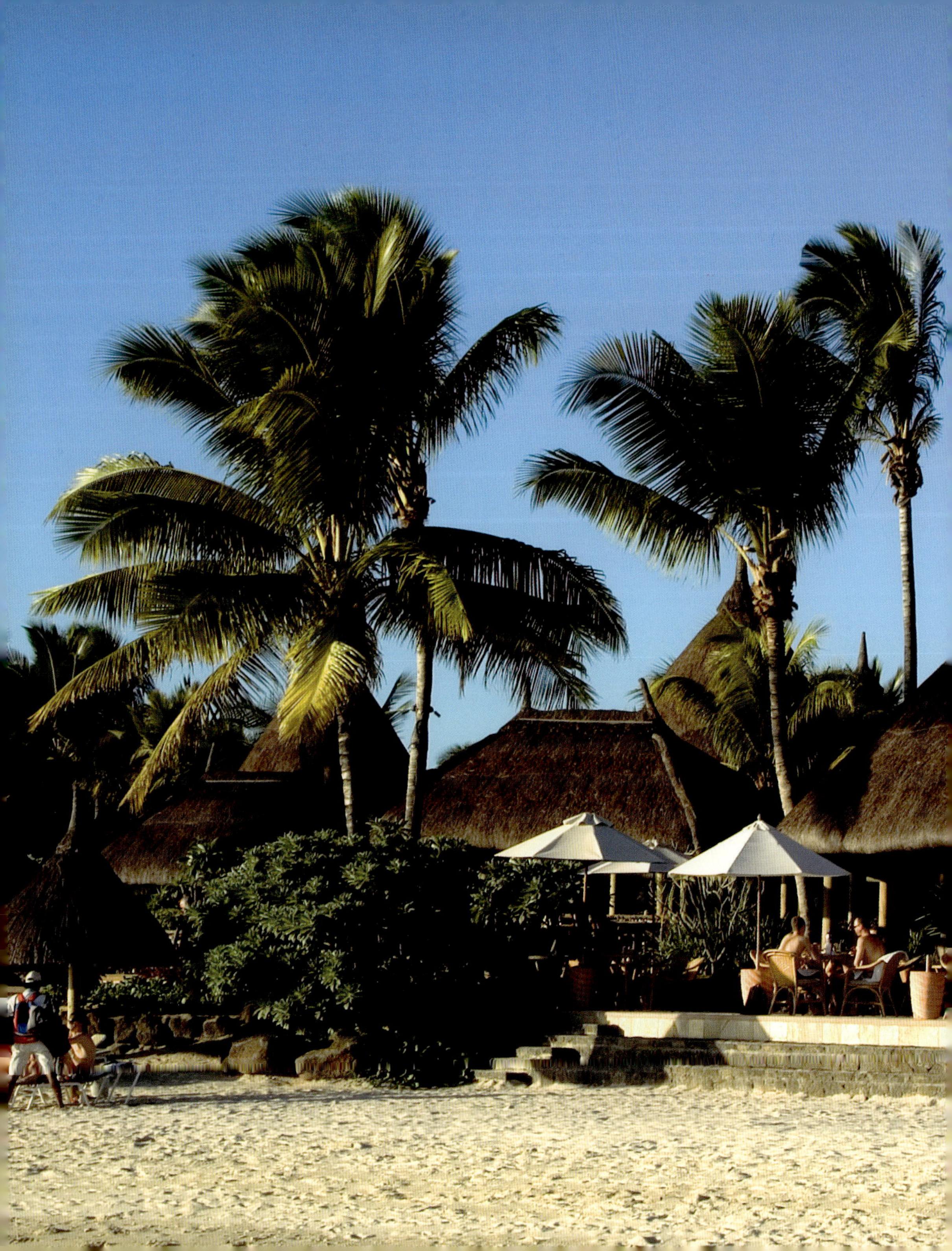

Island Getaways

Left: Find a seat at the bar and enjoy a drink while waiting for the glorious Mauritian sunset at Le Paradis Hotel and Golf Club.

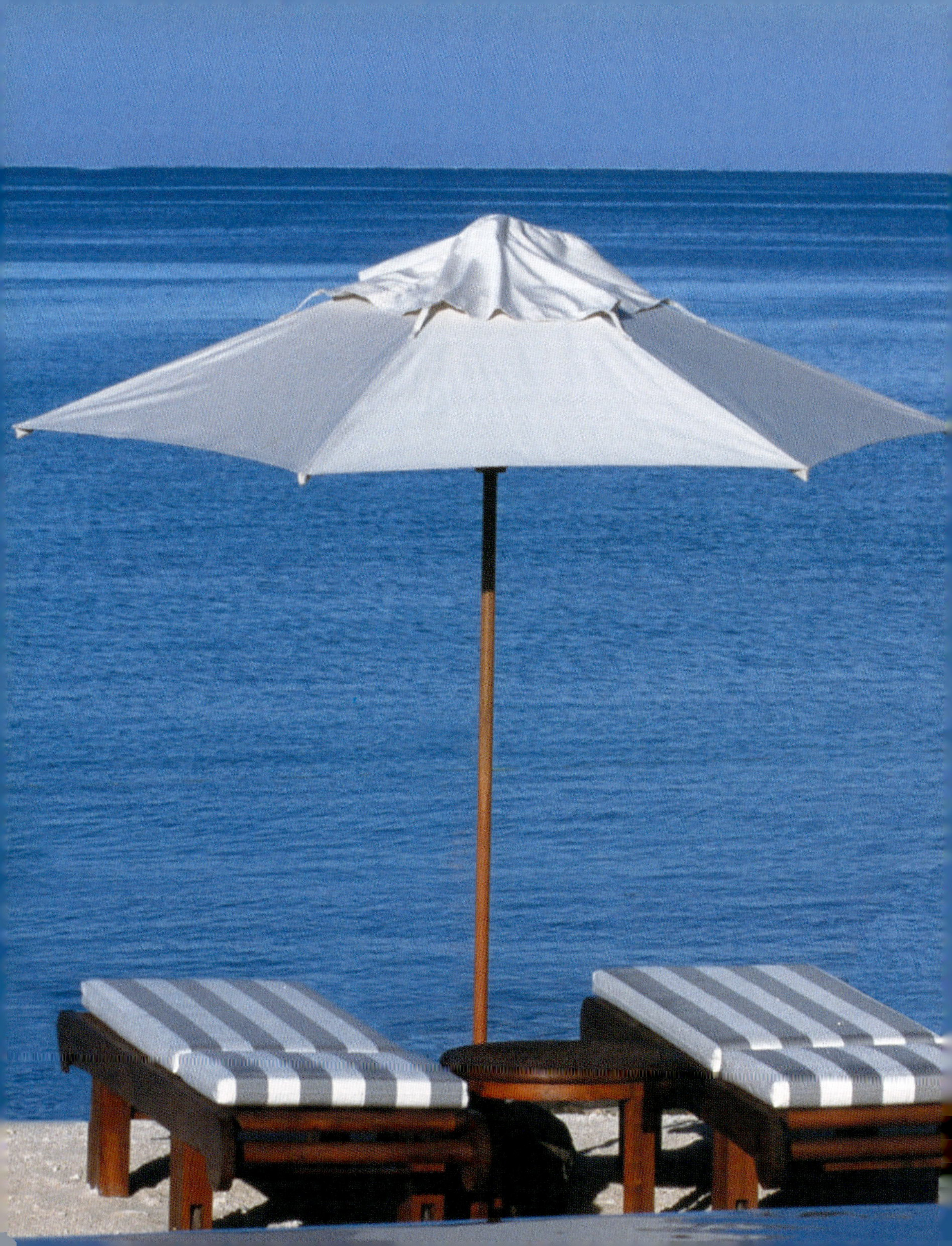

Where to Stay

Five-star resorts can be found all across Mauritius and many offer facilities so complete that guests don't have to leave the well-manicured grounds. However, if you do want a little excitement beyond the confines of the hotel, here's a little more information to help you choose the most suitable location.

For short transfers, the Blue Bay/Mahébourg region can't be beaten, though the disadvantage is a little airport noise. The Morne Peninsula has some very fine and large properties but there's not a lot of infrastructure beyond the gates, so an all-inclusive package would make sense here. Flic en Flac is a growing resort area with a range of restaurants and shops, so a stay here would give you the opportunity to do a little shopping or have lunch. Even better for this is Grand Baie, the largest resort on Mauritius, with restaurants, shops and tour operators strung out along the coastal Royal Road. It's only a short taxi ride to Grand Baie from Trou aux Biches or Mont Choisy, but these two small resorts do have a selection of eateries and bars. The hotels of Belle Mare string north and south of the village so there's no resort centre as such but it's only a hop into Centre du Flacq for genuine Mauritian atmosphere and some delicious street food.

The longest transfer – airport to hotel – is to resorts in the northeast of the island, but even these are only an hour by taxi – not too much of a sacrifice considering you'll be checking in to paradise.

Royal Palm

The gleaming Rolls Royce Phantom that's at the disposal of guests sums up the ethos at the Royal Palm – it epitomizes luxury and does the job effortlessly, completely at one with its role. Although not the longest established resort on the island, the Royal Palm could be considered the 'pride' of Mauritius hotels. Standards here are reassuringly high.

It's definitely the most formal of the many quality hotels here and makes no apology for its dress code and mobile phone policy (not in public areas). Being a stickler for these rules is part of the reason for the Royal Palm's many loyal regulars. It's less a hotel, perhaps,

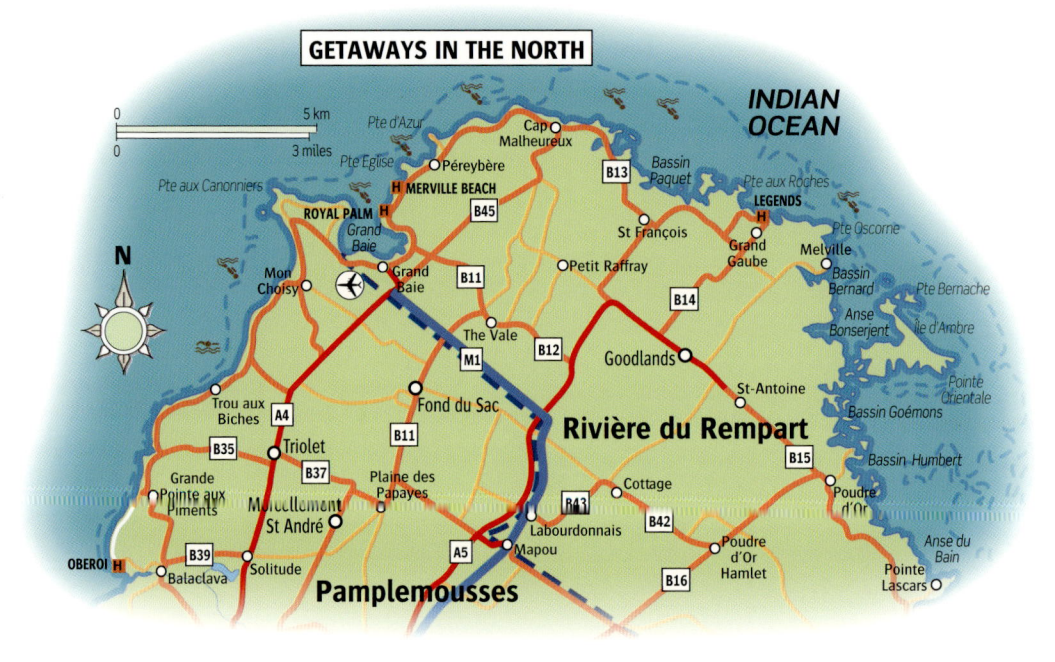

You'll find more than a fair share of high-class resorts on Mauritius. Even as the concept of mass tourism was being born, the island had the foresight to eschew high-volume tourism for quality and set about designing the hotels to attract a more demanding clientele.

Incredible beaches and seemingly endless sunshine were, of course, nature's contribution to the equation, but the cognoscenti point to the hoteliers' attention to detail in resort styling and facilities and the legendary Mauritian service – always attentive and gracious – as other elements that add up to luxury.

A favourite destination for weddings and honeymoons, the island has a bunch of celebrity fans but it is the ability to make every guest feel like a star that keeps Mauritius hotels at the top of the 'best of' lists.

Left: *What better place to spend another warm sunny day in Mauritius.*

Where to Stay

Five-star resorts can be found all across Mauritius and many offer facilities so complete that guests don't have to leave the well-manicured grounds. However, if you do want a little excitement beyond the confines of the hotel, here's a little more information to help you choose the most suitable location.

For short transfers, the Blue Bay/Mahébourg region can't be beaten, though the disadvantage is a little airport noise. The Morne Peninsula has some very fine and large properties but there's not a lot of infrastructure beyond the gates, so an all-inclusive package would make sense here. Flic en Flac is a growing resort area with a range of restaurants and shops, so a stay here would give you the opportunity to do a little shopping or have lunch. Even better for this is Grand Baie, the largest resort on Mauritius, with restaurants, shops and tour operators strung out along the coastal Royal Road. It's only a short taxi ride to Grand Baie from Trou aux Biches or Mont Choisy, but these two small resorts do have a selection of eateries and bars. The hotels of Belle Mare string north and south of the village so there's no resort centre as such but it's only a hop into Centre du Flacq for genuine Mauritian atmosphere and some delicious street food.

The longest transfer – airport to hotel – is to resorts in the northeast of the island, but even these are only an hour by taxi – not too much of a sacrifice considering you'll be checking in to paradise.

Royal Palm

The gleaming Rolls Royce Phantom that's at the disposal of guests sums up the ethos at the Royal Palm – it epitomizes luxury and does the job effortlessly, completely at one with its role. Although not the longest established resort on the island, the Royal Palm could be considered the 'pride' of Mauritius hotels. Standards here are reassuringly high.

It's definitely the most formal of the many quality hotels here and makes no apology for its dress code and mobile phone policy (not in public areas). Being a stickler for these rules is part of the reason for the Royal Palm's many loyal regulars. It's less a hotel, perhaps,

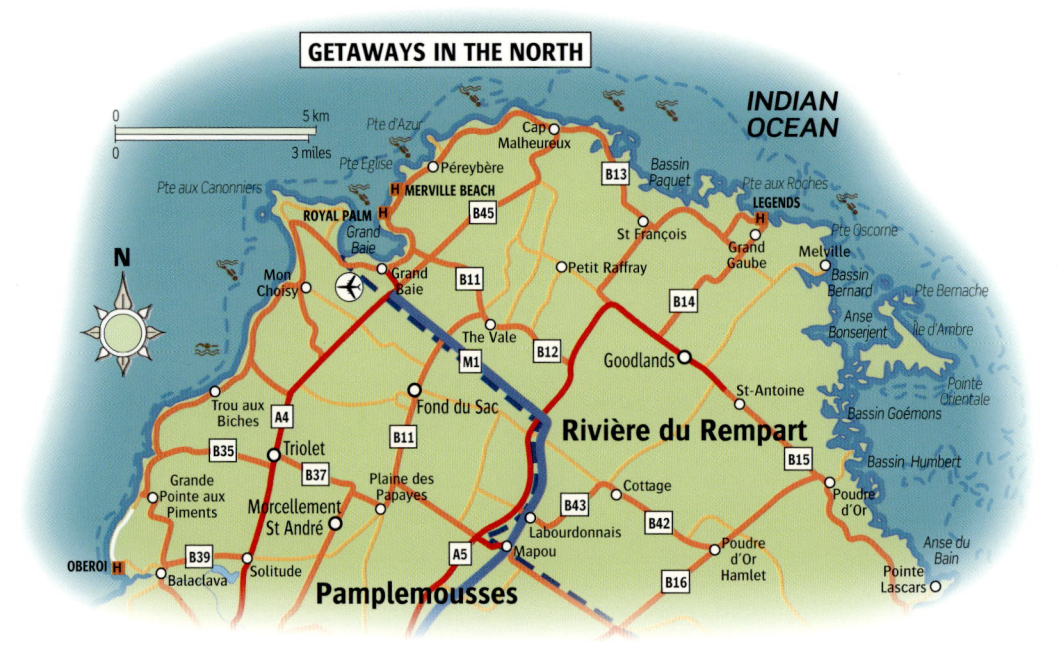

Above: *The glorious shaded beach at the Royal Palm sits only a few metres from every room in the resort; it's the perfect location for a day of utter relaxation.*

than a country club where the tranquillity is broken only by the arrival of your cooling cocktail. Staff are always on hand if needed but are never intrusive or over familiar, and there is no ebullient entertainment team to cajole and 'jolly' the guests. That's not to say that the atmosphere is stiff or that the staff don't display the legendary Mauritian friendliness: they do, but they very much cater to the needs of the guest and if you want privacy and anonymity with your six-star service (yes – they claim an extra star), you'll certainly be allowed to enjoy it.

The country club feel is further enhanced by the fact that this isn't a large property so everything is close at hand. The 84 spacious suites are set in verdant but not expansive grounds. All benefit from impressive sea views from their very generous balconies or terraces, and all are within seven or eight metres of the beach – a fine stretch of sand which in some unexplained way remains remarkably free of the beach vendors that are by Mauritian law allowed to range free on the high-water line all across the island.

The styling of the public areas is typically 'Mauritian tropical', with vast thatched roofs covering bars and restaurants. The rooms are decorated in a contrasting style that could be called 'conservative modern colonial', with natural neutral shades and solid pieces of furniture imported from Bali and India, including the enormous beds, all beautifully accented with richly coloured accessories.

La Goelette, overlooking the waters of Grand Baie, is an exceptional location for breakfast – though many guests prefer to have this delivered to their rooms – but really comes into its own in the evenings as a gastronomic silver service a-la-carte restaurant. The alternative evening eatery is the waterside Natureaty, which serves light, nutritionally balanced cuisine with influences from around the world.

The piano bar forms the focus of evening entertainment, with a live band nightly and a couple of shows a week, but the emphasis isn't on 'let your hair down' activities. It's much more suited to genteel conversation or romantic after-dinner drinks.

The Royal Palm is ideal for clients who want a luxury retreat with refined service and who don't want a list of daily activities as part of their welcome package.

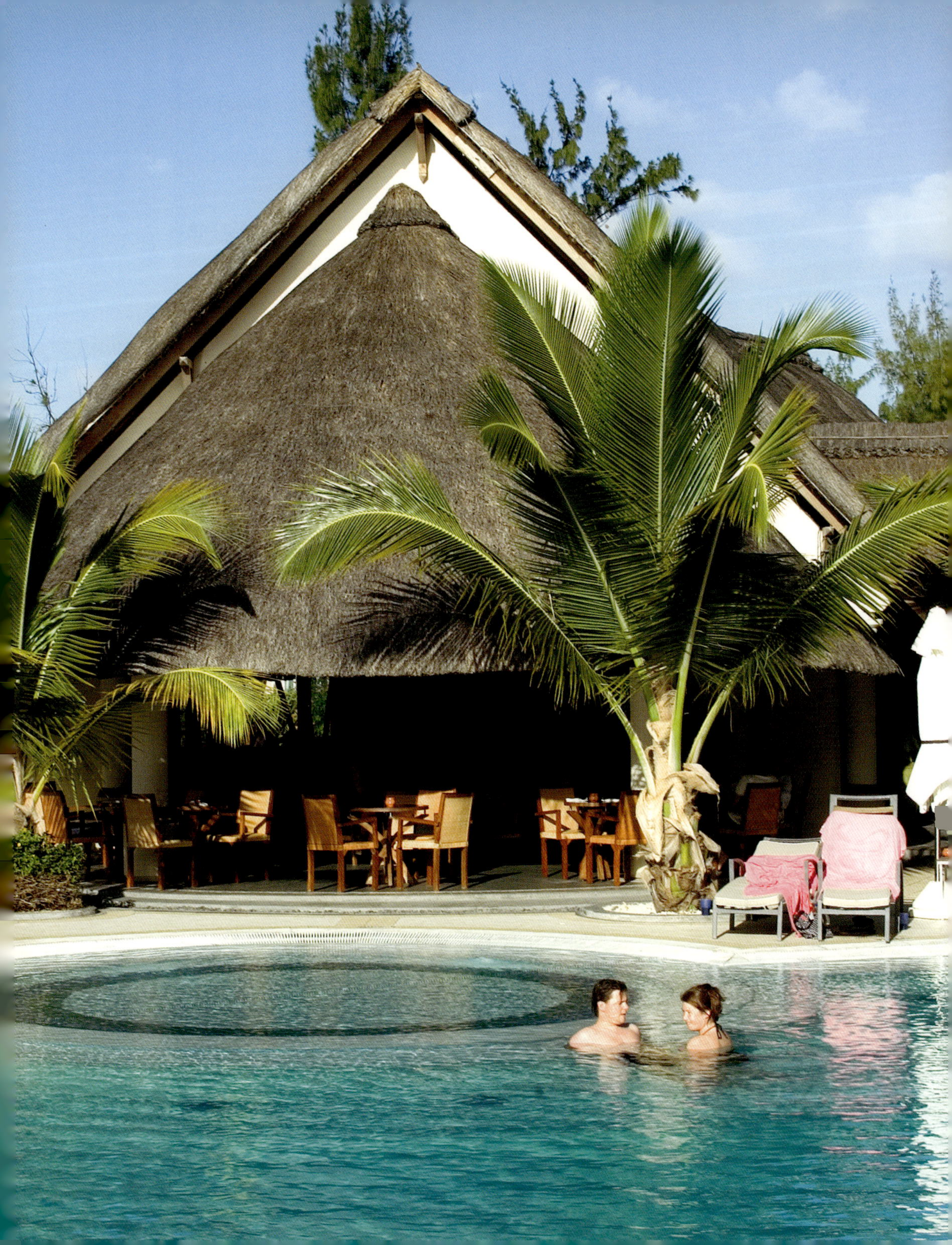

Legends

In a highly competitive marketplace, Naïade Hotels wanted to take a different approach for its most recent hotel refurbishment and they found it in feng shui – the Chinese principle of managing the environment to promote harmony and wellbeing. An Asian feng shui Grand Master was contracted to advise the designers during the planning and building stages, and one of the management team is a qualified feng shui practitioner who monitors the property on a day-to-day basis.

Feng shui has influenced all areas of the hotel design, from the long slim dragon shape of the whole property (very positive) and the curved surfaces and pathways (to enable chi, a form of energy, to flow around the hotel) to simple decorative ornaments designed to please the eye. Rooms have been designed and decorated with regard for the fundamental 'elements' of feng shui philosophy – wood, water, metal, fire and earth – with metal being the theme of the superior rooms and wood providing a warm tropical ambience in the junior suites.

Of course feng shui alone couldn't guarantee the success of any hotel, and Legends has one immediate advantage, supplied by Mother Nature, that is fundamental to any tropical island resort – the beach. Although it sits on the predominantly rocky north shore, the property's main beach is a perfect crescent of pristine white sand back by palms and casuarina trees, with a shallow azure bay providing ideal conditions for swimming and water sports. Offshore the horizon is broken by the island nature reserves of Île Ronde, Île aux Serpents, Îlot Gabriel and Île Plate and these are best viewed from La Bastide, a Mediterranean-style bistro set on a rocky outcrop at the easternmost tip of the beach. The main restaurant overlooks the vast pool on the western flank, above which you'll find Karma House (*see* page 143), the hotel's gastronomic Franco-Asian showcase.

The hotel has a kids' club and TNT, a club that runs a range of activities for 11–17-year-olds until 23:30. The Source is a combined thalasso (sea-water treatment) centre and spa with a gym and saltwater swimming pool. The signature treatment here is the four-handed ylang-ylang massage, a supremely relaxing experience. One unique feature of the hotel is the 60-seat cinema room where you can watch the latest movie releases or unmissable sporting events.

Clients don't have to be into feng shui to enjoy Legends; the concepts are never forced down one's throat and the room décor in all classes certainly pleases the eye with simple concepts and clean lines – but for those who want to delve deeper into the art ...?

Zen Sundays

If you want to find out more about the Oriental philosophies and lifestyles, Sundays at Legends are for you. A special programme of events and activities provides an introduction, with food options at every meal. During your feng shui breakfast the restaurant manager will be on hand to offer dietary advice that will improve the flow of positive energy through the body and alleviate the damaging effects of our modern lifestyle. At 11:00 the senior staff give a presentation entitled 'What is Feng Shui' in the hotel cinema, where you can begin your exploration of this fascinating and complex issue.

Dim sum is served at lunch time, then at 16:00 you can partake of tea and Chinese pastries where a selection of books on feng shui is provided. There's also a Chinese calligraphist who'll write your name or message in beautiful Oriental script. A meditation and t'ai chi session takes place at 17:00 after which you can prepare for dinner – a sumptuous Chinese buffet at Ginko restaurant followed by a Fusion floor show combining eastern and western dance elements. At the end of the day you'll find that your Chinese horoscope has been delivered to your room; a little light reading before bed time.

Left: The free-form swimming pool at Legends is designed to promote harmony and wellbeing through management of one's surroundings. It has no harsh, straight boundaries, which allows positive energy to flow – plus it's only a couple of wet footsteps to the bar for a well-earned cooling cocktail!

Oberoi Mauritius

More of a sanctuary than a hotel, this bijou property is a must for anyone who wants to enjoy a boutique feel, a tranquil atmosphere and the finest quality five-star service. The Oberoi has only 72 pavilions and a small selection of villas, allowing every guest to feel like a VIP and offering a totally different ambience to the larger high-class resorts.

The overall design of the Oberoi brings Bali to Mauritius – with styling details influenced by Balinese religious architecture. Grand carved archways and stone statues mark the transition between various sections of the grounds and these are interspersed with cooling pools and fountains. The 20-hectare resort footprint is small by island standards but the clever design and wonderful tropical gardens give one a feeling of both space and cosiness, creating many quiet corners for meditation and reflection.

Everything at the Oberoi is designed to promote a sense of relaxed serenity. The spa (see page 161) is one of the highlights of the resort and has recently been added to the ranks of the 'Leading Spas of the World', one of only 85 worldwide. There's no vast programme of sports and activities – though the boat dock has water sports – and evening entertainment is low-key, with jazz or other live music in the bar area. For these reasons it certainly has more of a couples feel than a family feel, though there isn't a 'no children' policy. It simply caters better to clients looking for somewhere to recharge the internal batteries.

The 72 thatched terrace pavilion rooms are beautifully designed with large windows to take in the fantastic views. The high wooden-slatted ceilings and neutral coloured walls meld into a colonial tea-plantation type of feel. Every room features a four-poster bed and a sunken marble bath for a little romance. The villas offer the ultimate in privacy, having walled gardens and private garden gazebos for dining.

The Oberoi beach is not the most extensive on the island but it is a good quality stretch of sand backed by shady trees and, most importantly, only a few steps away from refreshment at the hotel beach bar. Even so, cold towels and slices of refreshing melon are delivered regularly to keep you cool.

The Oberoi has only one restaurant for dinner, overseen with great care and dedication by Pierre Burgarde and offering exceptional cuisine and fantastic views across the lagoon. In the evening the neighbouring poolside area is lit by candles for a most romantic effect.

Below: *The Asian-influenced Oberoi is the island's smallest luxury property.*

Labourdonnais Waterfront Hotel

Port Louis's only five-star option, the Labourdonnais Waterfront was planned as an integral element in the regeneration of the Caudan Waterfront, the most prestigious shopping and tourism complex in the city. It's a high-rise building whose upper rooms offer panoramic views across the cityscape or out over Port Louis harbour.

The rooms are designed around a central atrium with glass lifts rising up through the middle of the tower, and could be termed 'international classic' in feel. The open-plan reception area features a restaurant, bar and terrace area that's usually frequented by Mauritian and international businessmen.

La Rose des Vents restaurant is one of the gastronomic highlights of the capital and is particularly known for its 'degustation' menus – selections that allow you to explore a meal of several courses accompanied by specially selected wines to complement the food. Other facilities include a gym and a plunge pool. Management arrange for boat trips along the coast so guests can enjoy the beaches at the Maritim Hotel, and there's the option of eating at the Labourdonnais's sister hotel, Le Suffren, just across the yacht basin.

The main advantage of the Labourdonnais Waterfront is that the delights of Port Louis are just on the doorstep – you can shop at the market, explore the museums or have a day at the races and then head back to the hotel for refreshment or a rest. It's the perfect property for a two-centre trip in combination with one of the other recommended resorts.

Above: The Labourdonnais Waterfront is the only five-star option in Port Louis and the island's premier business hotel. Set on the newly developed Caudan Waterfront and surrounded by shops and restaurants, it's within strolling distance of everything the capital has to offer, from the museums to the market.

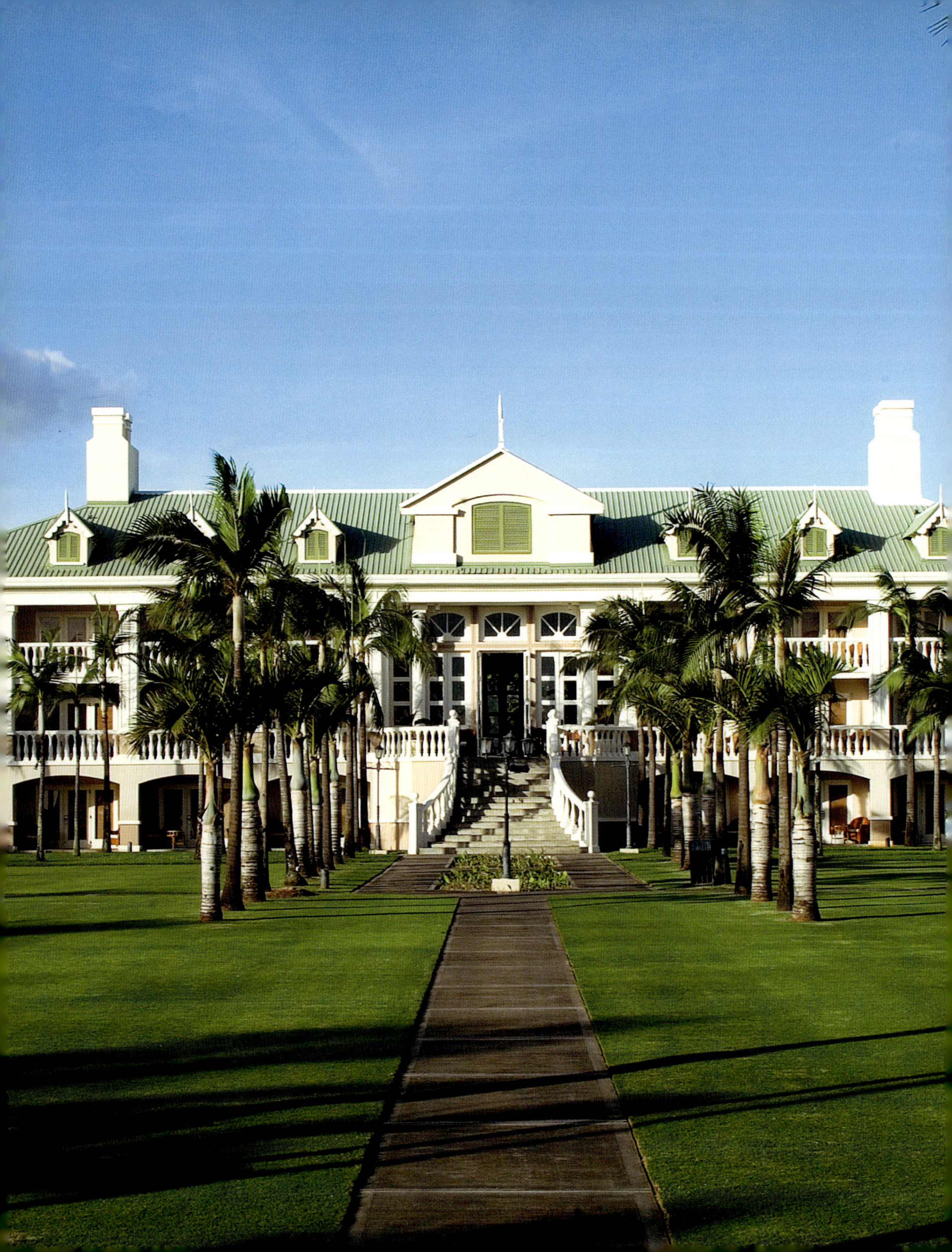

Sugar Beach Resort

Colonial splendour meets Mauritian hospitality at the Sugar Beach Resort on the west coast, where designers set out to capture the grandeur of the era of rubbers of bridge and afternoon tea on the veranda while the sugar ripened under the tropical sun. Whitewashed classical façades offset by lime-washed cane furniture evoke the atmosphere of the informal family life of the sugar-cane barons, while the boathouse with its water sports, the vast swimming pool and the long stretch of sandy beach offer the accessories expected by today's demanding clients.

Guests get an immediate feel of the styling as soon as they are shown to their rooms via a grand double-bow staircase leading down from the reception atrium into the grounds. The heart of the resort holds a substantial classically styled sugar mansion, like something stolen away from the set of *Gone with the Wind*, fronted by formal gardens and a croquet lawn. The two vast wings house 83 rooms, many of them interconnected and ideal for families, and in the evening the central atrium is transformed into a rum-sipping area and cigar bar, where the menfolk might have sat and relaxed in days gone by.

Scattered around the ample grounds lie smaller villa-type buildings designed to mimic an old plantation village. Each villa is named after one of the old Mauritian sugar-cane plantations, including Médine close by, and consists of a block of 10 rooms and suites. Beachfront rooms really are only a few steps from the sand, while others rest in amongst manicured greenery. Room styling draws influences from the colours and patterns of Provence in southern France to add a contemporary continental touch to the main design theme.

The Sugar Beach Resort offers an excellent range of activities. The Sugar Club sports complex is particularly strong on tennis but includes a good gym and a full programme of activities from yoga to VTT (*velo toutes terrains* or mountain biking) tours, while the Fun Kids' Club with a staff of 17 is well equipped to cater for children of all ages. There's also a Teens' Club.

Guests of the Sugar Beach Resort also have all the facilities of the neighbouring and sister resort, La Pirogue Hotel (home of the famed Marlin World Cup sport-fishing contest), at their disposal. The island's most traditionally Mauritian hotel in style, La Pirogue makes a wonderful contrast to the Sugar Beach Resort and offers a combined total of 1km of pristine Flic en Flac beach, plus numerous extra dining and entertainment possibilities including, arguably, the best sunset bar on the coast.

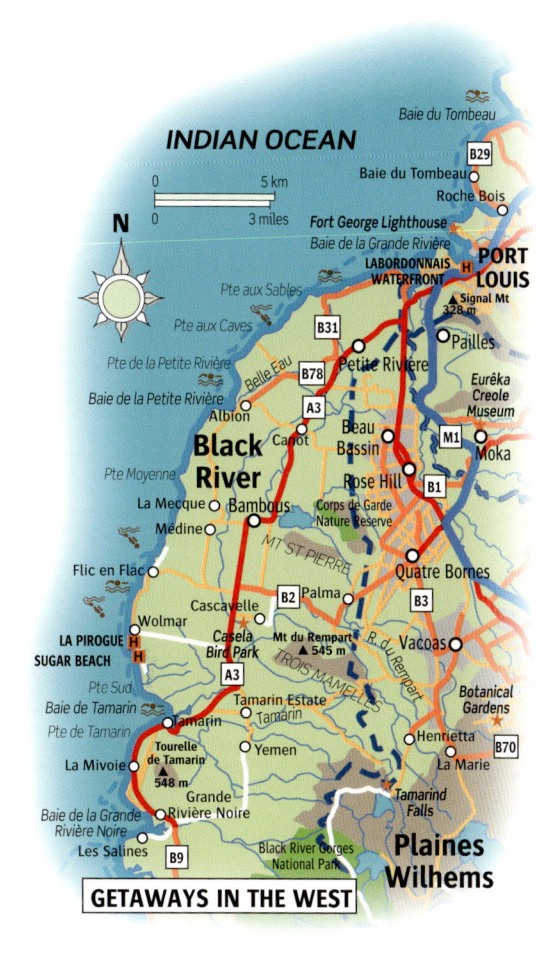

Left: *The colonial styling of the main building at the Sugar Beach Resort puts one in mind of antebellum mansions in the deep south of the United States. The formal lawns in the foreground lead directly to the fine sandy beach.*

Dinarobin Hotel Golf & Spa

The Arabs named Mauritius Dinarobin or Silver Island on their 12th-century maps, and Beachcomber hotels pay homage to the original island moniker in this 30-million-euro hotel, which opened in 2001. With a dramatic location at the foot of the looming Morne Brabant and benefiting from a long ribbon of immaculate white sand, the setting is one of the finest in southern Mauritius.

The hotel offers spacious all-suite accommodation. The upper suites have high cathedral ceilings and both of the two floors are bathed in light from large bow windows. Creams and neutral fabrics act as perfect counterpoints to the dark wood of the fixtures to give an opulent feel, and French windows lead out to a spacious private balcony or patio styled to act as an extra room rather than just an open-air seating area. At Dinarobin it's as if you are staying in a private serviced apartment. A doorbell by the balcony door is a nice little touch in that direction – announcing visitors, or your room service order.

The thatched public areas sit at the southern end of the resort, making it quite a hike to the most northerly rooms; however, you have a limousine golf cart service just a phone call away. Designed with a kind of 'Zen meets New Mexican adobe' theme, the open-plan reception area flows through to the bar, with tropical pools providing natural transitions without overshadowing the feeling of space. Huge rattan sofas bedecked with comfy cushions invite guests to spend a little time here.

Those who want a little extra luxury or privacy can use the 'Club at Dinarobin', currently the only 'executive' facility in Mauritius, where private buffet breakfasts, an exclusive bar (Le Martello), newspapers, Internet access and a personal concierge come as part of the package.

Set in attractive tropical gardens, the diminutive Clarins spa is designed with an East Asian theme and has a relaxing internal courtyard with a plunge pool and several treatment rooms. The hotel has three restaurants including the gastronomic Saveurs des Îles. But what about the golf course? Well, it's something of an overstatement to call the Dinarobin a golf resort; technically the course, which runs along the length of the property on the landward side, belongs to Le Paradis, the neighbouring sister hotel, along with other great sports facilities. However, guests can use the extensive amenities of both hotels freely, whichever one they book into, making this one of the most flexible holiday options on the island.

Right: *The Mauritian-style thatched Dinarobin sits amongst lush grounds in the shade of the dramatic Morne Brabant Mountain. From here it's possible to walk along seven kilometres of sandy beach, and the sunsets are spectacular.*

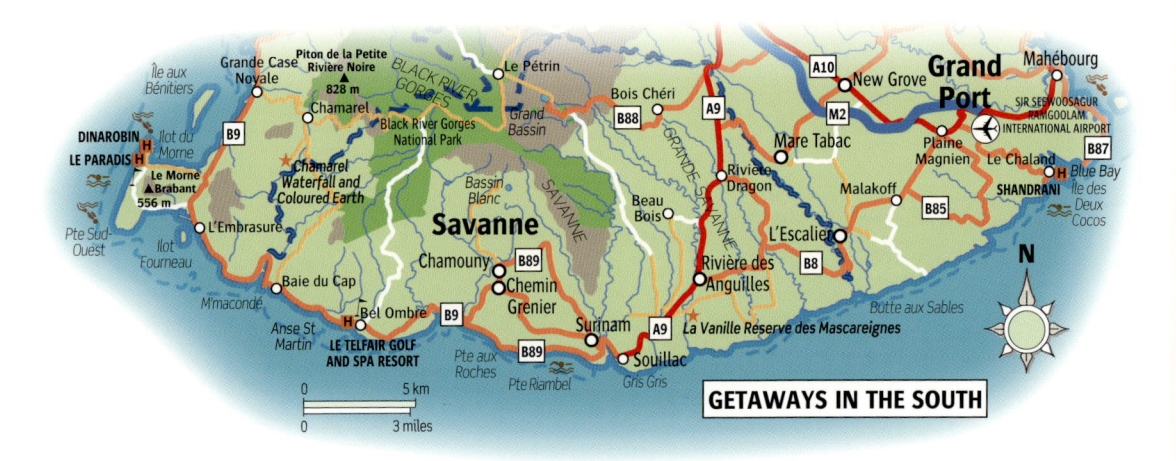

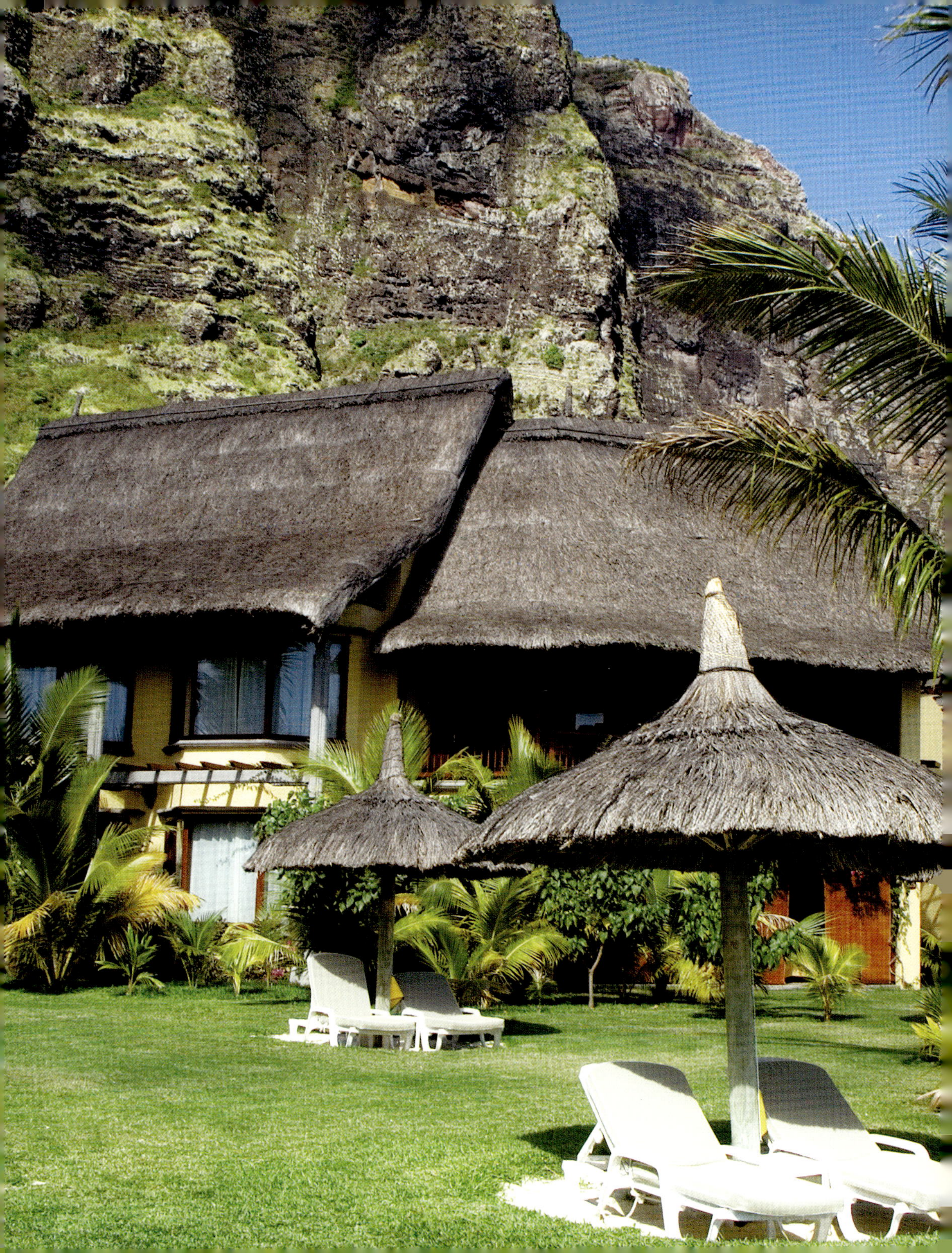

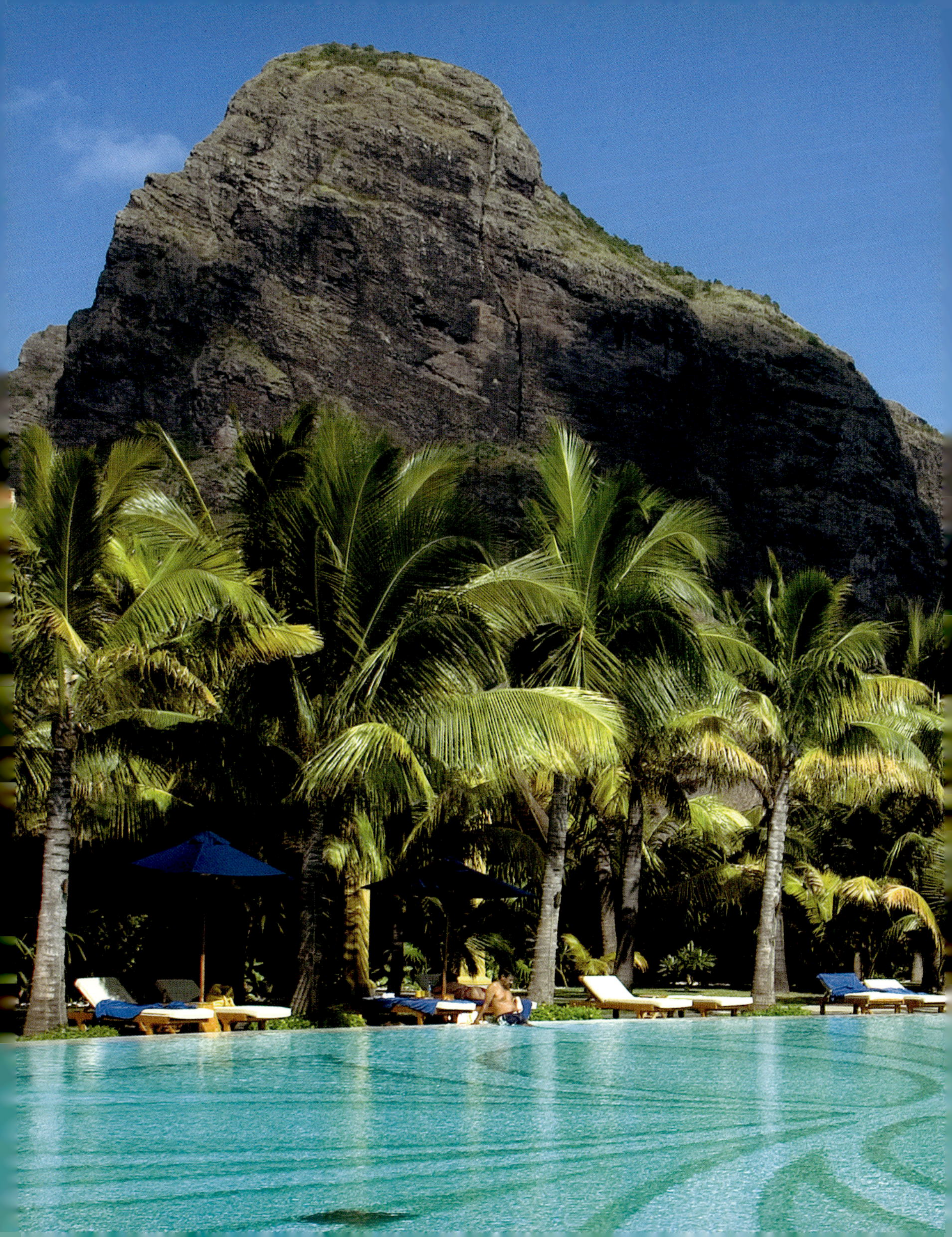

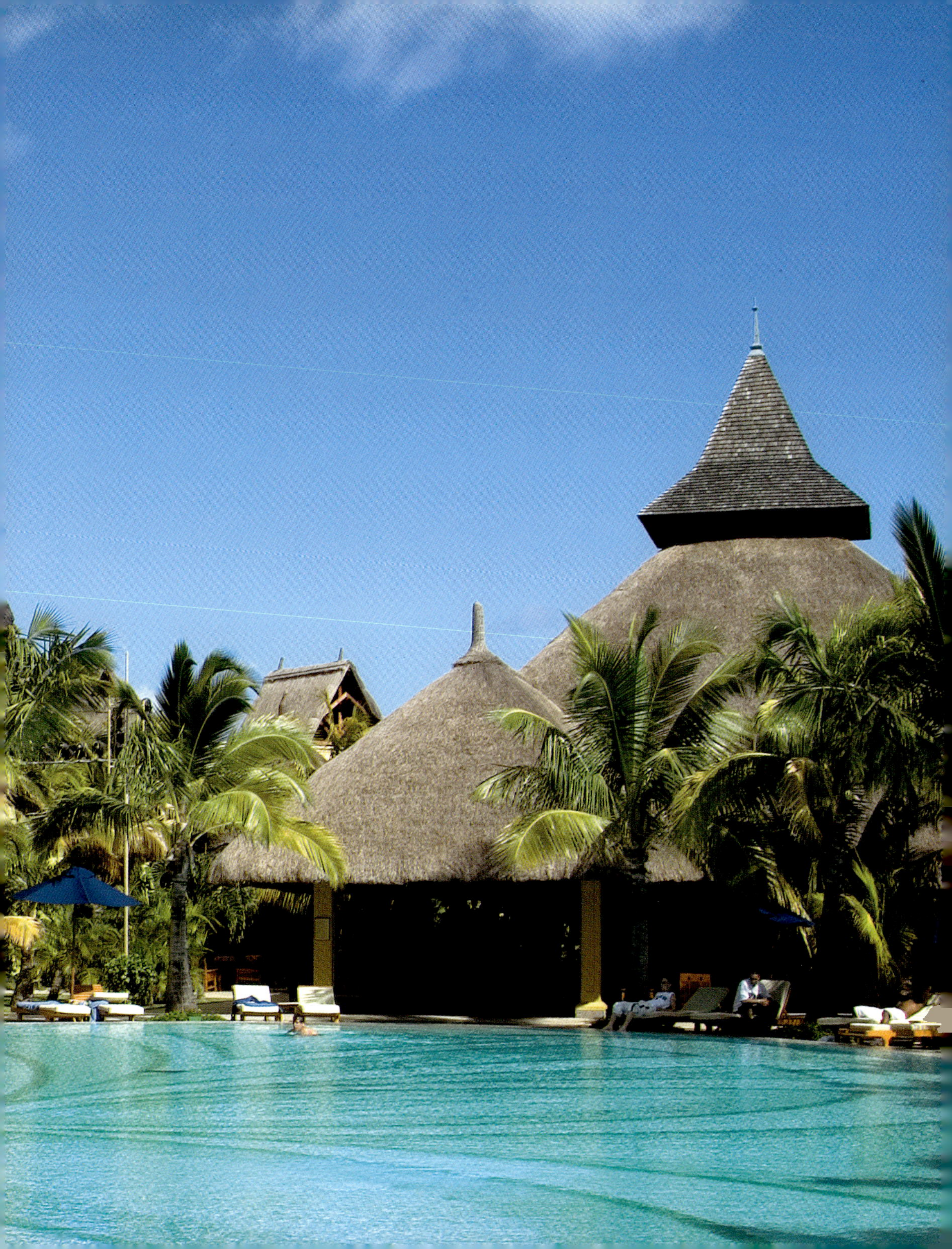

Le Paradis Hotel and Golf Club

Le Paradis Hotel and Golf Club could be classed as the most rounded five-star resort in Mauritius. With the wide range of amenities on offer for the whole family combined with the excellent levels of service, it's very difficult to beat.

The setting is also spectacular, occupying the whole of the northern nub of the Morne Peninsula – that's 150 hectares – with fabulous stretches of beach on two flanks and the Morne Brabant mountain dominating the landscape to the immediate southeast.

The resort is without doubt the biggest on Mauritius but the public areas – reception, bar and restaurants – sit at the heart of the site, limiting long strolls to the bar from either end of the resort. There's also the golf cart transfer to whisk tired legs or sleepy heads back to the room at the end of the evening.

The sporting facilities at Le Paradis have something for everyone, not least of which is the golf course (*see* page 169), a par 72, 5899m, with a back nine that includes five water hazards. The golf school here is the perfect place for beginners and is well recommended for a child's first swing. Hire a bike to cycle around the grounds – again safe for children since there are few vehicles beyond the main entrance roads; take to the tennis courts, or charter a boat and head to the marlin fishing grounds just out to the west. The Karma-influenced spa (*see* page 163) is one of the largest on any hotel property in Mauritius, with a wide range of treatments on offer.

Superior and de luxe rooms spread out across the very northern tip of the Morne, with a series of small blocks of beachside junior suites on the southern flank of the reception and restaurants. The clever design of these blocks means that suites back on to suites and these can easily be combined to produce spacious accommodation for families. Styling varies over the ten different room types, though 'tropical elegance' is the watch phrase, whether you book the superior room or the executive villa, with neutral colours embellished with splashes of colour used throughout.

Le Paradis has four restaurants including Le Blue Marlin with its excellent seafood and the Italian-influenced La Palma, but the romantic La Ravanne (*see* page 143) is the showpiece, and perfect for that special evening under the stars.

Hotel clients can also take advantage of facilities at the slightly more genteel *Out of Africa*-styled sister resort, neighbouring Dinarobin Hotel Golf and Spa, with its three restaurants and more intimate spa.

Private Villas

Le Paradis has more private villas than any other hotel on Mauritius. All 13 received a comprehensive renovation and redecoration in 2005–06. Nestled on the lagoon side within tropical gardens and each with its own private beach, they offer the ultimate luxury for families, friends or couples. The styling is decidedly contemporary with more than a hint of the tropics. Thatch and rattan bring a colonial touch to the colour scheme of beige and honey, and splashes of bright colour are added in the soft furnishings.

A central lounge opens out onto a generous terrace with six-place dining table and outside seating area. Three bedrooms carry on the neutral colour scheme but decorative elements are drawn from Southeast Asian feng shui and Zen – crimson and chocolate accents along with wood and metal accessories are carefully chosen and placed to aid restful sleep. The two double bedrooms each has a splendid bathroom complete with private open-air shower, indoor shower and tub. A third twin-bedded room has an en-suite bathroom and makes an ideal children's bolthole.

Although the choice of restaurants at Le Paradis is unsurpassed by any resort save neighbouring Dinarobin, your villa has a fully equipped kitchen and your personal chef will cook your choice of meal and serve it on the terrace. A personal butler is on call to cater to your every whim and you'll have the use of a golf cart to get you around the resort.

Previous page: *The water of the vast main pool at Le Paradis looks cool and inviting, and the view, with the Morne Brabant and the palms, is spectacular.*

One&Only Le Touessrok

Beloved of the high-class travel magazines, Le Touessrok has been a regular in the 'world's best hotels' list since it's conception and this reputation has been further bolstered by a comprehensive $50 million renovation programme that was completed in 2002.

The setting of the hotel couldn't be better. Rooms flank a pristine sandy bay or nestle on diminutive Frangipani Island linked to the mainland by a covered wooden bridge. Several sandy inlets can become your private beach for the day and just offshore you'll be able to explore one of Mauritius's most famous playgrounds, the Île aux Cerfs, where One&Only have gilded the lily with their restaurants and water sports, or Îlot Mangenie, where the hotel operates a 'desert island' retreat for One&Only clients.

Today the overall feel of Le Touessrok is one of cool, contemporary sophistication – it's the hippest hotel on the island by far. The designers have taken a deliberate departure from traditional tropical styling without ignoring the many inspirations suggested by this island paradise location. Travertine marble and ivory stucco grace the public spaces, providing a neutral yet luxurious canvas against which are set accents of rich purples and reds. Rooms follow this same albescent colour theme through the use of Indian quartzite and porcelain. A huge marble and concrete bath dominates the bathroom, offering a hint of 'let yourself go' naughtiness. Of course hi-tech toys make an appearance, with expansive plasma screen TVs for late-night movies in bed or games on the PC, and even an espresso/cappuccino machine for a caffeine hit if you don't want to raid the mini-bar.

__Below__ Want refreshment while building your tan? At One&Only Le Touessrok you simply raise a flag and a beach butler will be on hand to take and deliver your order, be it a picnic lunch or champagne cocktail. If you want privacy for a mid-afternoon nap simply raise your 'do not disturb' flag.

Dining meets performance art at the hotel's main restaurant, the tri-level Three-Nine-Eight, which is designed around no fewer than eight open kitchens. Michelin-starred chef Viteen Bhatia, the first Indian chef to receive the accolade, also delights at Safran where he presides over the aromatic dishes of the subcontinent.

Frangipani Island, styled with more than a passing reference to a small Aegean Island village, offers a refuge for adults with its heated travertine pool and no-noise policy. You'll also find the Givenchy Spa here (see page 162), a haven of peace and relaxation.

Since the rebirth of Le Touessrok, One&Only haven't stood still here. The magnificent Bernhard Langer designed Île aux Cerfs golf course teed off in 2003 and a trio of stunning waterfront villas were unveiled in 2005. Some things don't change, however. Barlen Ramsamy has been a staff member here for over 25 years, starting as a waiter. Today he runs Barlen's, the trendy Mauritian restaurant on the property.

Le Touessrok guests can double their enjoyment by spending time at the sister resort, Le Saint Géran (see below), just a twenty-minute transfer away. You'll get the same quality service here, though the styling and atmosphere is a little more conservative.

One&Only Le Saint Géran

The 'Grand Dame' of Mauritius hotels, One&Only Le Saint Géran celebrated its thirtieth birthday in 2005 in lavish style. From the very moment you are welcomed here, it's clear that there's nothing staid or dated about this property, whose suites have seen a steady stream of renowned clients including royalty, world leaders and more instantly recognizable celebrities since its very early days.

Rambling across a 24-hectare peninsula in ample private grounds, the hotel is the embodiment of timeless elegance with calming neutral shades throughout the public areas and the generously sized suites. Rattan, bamboo and light hardwoods add to the sense of space and give an overall impression of a conservative tropical ambience. Winding through the public spaces is a verdant tropical garden of ponds and cascades replete with

***Above**: Privacy is guaranteed at Le Saint Géran, where the sun beds are spread out around the peninsula. Those overlooking the magnificent beach are most popular, but the shady spots by the landward lagoon offer a perfect retreat.*

waterfowl and ducks. Manicured lawns dotted with palms stretch out around the main accommodation wings and a magnificent beach runs the whole length of the property.

Service at the One&Only Le Saint Géran is the stuff of legend. The hotel pioneered butler service in all its rooms and is proud of its reputation for attention to detail, even down to polishing your sunglasses for you when the need arises. Your assigned butler is your personal concierge, tour-operator and packing service – and might even become a long-standing friend.

The butler-training programme was devised by Ivor Spencer who had many years of service at Buckingham Palace looking after the British Royal family – what better credentials? So attentiveness and discretion have become watchwords here.

The 696m^2 Givenchy spa (*see* page 162) is an innovation that's been adopted in similar fashion by hoteliers across the island. In the world's top five, the lap pool is the epitome of tropical chic and has appeared in many a magazine fashion spread draped with stylish beauties.

One&Only have formed an alliance with one of gastronomy's leading men, French three-star Michelin chef Alain Ducasse, to push culinary boundaries at the signature Spoon des Îles (*see* page 142), while the Paul et Virginie with its lagoon-side deck is a wonderful location for a relaxing lunch or dinner.

For sports enthusiasts, there's a Peter Burwash tennis centre where you can take lessons – *ab initio* to competition standard; a renowned Gary Player-designed nine-hole golf course, and an excellent water-sports centre on the landward inlet offering great conditions for sailing and waterskiing.

Le Saint Géran guests are also welcome to use the facilities at its sister hotel Le Touessrok, where cool chic is a byword. The delights of the Île aux Cerfs, with its fantastic beaches and world-famous 18-hole golf course, and Îlot Mangenie, with a private One&Only beach, can both be visited by private boat transfer. A free shuttle service links the two resorts which lie about 20 minutes apart.

Beau Rivage

A dazzling free-form infinity pool is the signature feature at Beau Rivage. Shimmering in the sunshine, defined by graceful curves and backed by swaying palms, it captures the essence of the luxury island getaway.

Naïade's flagship property sits on a stunning little headland along the Belle Mare coast where nature has provided a wide tract of sand, pointing out like an arrowhead into the lagoon. It's a glorious place to swim and provides excellent snorkelling right on the doorstep.

A vast thatched central atrium brings together Indian, Southeast Asian and Balinese elements in a 'luxury colonial' meets 'cultural crossroads' central design theme. Oriental wood and rattan screens divide the larger communal spaces into intimate corners where comfortable sofas invite repose. Ceremonial masks and immense wall hangings dress up walls of soft terracotta and turmeric.

The hotel sits in compact grounds and has three storeys throughout but careful design means the rooms don't feel tightly packed. The accommodations are spacious, an impression enhanced by the minimalist pale floor tiling and walls. This canvas is accessorized with warm solid wood fittings and accented by rich reds and golds on drapes and soft furnishings. The Maharajah Suite – the hotel's most luxurious option – is a palace fit for an Indian prince.

The Beau Rivage's restaurants and bars carry on the Eastern theme under a canopy of sugar-cane thatch, and the property looks particularly inviting after nightfall.

The capacious sofas at the Monsoon Bar make the most inviting location for a pre-dinner drink, surrounded by sensuous cashmere throws and gold braided drapes – styling influenced by the destinations that linked the ancient Silk Route, from Asia Minor, through Persia and east to China – but you'll move to Africa for the décor inspiration of Club Savanne, an intimate jazz bar where you can enjoy an postprandial brandy and cigar.

The attentiveness of the staff is first rate, with a cheery hello from your concierge staff and conversation with your wait staff. Despite a dress code in the evenings this may just be the least formal five-star hotel on the island – a hit with families and those who want luxury amenities while still enjoying a relaxed atmosphere. There's themed entertainment each day and the majority of the dinners in the main restaurant are buffet or gala style.

The property benefits from the Aphrodite Spa with a range of treatments and a relaxing plunge pool area, and even a wedding gazebo for those intending to tie the knot.

A Cut Above

One of the more unusual activities that guests can take part in at the Beau Rivage is the chance to be initiated into champagne *sabrage*, the technique of opening a champagne bottle with a razor-sharp sabre. This simple activity is an act surrounded by pomp and was made popular by officers of Napoleon's armies in the early 1800s. A team of hotel food and beverage staff are trained *chevaliers* of the Confrérie du Sabre d'Or, an organization whose aim is to promote safe and professional *sabrage*, and they will guide you in the historic skill and all its associated rituals.

The skill of the *sabrage* is in the angle of the blade and just the right amount of force hitting the annulus, the slight bulge at the neck of the bottle. Do it correctly and the top of the bottle, complete with cork, will break clean away and the champagne is ready to pour.

Guests are invited to perform their *sabrage* and successful candidates are welcomed into the Confrérie with a Sabreur diploma. The head wine waiter will provide a selection of the finest champagnes for the occasion.

Right: The dramatic two-tier free-form pool is the centrepiece of the Beau Rivage, linking the reception atrium and the restaurant and bar areas with the beachfront. The lines of beach umbrellas and palm trees add an almost architectural feel to the vista, while the slender dividing wall attracts the eye with its sensuous, constantly moving curve.

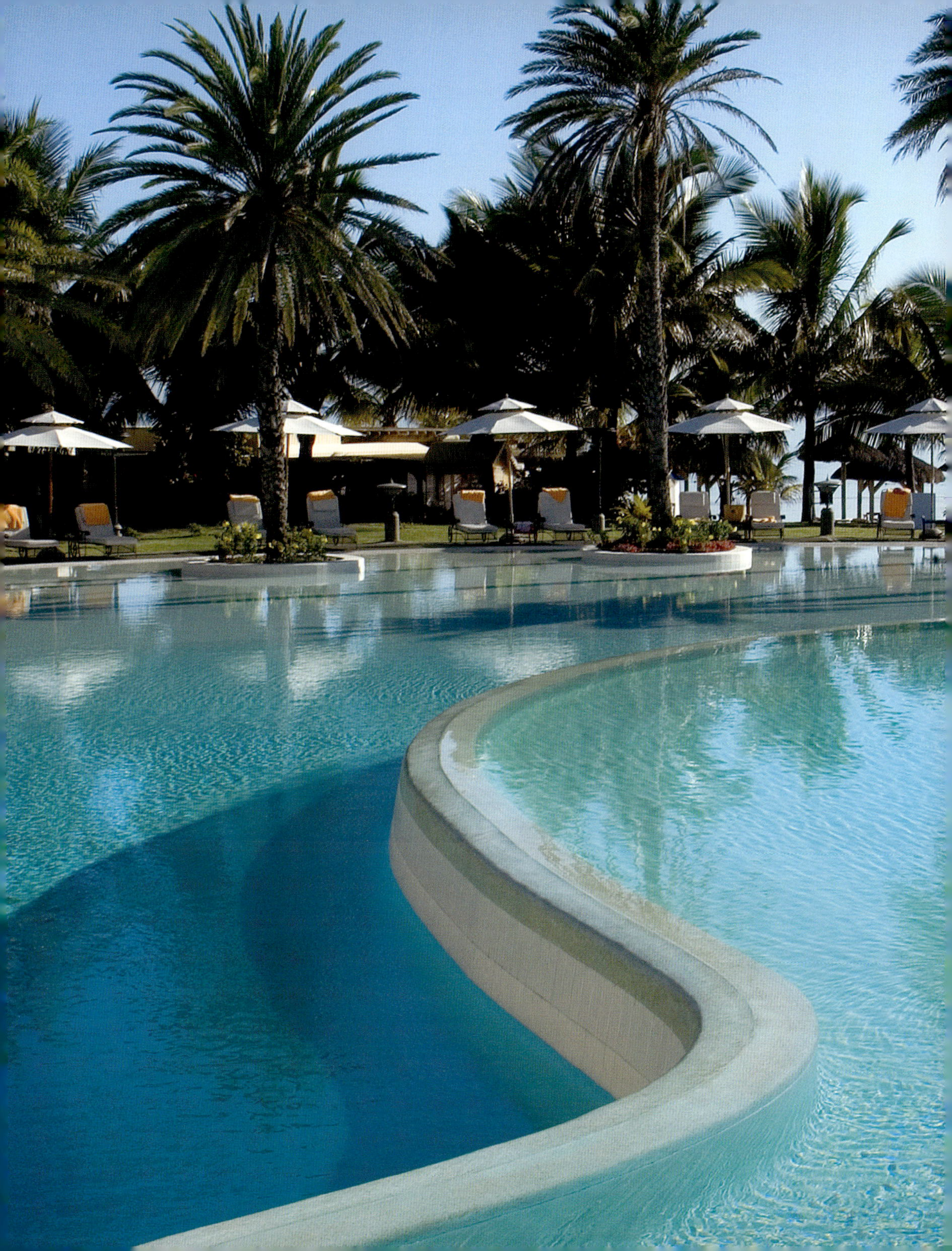

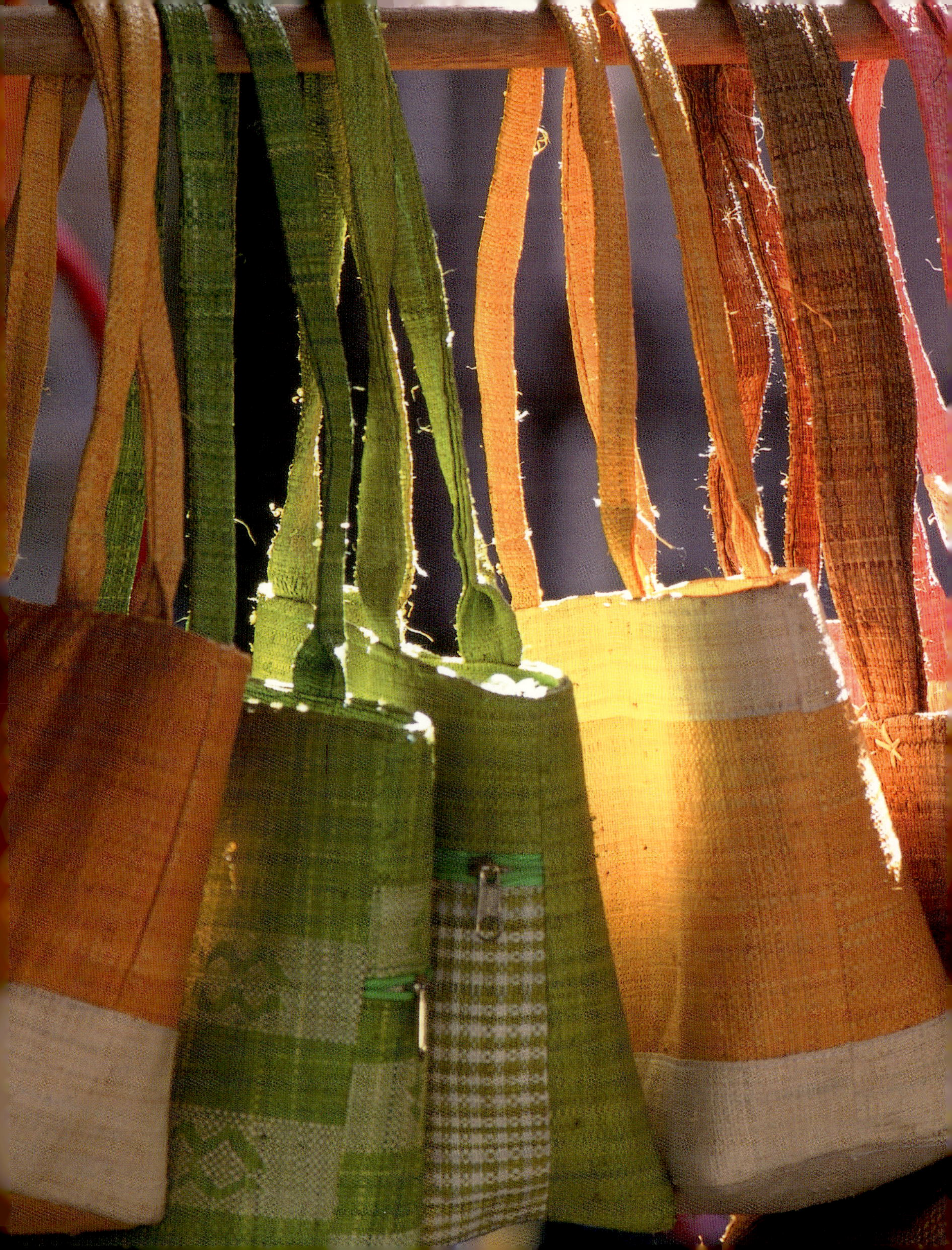

Shopping and Markets

Left: *Colourful raffia bags and baskets are for sale all over the island and make an inexpensive and practical souvenir. Use them during your stay to carry towels and sun tan lotions, or any souvenirs that take your fancy.*

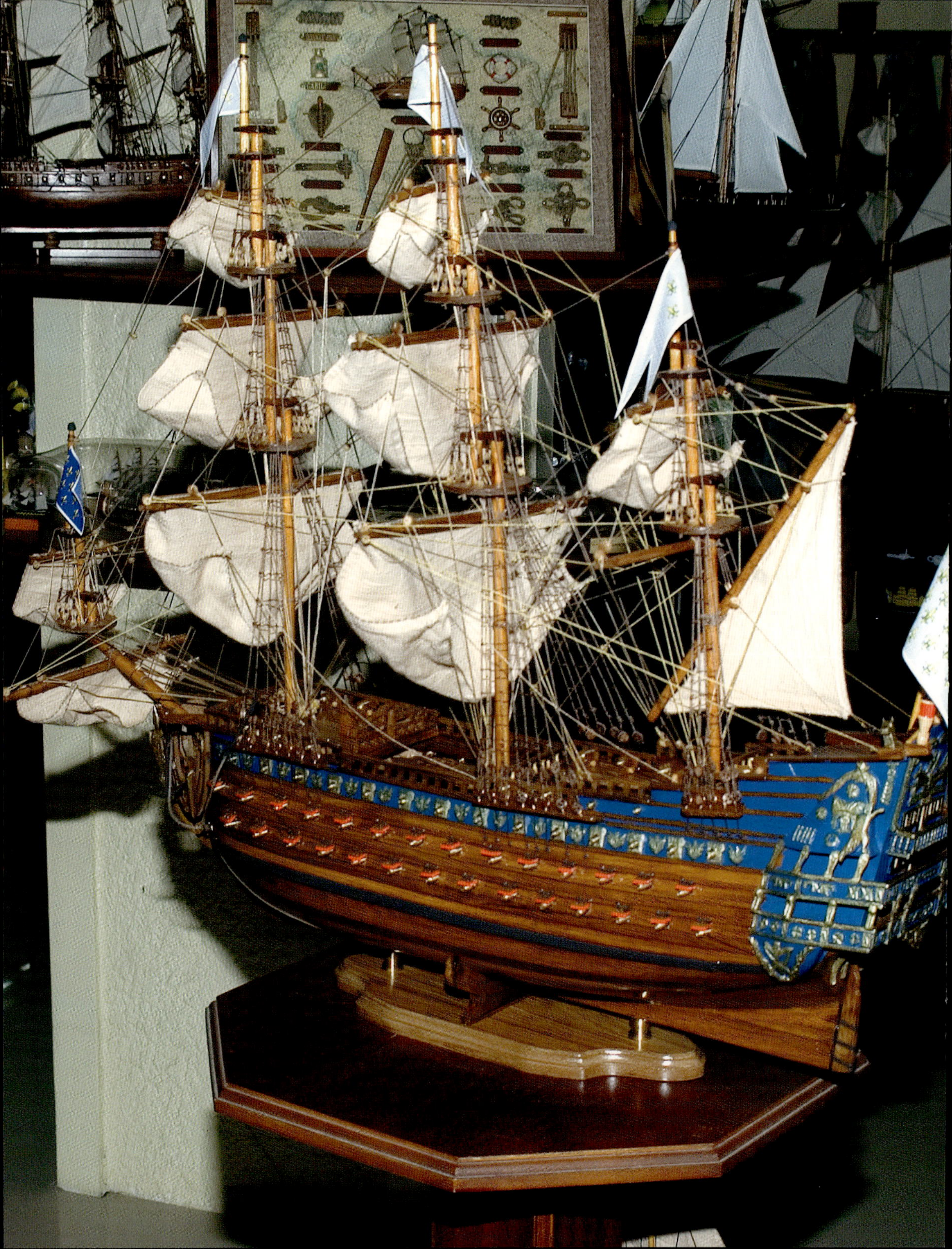

From everyday items to once-in-a-lifetime treats, shopping in Mauritius caters to both your most basic needs and your most intimate desires, with luxury goods being high on the agenda at very advantageous prices.

The island runs the full gamut of emporia. The pleasure of browsing in a high-class air-conditioned boutique can be followed by the excitement of strolling through a rustic street market. The same is true for budgets. It's possible to have fun with very few rupees or max out the highest limit on any credit card.

A plethora of designer names entice those with an eye for instantly recognizable quality, but it's the wonderfully colourful crafts and clothing that most reflect the spirit of this unique tropical isle.

Left: *Hand-built scale model sailing vessels are a Mauritian speciality, but don't expect to take this example as carry-on baggage on your return flight!*

What to Buy – Best Buys

If you love shopping, you'll be in heaven in Mauritius. Whatever your budget there's such a range of goods available that you can spend more than a few hours comparing quality and price to seek out that perfect souvenir.

Diamonds

Mauritius doesn't mine diamonds, but its close neighbour South Africa has one of the world's largest reserves. Since the 1970s several diamond-polishing houses have become established on the island and jewellery has become big business, with the rough diamonds arriving direct from the diamond auction houses and being transformed into brilliant gems. The polisher must use his skill to decide how best to shape each one, taking into account the size, the shape of the mined base stone and any flaws within it. You can buy loose stones in a variety of cuts and finished jewellery pieces, or you could have a bespoke piece made within a few days. Prices are competitive, especially with the additional 15 per cent duty-free discount (*see* page 128).

Diamonds are priced according to the balance of four main criteria – colour, clarity, cut and size – so a bigger stone with flaws may cost less than a smaller but 'cleaner' stone. When buying diamonds you should be given detailed information about the quality of the stone you are buying and a certificate of authenticity to accompany any purchase.

Cledor was the first diamond polishing company on the island but it was closely followed by Adamas (the name is Greek for diamond). Both companies concentrate on fine gem jewellery. Other companies include Vendome, who sell a good range of designer watches in addition to jewellery; Poncini and Parure.

Textiles

From cotton to cashmere, Mauritius supplies some of the major fashion houses and high street names with fin-

Right: *Textile production is a major industry on Mauritius and cloth is an excellent buy.*
Below: *Gem jewellery – particularly diamonds – and designer watches are good value. The quality of the craftsmanship is high and prices are tax-free.*

What to Buy – Best Buys

SHOPPING IN PORT LOUIS

ished clothing items, and 'Made in Mauritius' is a benchmark of quality that you can trust. The most up-market brand has to be Cerruti 1881, part of the Italian *haute couture* empire, but fashion names such as Guess, Gant and Burberry feature prominently. Although the bulk of the finished products head out of the island to hit stores worldwide, the factory can sell production overruns and 'duty-free' shops have sprung up across Mauritius selling genuine branded clothing at attractive prices.

Be aware that the counterfeit market is as rife here as in other textile-producing countries, so the shirts, shorts and other clothing with these same brand names found in markets for very little money will, in all probability, be forgeries.

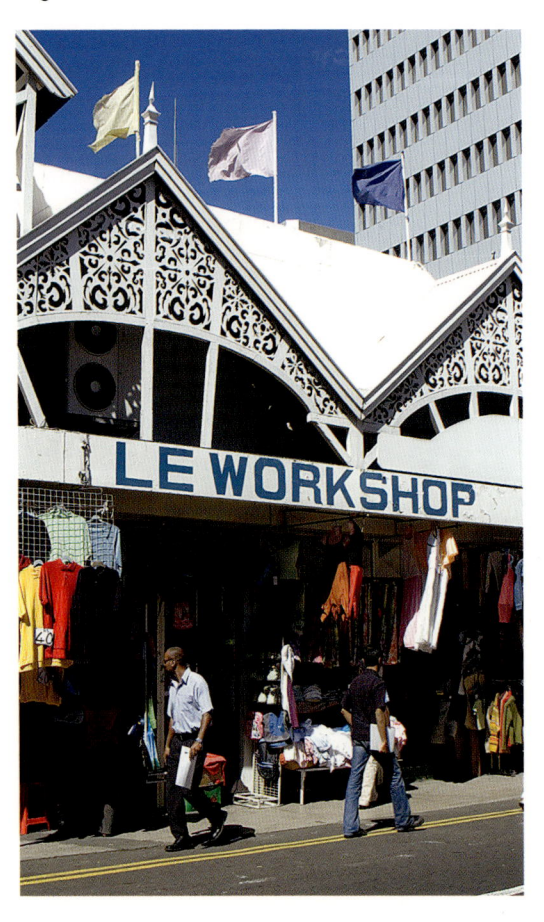

> ### The Duty-free Scheme
> Mauritius has a well-organized duty-free scheme for tourists that means you don't pay the 15 per cent VAT added to the price of goods on the island.
>
> Specialist duty-free shops are open only to foreign nationals and these offer high quality products such as jewellery and designer watches. The prices for these goods do not include the VAT element – i.e. they never enter the duty system in Mauritius – but, because of this, you will not be allowed to take them from the shop on the day you purchase them. They will be delivered to the airport and you pick them up at the Chamber of Industry and Commerce desk before you check in for your flight off the island.
>
> In order to purchase at a duty-free shop you will need to have your passport and return flight tickets with you. This is to prove that you will indeed be leaving the island and to confirm your flight details so that delivery goes smoothly. You must also pay in foreign currency – by cash, card or traveller's cheque.
>
> In an extension to the duty-free scheme, items such as textiles, leatherwear, art and photographic equipment can also be exported duty-free. Pay VAT at the time of purchase and get a refund at the airport when you leave by showing the goods and your receipt.

There are also a growing number of clothing designers and reliable trade names not seen outside the island. Karl Kaiser is the major outlet for Cerruti and other formal tailoring and you can buy off the peg or have a made-to-measure suit made during your stay. Both Harpers and Café Coton specialize in men's formal cotton shirts, while Maille Street/In'Am boutiques specialize in cashmere. The factory outlets for major

***Left**: Small family-owned workshops all across the island produce inexpensive clothing for local people and can make you a shirt or pair of trousers in a day or two. You can take home many inexpensive copies of your favourite outfit.*

What to Buy – Best Buys

producers at Floréal, Vacoas and Curepipe are good bargain-hunting territory. The most popular halt for organized day-tour buses is the Floréal Square Shopping Centre at Floréal which has several duty-free and factory stores in one complex.

Branded goods aren't the only quality clothing buys, however. Mauritius has hundreds of small family-run workshops that will copy your favourite shirt or run you up a made-to-measure suit at a fraction of the cost at home. Simply bring the article or a picture with you and, after choosing your fabric, the replica will be completed in a couple of days.

Food and Drink

Wherever there's sugar cane, there's rum – it's a fact of life. In the early days rum soothed the daily grind for slaves working in the fields and fuelled the hot tempo of the sega (see page 78) they danced in the evenings. Today the basic white rum (or *rhum agricole*) makes an ideal base for the thousands of cocktails served at beach bars every day, while distilleries have also developed a finer product, 'aged' rum, to compete with the fine cognacs and other European *digestifs* (after-dinner drinks). Aged Mauritian rum is a little sweeter than its counterparts in the Caribbean and is often flavoured with a hint of vanilla. You can try a tot at various domaines around the island including St Aubin, Domaine Les Pailles and at Eureka colonial house and buy direct if you like what you taste. Green Island and Goodwill are the main commercial producers, and their products, including a tasty Green Island Spice, are sold in all shops and supermarkets.

Very little Mauritian tea is exported, so if you enjoy this particular brew, you'll need to stock up while you are here. Most Mauritians buy loose tea in kilogram packets, but producers like Bois Cheri also make tea bags and infuse plain black tea with flavours such as vanilla and mint.

Pickles, chutneys and preserved spices can add a zest to your cuisine and you can buy prettily packaged examples in souvenir shops across the island.

Art

The colours of Mauritius can't fail to inspire the artist. Azure seascapes, palm-fringed beach scenes and heady sunsets challenge the palette, while the cultural kaleidoscope is a constant stimulation. There are several commercial galleries offering a range of tropical-themed art.

Vaco Baissac is a Mauritian artist who captures the essence of the island through his colourful naïve canvases. Fish feature prominently in his still-life paintings, while daily life is his second major inspiration; his style uses vibrant blocks of colour to build the finished piece.

Royal Road between Point aux Canonniers and Grand

Below: Dark sipping rum is aged in oak casks for five years before it's bottled and takes on the warmth of a cognac. Sold at various distilleries on Mauritius, the bottles below can be bought from L'Aventure du Sucre complete with a small sample of a specially developed sugar which, when added to the glass, further improves the taste of the rum.

Baie is certainly a hot spot for art buyers and you could spend a leisurely day exploring the several commercial galleries along the route. Galerie Helene de Senneville has an excellent reputation for island art and nearby is Galerie Raphael, while further north towards Grand Baie you'll find Galerie Françoise Vrot 'Chane Cane'.

Oriental and Asian Arts and Crafts

The island's strong connection with the Indian sub-continent and China extends to its shopping. Imports of the finest Indian and Chinese handicrafts cater to the demands of discerning Indo- and Sino-Mauritians, to the advantage of tourists who can find the treasures of the Orient here.

Hand-woven silk carpets make an exquisite souvenir, with their rich patterns and luxuriant, supple texture. Delicate silks and satins, some woven with gold thread, make excellent accent drapes or throws, while hand-carved brassware is fashioned into pots and mirror frames and intricately decorated fine porcelain adds an accent of decadence. Shops such as Macumba, Silk & Persian and Etoile d'Orient have an extensive choice.

In addition to truly western-style clothing there are some exquisite Indian-influenced fashions on the market and silk *churidar* pants or a *kameez* (tunic) make very wearable additions to your wardrobe, or you can invest in a beautiful sari (draped dress made of one long length of fabric and worn by Hindu women). Pushkaar boutique is particularly known for its modern Indian designer fashions.

If you have an interest in feng shui, the Chinese stores in Port Louis sell all manner of tokens and trinkets designed to improve the flow of chi or enhance luck and wellbeing.

Traditional Crafts

A little like the dodo, most traditional crafts haven't survived on Mauritius, but recently unusual modern crafts have taken their place and these have developed a particular tie to the island.

If you want to be sure of buying genuine local handicrafts, visit the shops of the National Handicrafts Promotions Agency (NHPA). The agency was formed by government statute in 1998 to promote crafts from Mauritius and Rodrigues so all items here are home-produced and most of the money you pay goes directly to the artisans concerned.

Basketware and Wicker

Natural fibres are readily available in the form of coconut, aloe and banana, and the production of

Left: *Beach vendors bring a souvenir stall to you at your sun-lounger, so no need to make a shopping trip. Just remember to haggle for a good price.*

basketware, place mats and other practical household items is one tradition that has survived. Colourful baskets of all sizes are piled high at the main markets and at souvenir stalls and shops around the island. Buy one at the start of your trip because they make great beach bags and you'll have had your money's worth even before you take it home.

Model Ships

Mauritius is known throughout the world for the quality of its hand-made model ships and the industry has grown very quickly. A handful of like-minded men made the first exact scale copies of classic sailing ships as a labour of love, but their magnificent craftwork caught the imagination of visitors during the 1970s and today there are several workshops where specialist artisans work on such craft as the *Mayflower*, *Cutty Sark* or *Golden Hind*. It's worthwhile visiting to watch the ships being made because it really brings home exactly how many hours worth of work it takes to complete even the smallest example of a model ship. The attention to detail is impressive, with specialist woods used for each element of the superstructure as they were in times of yore. Recently the industry has branched out to produce scale cross-sections of these same ships, showing the cargoes stacked on the lower decks and the ballast in the keel.

All the workshops are expert in packing the craft for transportation. Up to a certain size the ships can be carried as hand luggage or, if you opt for a super-sized example, they will arrange shipping. Most workshops are found in the Curepipe area, with Comajora, La Flotte and La Pirogue Maquettes de Bateaux being based there, though Historic Marine is based in Goodlands in the north.

Recycled Glass

The Mauritius Glass Gallery uses 100 per cent recycled glass for all its products. Its location close to the Phoenix brewery means there's certainly a ready supply of the raw material, but collections from around the island also stop other types of glass from taking up space in the overstretched refuse system.

All the gallery's products are hand-blown and include small kitschy dodos (a very popular purchase) and drinking glasses, as well as larger objects like lamps. You can have bespoke items made — perhaps etched with your name or a special date like a birth, wedding anniversary or birthday.

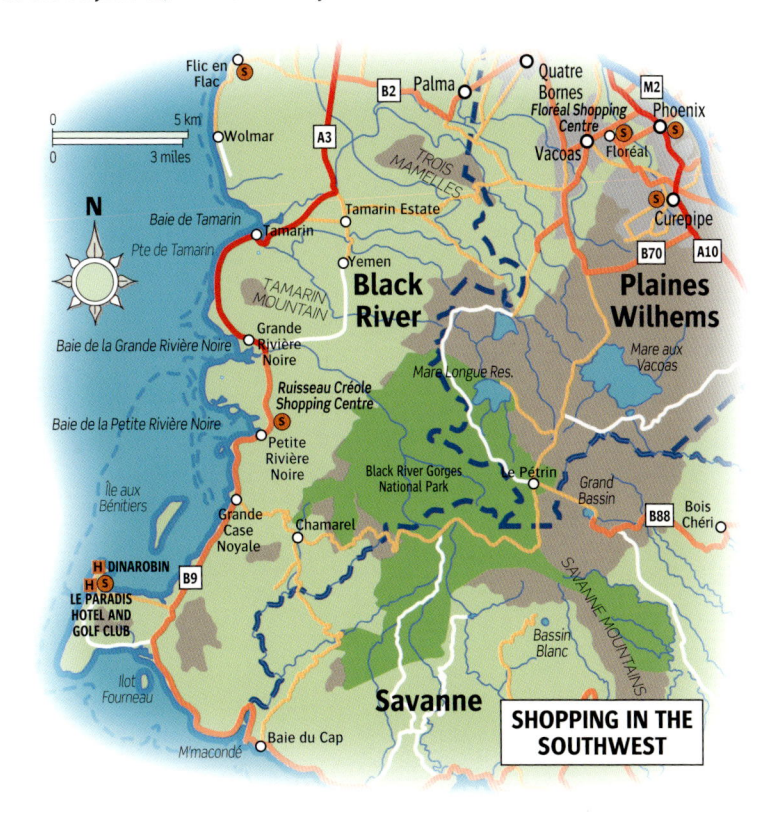

SHOPPING IN THE SOUTHWEST

Where to Buy
Markets
A trip to a Mauritian market assaults the senses: the smell of tropical fruits or incense wafting through the alleyways, colourful crafts and spices piled high in every direction and the hustle and bustle of hundreds of islanders hunting out a bargain and haggling for the lowest price.

Port Louis has the largest and best market and it's open every day with dedicated areas for food, meat and fish. The handicraft section of the market is replete with basketware, Hindu and Buddhist statuary, African wooden carvings, 'knock-off' T-shirts and other goods. It's a great place to check out what's available in the budget souvenir area, though the repeated sales pitches can become wearing.

Other markets around the island are less tourist-orientated and usually take place once or twice weekly. Try Centre de Flacq on a Wednesday or Sunday, or Mahébourg on a Monday.

Malls
Several small modern malls offer a contrasting atmosphere to the bustle of the market. The Port Louis harbour was transformed in the 1990s when the Caudan Waterfront complex was opened. It has a range of shopping including several duty-free jewellers and a craft market, and there's regular live entertainment.

Comptoir des Mascareignes is designed like a repository of the French East Indies Company, with a collection

Below: Sunset Boulevard Shopping Centre in Grand Baie is a modern open-air shopping mall with the most comprehensive souvenir shopping on the island.

Where to Buy

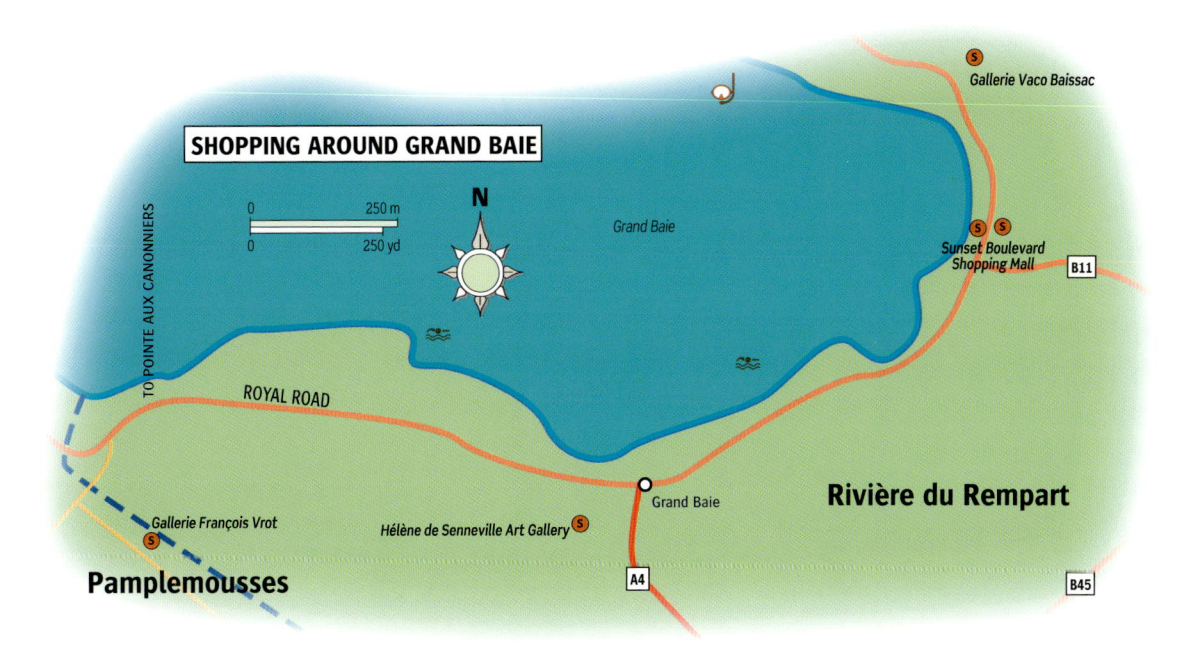

of individual boutiques selling traditional souvenirs, unique art work, jewellery or model ships. There's also a café on site.

Right at the heart of Grand Baie, Sunset Boulevard spans Royal Road and brings together a range of souvenir and clothing stores in a tree-lined open-air mall. Floréal Square Shopping Centre is small complex of twelve duty-free and factory outlets offering a one-stop shop for the best of everything souvenir-wise. Consequently it's on many tour bus schedules.

The island's newest complex, ultra-modern Ruisseau Creole, combines shopping with eateries, cafés, office space and modern loft-living style apartments. The accent here is on the up-market and many of the goods are imported for well-to-do locals, but here's also a craft market.

Beach Hawkers

In Mauritius the beach up to the high-tide mark is public property and it's the domain of the beach hawker. Some see them as a nuisance, but they do bring a range of budget souvenirs direct to your sun bed and a polite 'no thanks' is usually all it takes for them to move to the next prospective customer.

To Haggle or Not to Haggle?

Haggling is common in Mauritius. It's most widespread in the markets or on the beach, where you should never pay the first price asked. In shops, prices may seem to be fixed but it can't hurt to ask for a discount, especially if you are buying a high-value item or more than a single item. If business is slow – at the beginning or end of the season for example – traders may be more flexible on price. If you feel uneasy about haggling here are a few guidelines to ease the way:

Remember that haggling should be a friendly process through which a mutually satisfactory price is agreed upon. It's not a form of verbal combat. Try not to show too much interest in the item you want – feign disinterest. When a vendor offers you a price, counter with an offer of around half this sum. When the vendor counters with another price, counter again with a lower offer. You'll normally end up agreeing at around 75% of the vendor's original offer price.

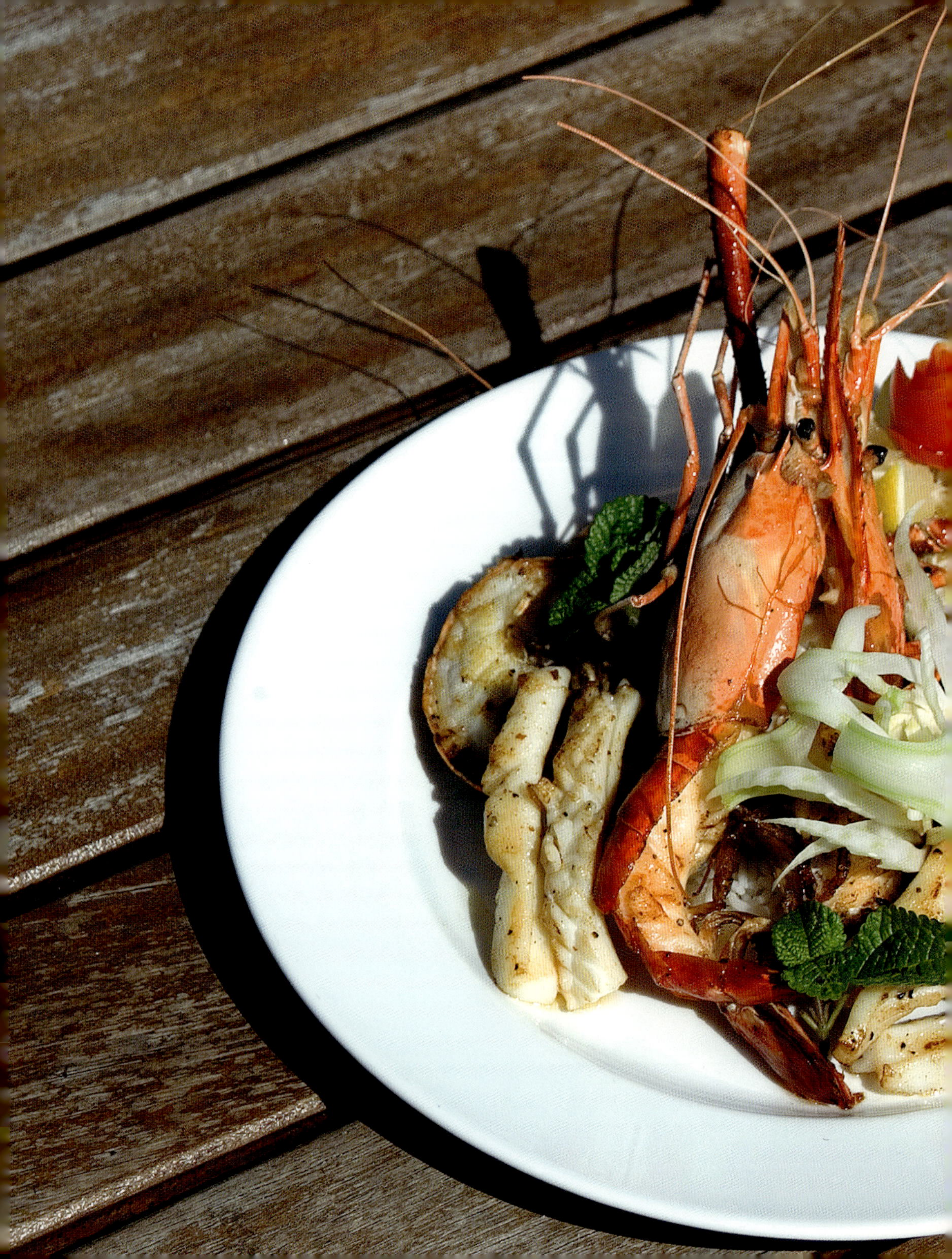

Island Cuisine

Left: *You'll find delicious fresh seafood everywhere on Mauritius, such as this delicately arranged seafood platter served at the Paul et Virginie Restaurant at One&Only Le Saint Géran.*

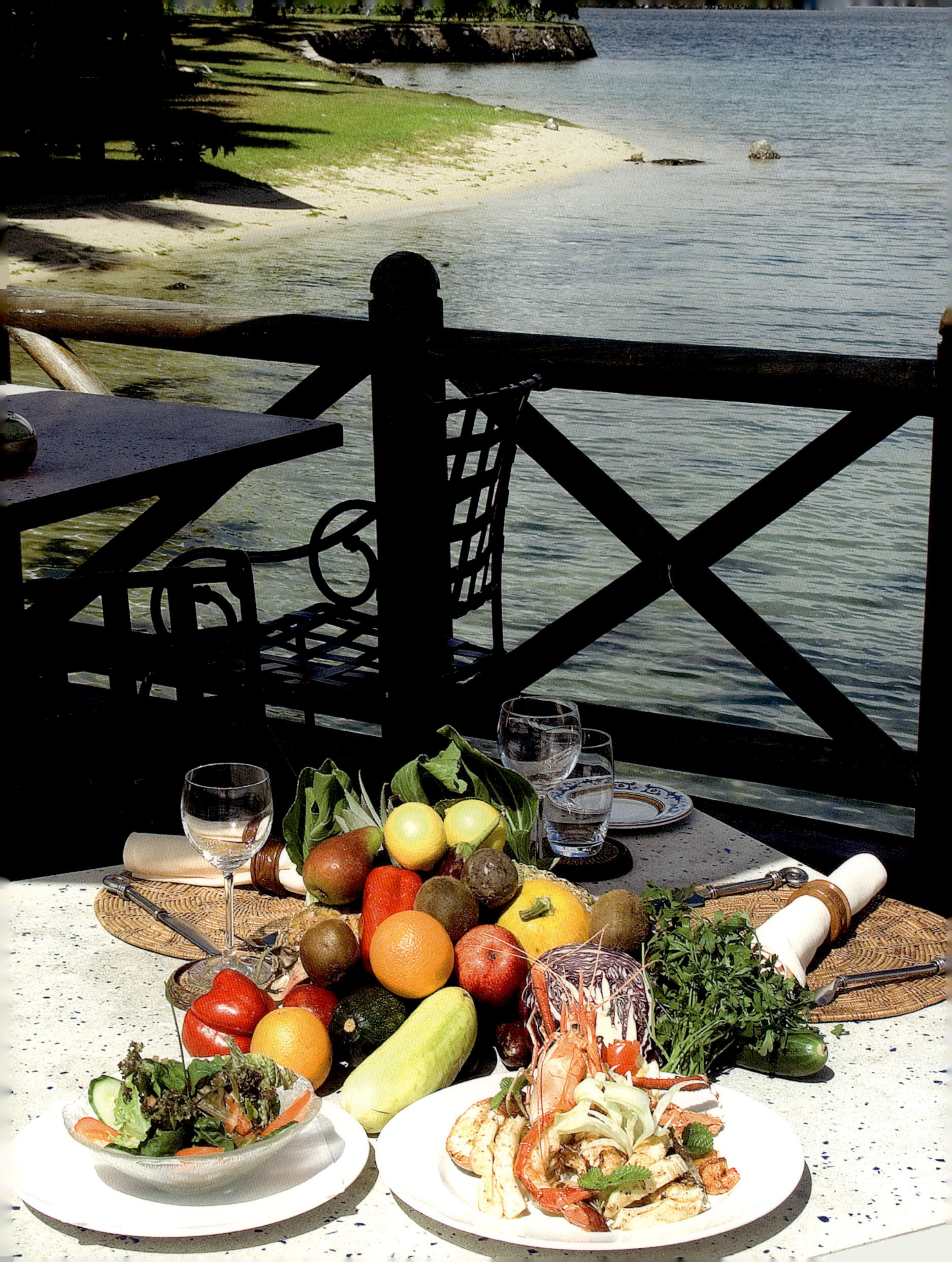

The recipe reads like this: take first-class ingredients from a tropical island. Mix them with the finest others imported from around the world. Add a touch of spice. Put this combination in the hands of some of the most inventive chefs in the business, including more than a sprinkling of gastronomic superstars. Dress the plate with creativity and flair, uncork an excellent vintage, then serve both accompanied by a warm smile against a fantastic island backdrop – *et voila!* Welcome to dinner in Mauritius.

From the tastiest freshly grilled lobster to the juiciest steak, your dish will be a delight to the taste buds and to the eye.

Left: *Tropical food at Paul et Virginie Restaurant, One&Only Le Saint Géran.*

Mauritian Cuisine

The higher-class hotels in Mauritius work hard on their cuisine. They know that the quality and variety of their food will have a major impact on the satisfaction each client has with their holiday, so attention to detail is vital. All the large properties have a choice of places to eat, with a main restaurant generally serving buffet or gala-style dinners, plus a choice of one or more specialist restaurants offering a more intimate dining experience with the flavours of the Mediterranean basin, France, India or Asia served in beautifully designed surroundings.

Hotel executive chefs are kings of the kitchen and have vast experience of world cuisine. They add their inspirations to the culinary mix and import the latest trends to keep the taste and presentation fresh and up-to-date. Several chefs have received that most coveted of culinary accolades – one or more stars in the Michelin Red Guide (see page 141) – and Alain Ducasse, one of France's most accomplished restaurateurs, oversees, arguably, the most prestigious restaurant on the island, the Spoon des Îles, at the One&Only Le Saint Géran Hotel.

The eclectic cultural mix that is Mauritius carries through to its traditional cuisine. A panoply of Indian spices, abundant tropical vegetables and fruits from Africa and Asia, game imported by the colonists and the bounty of the Indian Ocean combine to make your taste buds tingle.

The melange of Indian and African ingredients accompanied by just a dash of French *je ne sais quoi* can lay claim to being the world's first 'fusion' cuisine, a trend that didn't really take off anywhere else until the late 20th century. Several dishes form the basis of cuisine within most Mauritian households. All these are accompanied by rice, which is the staple carbohydrate, *brèdes* (various gardens greens such as cabbage or watercress stir-fried with onions, garlic and hot chillies), or *achard* (finely chopped vegetables pickled in wine vinegar and mixed with a spicy paste of slow-cooked finely sliced onion, mustard seed, garlic and saffron).

The most common meats in butcher's shops are goat, venison and chicken as all three can be eaten by all the religious groups on the island – pork is forbidden to Muslims, and Hindus eat neither beef nor pork. Wild boar is also popular, especially during the hunting season.

The chosen meat can then be cooked in one of a range of rich spicy sauces including *carri* (curry), which has a base of puréed onions, garlic and ginger with chilli, cumin, coriander and turmeric in various amounts; *daube*, a sauce featuring potatoes and peas; *kalya*, saffron, ginger and garlic; or *rougaille*, a rich tomato-based stew made with the native *pommes d'amour* – Mauritian tomatoes that are smaller, sweeter and have a more intense flavour than other varieties.

Several species of muscular fish can be substituted for meat, and octopus is especially prized, particularly in a *rougaille*. Fish *vindaye* is also a mainstay – soused in a spicy cider vinegar marinade that gives it a slightly tangy, sweet and sour taste. Freshwater crayfish are farmed on the island and taste delicious simply grilled with a squeeze of lemon. Smaller prawns are added to curry, often in conjunction with chicken.

Eating street food is a way of life for Mauritians, who always seem to be snacking. Prices are incredibly cheap because the street stalls cater to the ordinary working population. They stock up on *dholl purri* – wheat pancakes stuffed with a helping of *dholl* (mashed split peas) served with a side of tomato sauce – or a *samosa*, often spelt *samoosa* (a triangular pastry packet stuffed with spicy meat, vegetables or both).

Two dishes can be classed as island delicacies. Heart of palm has long been a traditional Mauritian celebratory food. A miniature palm tree species, the plant is grown for five years and the whole tree discarded for the soft white flesh at the base of the trunk. This is scooped out and put into fresh milk to stop it from discolouring, and just before serving it is finely sliced and dressed with a light oil and ground pepper. Or try smoked marlin; the meat of this muscular fish has a delicate flavour and is finely sliced in the same way as smoked salmon.

Mauritian Cuisine

Above: *Mauritian Creole cuisine is based on an aromatic mix of exotic spices and fragrant herbs, blended to perfection.*

Most hotels will offer a Mauritian buffet once a week – probably to coincide with a demonstration of traditional sega dancing – but though the ingredients are without doubt of a high quality, you'll find the rich spiciness of the genuine article has been tempered to cater to the blandest palate. Staff will always be able to supply you with hot sauce or fresh chillies if you want to give the food a bit more of a Mauritian kick.

International Cuisine

Major hotels will always have a range of international dishes to enjoy and the quality is outstanding. The finest ingredients – from extra virgin olive oil to olives, truffles or foie gras – are imported to provide an authentic flavour and many restaurants are styled with a wonderful attention to detail.

Salads are crisp and delicately dressed, pizzas oven baked and piping hot, and a simple steak served just as you ordered it.

Breakfasts on Mauritius are a revelation, especially at the open kitchens of hotels like One&Only Le Touessrok or Le Paradis, where staff will cook your English-style breakfast or prepare pancakes as you wait. Alternatively you can browse the vast buffets for fruits, cold meat and cheeses, smoked marlin and salmon, cereals or *viennoiserie*. You can even start the day with a buck's fizz!

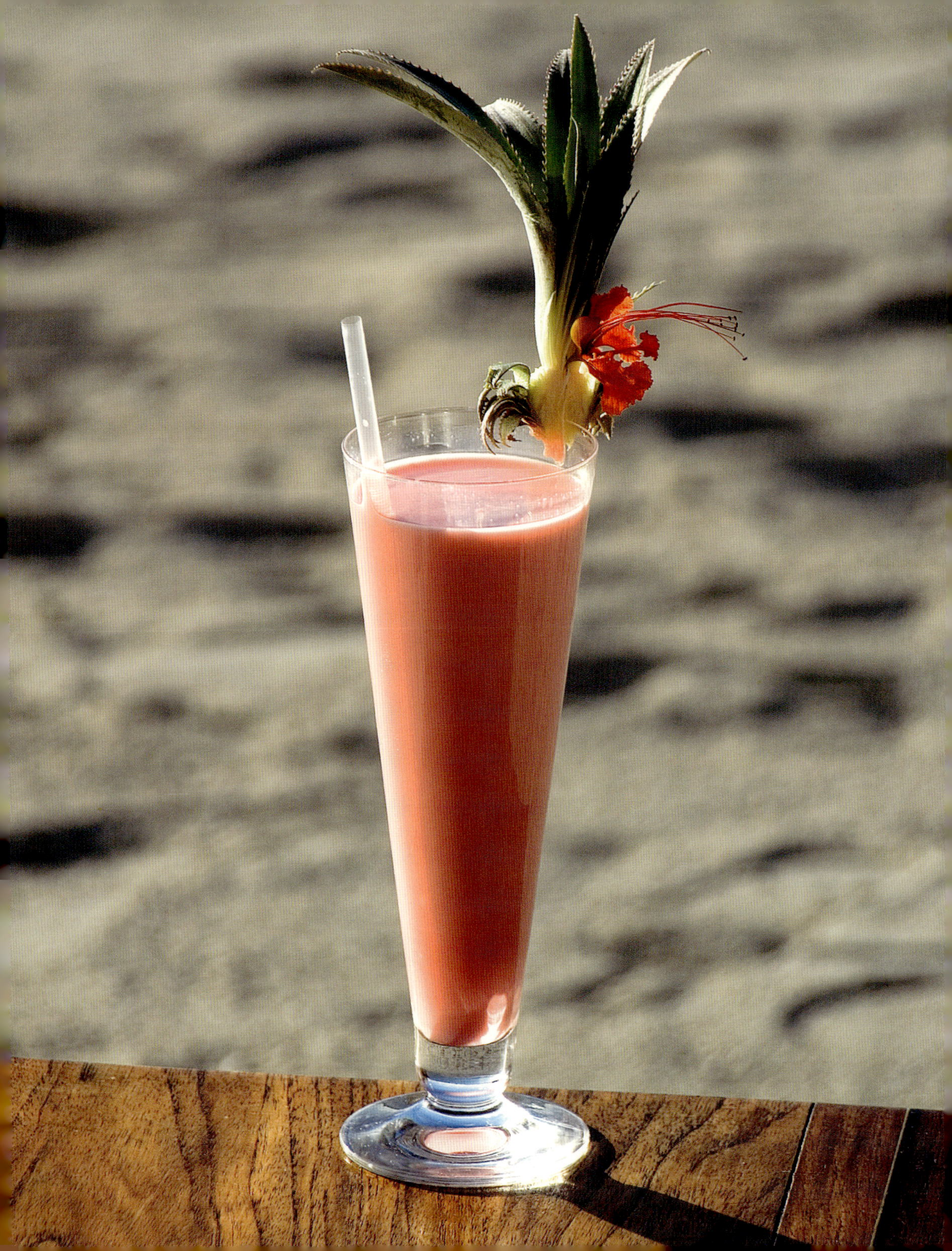

Drinks

Rum is part of the social fabric of the island and has been since it was first distilled in the 1630s. The clear *rhum agricole* is the industry standard and there are a couple of commercial producers on Mauritius – Green Island and Goodwill. White rum can be a little 'raw' if taken neat but is perfect at the heart of tropical cocktails, the alcohol making a perfect base note to the fruity melody.

Aged rum is a different matter. Left to mature in oak casks for five years, the base note of the *rhum agricole* develops into a rich fine 'tone', with a grace equivalent to a French cognac, and takes on a golden colour from the tannin of the barrel. Some aged rums are flavoured with vanilla and this adds a slightly sweet tone to the finished drink, while others (such as *rhum arrange*) are infused with fruit juices, including pineapple or guava. Aged rums are perfect as an after-dinner drink with coffee, or to accompany a fine cigar. Try them at St Aubin, Domaine Les Pailles, Eureka and at L'Aventure du Sucre, where a special sugar has been developed to complement the rum.

Mauritius also produces very tasty lager-type beer that is served at every bar across the island. Phoenix is the most popular brand and has been on the market since the 1960s, but you can also find Blue Marlin, a brew that's a little stronger in alcohol content.

Despite a total lack of vines, Mauritius has a wine producer. Oxenham and Company was founded by Edward Clark Oxenham in 1932 and began maturing and bottling wine produced from imported raisins. Later the company moved on to production using concentrated grape juice along with domestic gin and vermouth. Today the staff complement at Oxenham and Company includes no fewer than three qualified oenologists – a testament to their quest for quality – and their wines are the leading brand on the domestic market.

Left: *What could be more tempting than a freshly prepared tropical cocktail delivered to your sun-lounger by a beach butler in a crisp uniform while you laze the afternoon away, enjoy a good book or work hard perfecting your tan!*

Oxenham wines don't appear on hotel wine lists, however. An extensive range of wines is imported from around the world to complement the international cuisine, including excellent labels from France, Italy and Australia. Because of the proximity of Mauritius to South Africa, wines from the Western Cape are well in evidence and often make the best value choices on lists where prices per bottle can rise to many thousands of Mauritius rupees. Bellingham and Morgenhof are two labels to look out for.

The Michelin Star Guide

The Michelin quality rating for restaurants is probably the most famous in the world, partly because the organization is based in France – the undisputed birthplace of gastronomy – and partly because throughout their history they have remained exclusive, with very few restaurateurs receiving the ultimate accolade of three stars (in Michelin parlance 'exceptional cuisine – worth a special journey').

Michelin began writing guidebooks in 1900. In 1920 they began offering independent quality assessments of the restaurants and hotels they included in their guides, and the rest – as they say – is history. Quite why the tyre manufacturer decided to diversify in this way is lost in the mists of time but it was a master stroke, and an immediate success with the Francophone public.

Michelin did the legwork for its readers, distilling the many thousands of restaurants across the country into a shortlist of the best and most innovative, awarding them between one and three stars. Before too long restaurateurs were clamouring for a Michelin star or two, and with clever marketing the reputation of the star system grew and grew. Today, a dedicated team of anonymous reviewers visit restaurants regularly (perhaps a candidate for the best job in the world?) and chefs must have ultimate dedication in order to keep or improve their rating.

Detractors complain about a bias towards French cuisine in the Michelin system, but for the public it remains a trustworthy badge of excellence.

Island Cuisine

Restaurants

The following selection features a range of the best eateries on the island. We've included a variety of hotel restaurants and private enterprises chosen for the quality of their cuisine, their ambience, and their setting. Most hotel restaurants are open to non-guests but you will need to make a reservation.

Spoon des Îles

Michelin three-star chef from the age of 33 and Michelin's first six-star restaurateur (having two individual three-star restaurants), Alain Ducasse has developed into a one-man gastronomic industry with legendary establishments in Monte Carlo, Paris and New York. The 'Spoon' restaurants are his idea and their mission statement is to 'make *haute cuisine* approachable and understood by everyone'.

The concept is simple: a unique modular menu combining innovative tastes and textures which at Spoon des Îles also brings Creole influences into the mix. It's a challenging concept that excites the taste buds, and the ultramodern blood red décor and Philippe Stark designed furniture is unlike anything else on Mauritius.

Citronella's Café

The Mediterranean meets Mauritius at this beachside restaurant, with its beautiful tiling putting one in mind of Tuscany or Provence. Sit at the bar to sip an aperitif or

Below: Phoenix beer has been produced on Mauritius since the 1960s. It's very refreshing when served ice cold.

Above: Citronella's Café at Sugar Beach Resort serves excellent dishes from around the Mediterranean.

relax in a comfy rattan chair while making your choices from the menu.

Executive chef Mauree puts a modern twist on cuisine from Southern Europe and North Africa, drawing from the staples of what is still regarded to be the healthiest cuisine in the world. Choose a delicious mezzeh platter (featuring Greek hummus and Tunisian tabouleh) or a refreshing goat's cheese salad dressed in balsamic vinegar and fragrant virgin olive oil to start your meal. Herbs such as thyme and rosemary flavour the meats of the entrées and there is always an exceptional seafood option.

La Ravanne

Surely a candidate for the most romantic restaurant on Mauritius, you can enjoy a beautifully prepared gastronomic meal while sitting barefoot in the sand under a thatch umbrella, listening to the sound of the lapping of the Indian Ocean in the background as wandering Creole minstrels serenade you at your table. The scene is set when you wait at the boat pier for a pirogue to whisk you across the water to the restaurant where you will be shown to your candle-lit table.

The surroundings shouldn't lull you into the assumption that this is any other beach bar – service is impeccable and the food a sublime mix of international and Creole influences backed by a wonderful wine list.

Karma House

Feng shui meets foie gras at Karma House, where the yin and yang are balanced by combining the finest elements in French cuisine with the freshness, colour and textures of the modern Asian style. The menu works to refresh rather than jade the palate with sauces that enhance, not smother, and vegetables that retain a crispiness sometimes lost in mainstream European restaurants.

Presentation is given as much attention as taste here, where the food is visually stimulating, and with an open kitchen you can watch the chefs at work. Beyond the food, the whole restaurant has been designed to enhance the eating experience, from the table settings to the precise placing of plants and accessories.

Niu

An ultra-contemporary Japanese/Asian restaurant, Niu is picking up trends in world cuisine and setting new style standards out on the street. The clean white lines of the walls and tiles extend to the Japanese designs of the staff uniforms and allow total concentration on the presentation of the finished dish.

The menu isn't extensive but includes signature dishes from Japan, China and several other Southeast Asian countries. Sushi and sashimi are freshly prepared at a separate open bar where clients can watch the intricate procedure performed with great professionalism. You can also eat outside at several terrace tables.

Namaste

The rich flavours of Indian cuisine are at their best at Namaste. Sit in the opulent Raj-inspired main dining area or on the narrow balcony where you can watch the nightly entertainment in the surrounding Caudan complex, but rest assured that the dishes you will be served will be the star of the show. The patient staff will explain your choices and will arrange for the spiciness of the dishes to be just to your taste. The main courses are inspired by the very varied cuisine of the subcontinent, with cool yoghurt curries vying with hotter Madras style, and you can balance these with rice or bread in various guises. Cooling raita and tart chutneys come as standard accompaniments. A piquant delight!

Varangue sur Morne

Originally a gamekeeper's lodge, the Varangue sur Morne has been transformed into a wonderful mountain restaurant that's well worth adding to your tour itinerary – French president Jacques Chirac did when he visited the island!

Below: Attention to presentation is as important as the quality of the food – this delicious Asian dish is a feast for the eyes.

Above: *A Mauritian* carri *(curry) comes with a seemingly bewildering array of extras, from cooling chopped cucumber to hot chutneys, plus of course a generous serving of rice and* dholl *(split pea) dip.*

The food has to be good to match the stunning views down to the coast or across the mountains from the open terrace. It doesn't disappoint, offering a range of Mauritian specialities alongside an à la carte menu influenced by classical French cuisine. You can try palm heart and smoked marlin and wild boar, opt for the Creole platter with a combination of shrimp, chicken, venison and octopus, or tuck into a simple steak.

La Dolce Vita

One of four restaurants to choose from at Domaine Les Pailles, La Dolce Vita is an Italian trattoria with a menu offering a range of pizza, pasta and salads plus more substantial Italian dishes. Tables are set outside under a vast shady canopy and there's a swimming pool where the kids can let off some steam and cool down after a morning at the museums or markets of Port Louis. The atmosphere is tremendously relaxed so it's a great option for families to break for lunch. The only problem might be that you spend the rest of the afternoon here!

La Pescatore

Pramod Gobin is one of a number of young Mauritian chefs who has eschewed the hotel kitchen route to success and opened his own restaurant instead. However, he doesn't have an insular attitude to cuisine and visits France regularly to collaborate with a Gallic restaurateur.

Seafood is a speciality here, which is appropriate given its coastal location, but everything on the menu is served with flair and is accompanied by a carefully selected range of southern hemisphere wines.

Seemingly perched atop the rocks above a sandy beach, the views from the terrace are stunning.

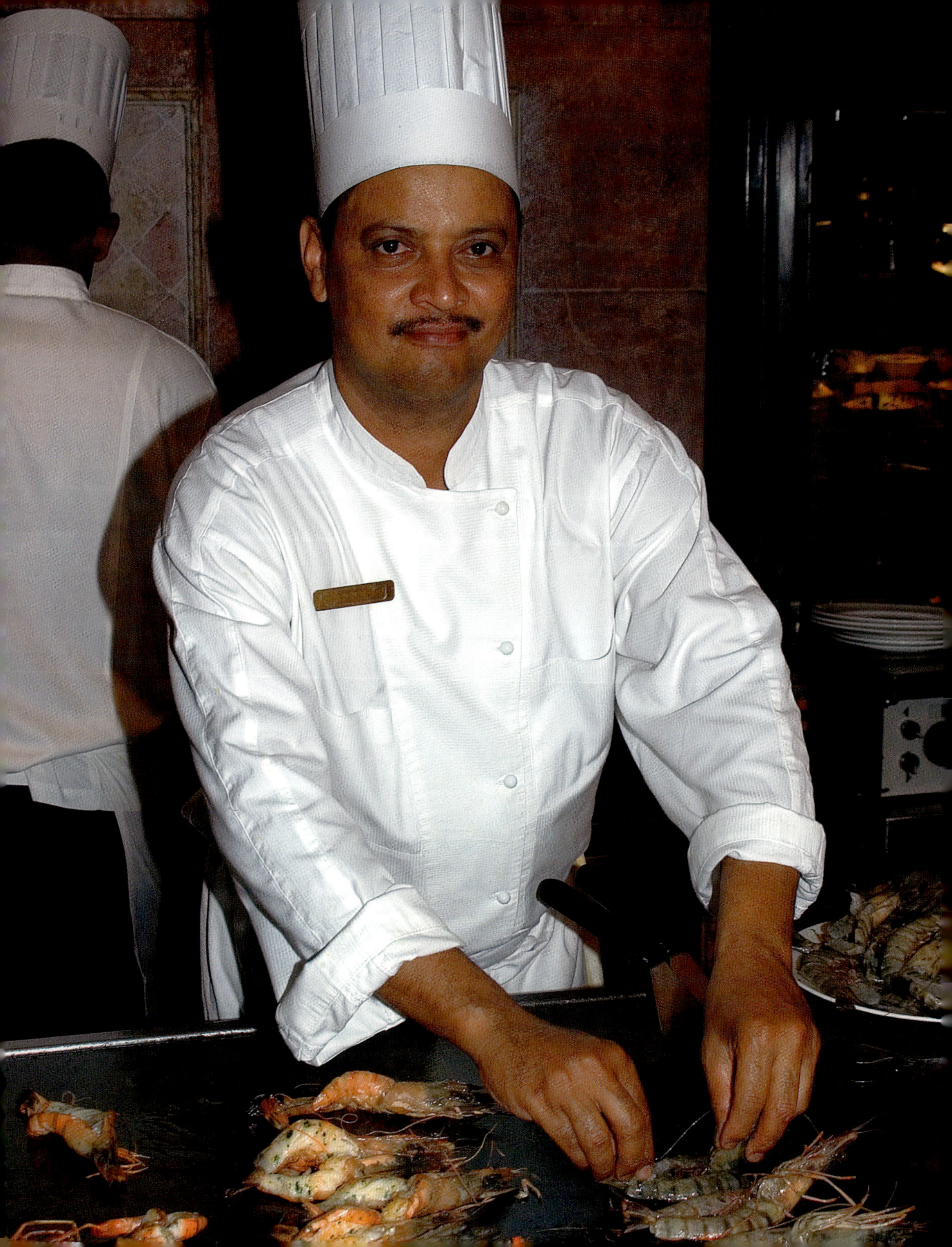

Chez Manuel

Run by husband-and-wife team Colette and Manuel, this restaurant has an island-wide reputation for excellent Chinese cuisine fused with Indian and Creole influences. Colette runs the kitchen and is a self-taught chef with a flair for innovation, though the traditional principles are never forgotten. Seafood dishes are a speciality.

Members of the minority ethnic Hakka Chinese community – a socially very conservative group originating around the Yellow River area of China, who are said to be descended from Chinese royalty – the couple will be happy to tell you a little about their customs and traditions.

Le Château de Bel Ombre

This genuine 19th-century mansion house, once the home of doctor and botanist Charles Edward Telfair, used to nestle amongst shimmering cane fields but now forms part of the new Le Telfair Hotel where it presides over the greens of the island's latest golf course. Inside, there's a grand wood-panelled dining room as befits this stately lady, and outside a magnificent veranda. You can enjoy a leisurely lunch, take afternoon tea complete with petit fours, or sit down to a sumptuous dinner. The cuisine is described as 'island international', mixing delicious Creole and classical French ingredients.

Le Barachois

Another candidate for 'most romantic restaurant', the Barachois is the signature restaurant at Le Prince Maurice Hotel. It's the only floating restaurant in Mauritius and sits on a wooden pontoon floating out on the lagoon and nestled amongst tropical mangrove. A wooden boardwalk leads you away from 21st-century Mauritius into the lush secret island of yesteryear, and

Left: At restaurants all across the island your friendly chef will grill the freshest seafood to perfection while you wait. Standards are high and the choice of tuna, lobster or shrimp is impressive. Enjoy it accompanied by the crispest chilled white wine, or perhaps a glass of bubbly.

the capacity of only 40 diners keeps the atmosphere intimate. The menu concentrates on grilled meats and seafood – what could be more simply delicious or more in keeping with the surroundings?

Café des Arts

This old 1840s sugar mill at Trou d'Eau Douce has been transformed into the most unusual restaurant in Mauritius. The owner, Jocelyn Gonzalez, is a first-class restaurateur but also an avid art collector, principally the works of Yvette Maniglier, an abstract painter and former pupil of the artist Henri Matisse. A chic gastronomic restaurant serving excellent French/Mauritian cuisine is its *raison d'être* but the dining room is stupendous, with Maniglier's vast modern canvasses lining the walls – adding visual stimulation to the culinary mix.

Where to Buy Food

If you are picnicking or self-catering you'll have no trouble finding a good range of foodstuffs, and preparing island cuisine means you'll be living healthily and cheaply because the prices of staple foodstuffs are incredibly low. Despite sugar cane staking a claim over the majority of the arable land, Mauritius still produces an amazing amount of fresh produce, and fruit and vegetables grow year-round.

The bustling markets of the major towns are fantastic places to buy your juicy fresh produce. Stalls are piled high with delicious pineapples, coconuts, sweet bananas and a massive choice of vegetables, from okra (ladies' fingers) and aubergine to sweet potatoes and tiny *pommes d'amour*, wonderfully sweet Mauritian tomatoes. Discerning shoppers crowd around picking out the produce that's perfectly ripe. Fruit and vegetables are picked fresh each day and it's only an hour at most to the market, but farmers will set up impromptu stalls just about anywhere – on street corners or at major road intersections – selling whatever is in season. Even a square of cloth can be turned into a sales area where ladies might spend all day selling a few kilos of tiny spicy chillies, ripe guavas, or bunches of fragrant herbs.

If you are buying meat, don't expect carcasses to be pre-butchered and laid out. The butcher will generally prepare your cuts for you at the time so you get exactly what you want. You'll also find that Mauritians are quite happy to use parts of the animals not popular in Europe, the USA or Australasia. Note that a lot of the meat sold on the island will be halal (slaughtered in ways approved by the Islamic faith).

Fish is on sale at the markets but is also sold by a vast fleet of mobile fishmongers who cycle around the villages in the late afternoon with their mobile scales, selling the fish just hours after it's been pulled from the ocean. Salesmen get their stocks at the fish landing docks, jostling around the tallyman as the catch is brought ashore in order to buy the finest looking specimens, then loading them into crates on their cycle handlebars. The fleets generally come in during late afternoon, and it's fascinating to get into the heart of the crowd as the bantering fishermen and two-wheeled sales force haggle jocularly over the price.

Mauritius also has a good number of modern supermarkets. You'll find a Winners supermarket in most major towns and there are Jumbo hypermarkets just north of Port Louis at Riche Terre Road and on the plains at Vacoas. There's a good-sized Leaderprice at the Barachois Shopping Mall at Tamarin, and a hangar-like Super U at Grand Baie. Supermarkets stock a vast range of imported goods, tinned products, pre-packaged fresh meats and wines and spirits – pretty much what you'd find at home.

One long-standing tradition passed down through the generations since French rule is good bread. Specialist bread stalls sell fresh, crispy baguettes and rounded loaves that could grace a Parisian *boulangerie*. Fresh croissants and a hot strong coffee make a delightful breakfast, and the continental pastries a tasty snack at any time of day.

Every village, no matter how small, will have a general store, often a colourful Creole-style building with brightly painted full length shutters. Stepping inside is like taking a step back in time, with the never-ending dark wooden shelves, old-fashioned high-topped counters, dusty bottles of liquor and the occasional family of free-range chickens strutting in and out.

Although full of atmosphere, the range of goods these stores carry is generally less useful to visitors than to local residents, consisting mainly of goods like rice sold by the 20kg sack or enough for a single meal, packets of biscuits, laundry powder and grass kitchen brushes – an eclectic mix for sure.

Left *Mauritius produces tonnes of crisp vegetables that form the basis of curries and rougaille around the island. The rich volcanic soil means crops grow well and many gardens have vegetable plots, with impromptu stalls selling piles of whatever is in season. Crops can be picked and be on the table within a few hours, ensuring optimum freshness and flavour.*
Right: *Markets are the main place to buy fruit and vegetables and a great place to do some picnic shopping and watch the world go by. Most small-scale farmers also sell their own crops rather than going through a middle-man, often only one or two sorts of fruit or vegetable depending on what's ripe at the time, though the main market in Port Louis has full-time professional stall holders with a range of fresh goods on display.*

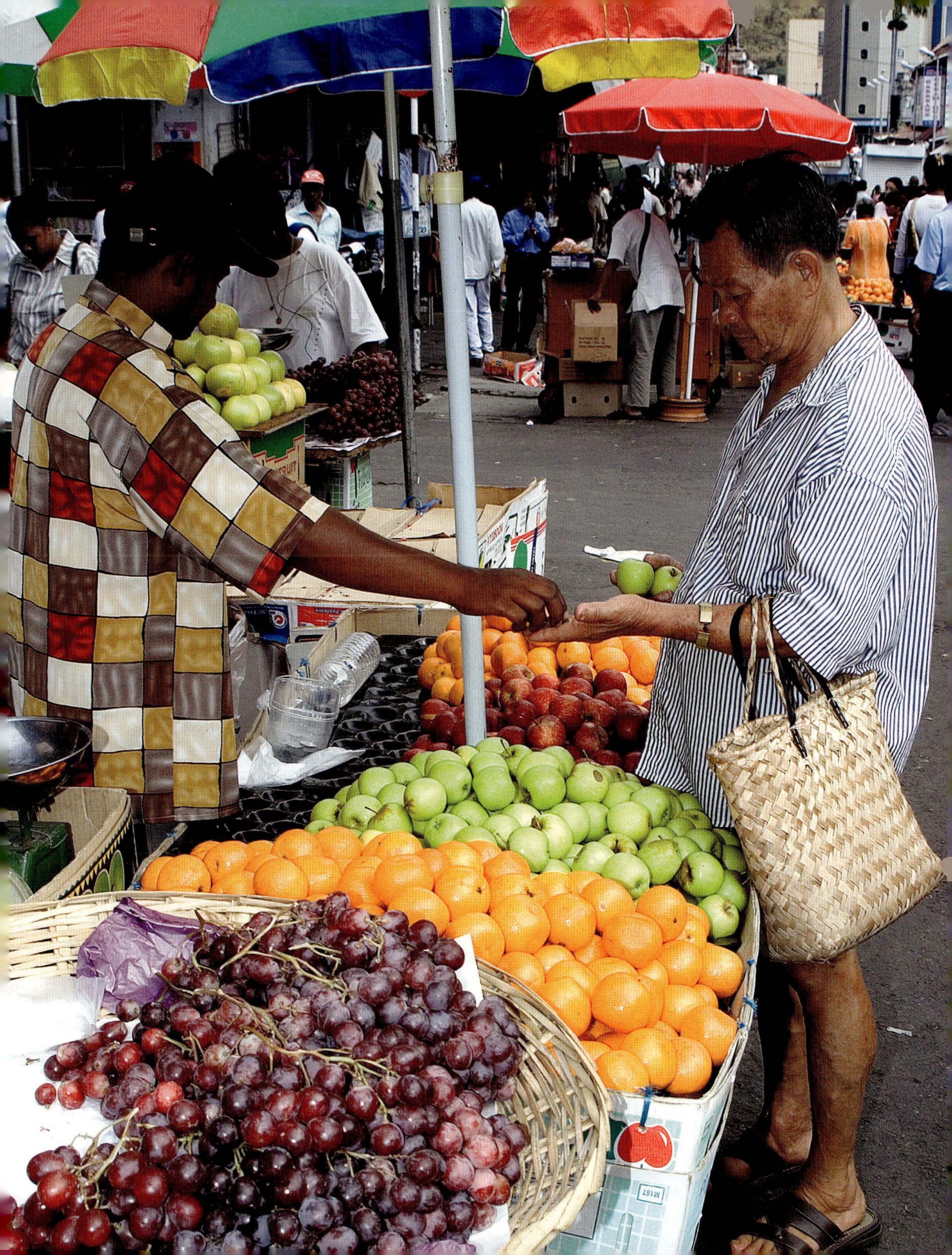

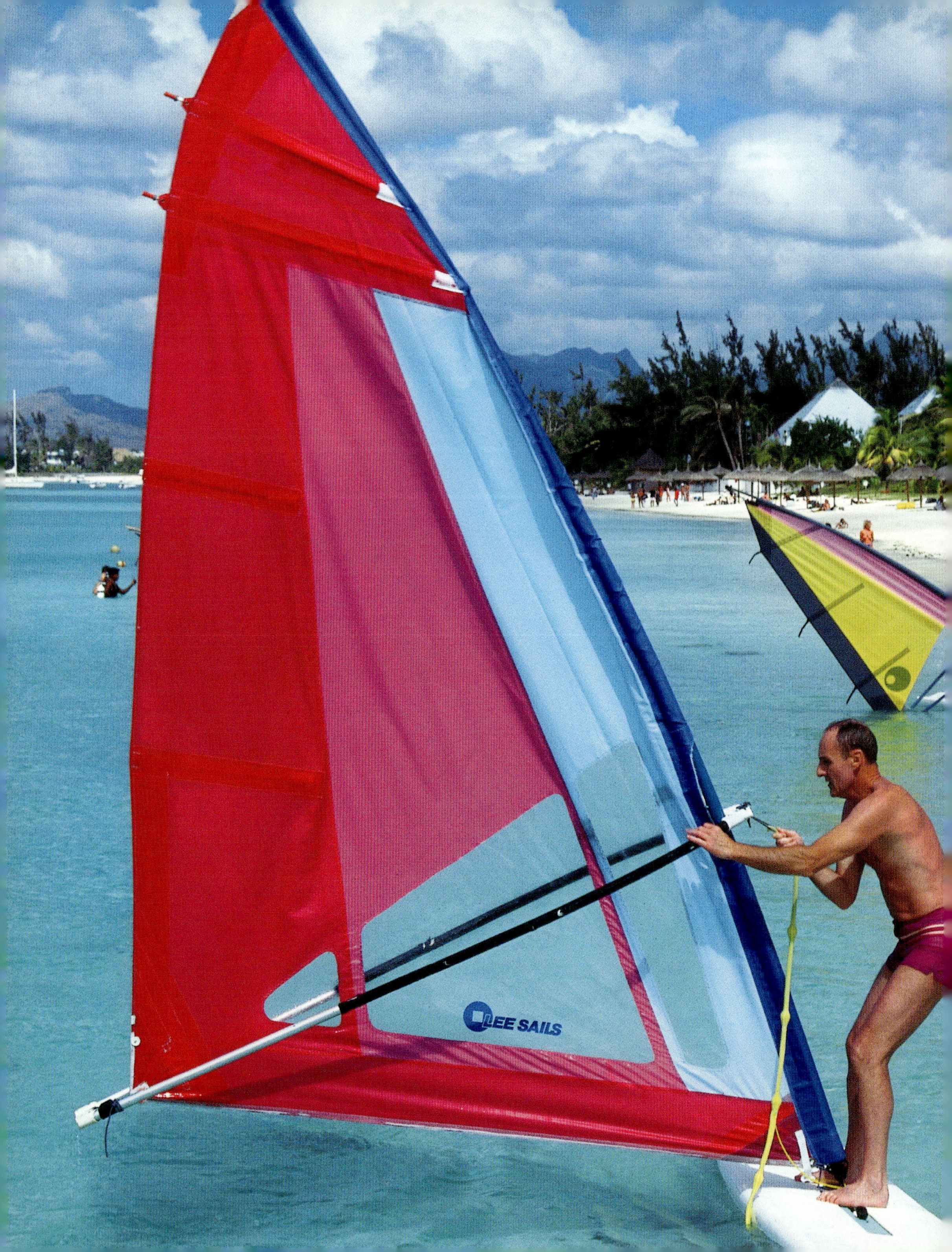
LEE SAILS

Surf and Turf

Left: The offshore lagoon is the perfect environment for windsurfing – for both beginners and experts.

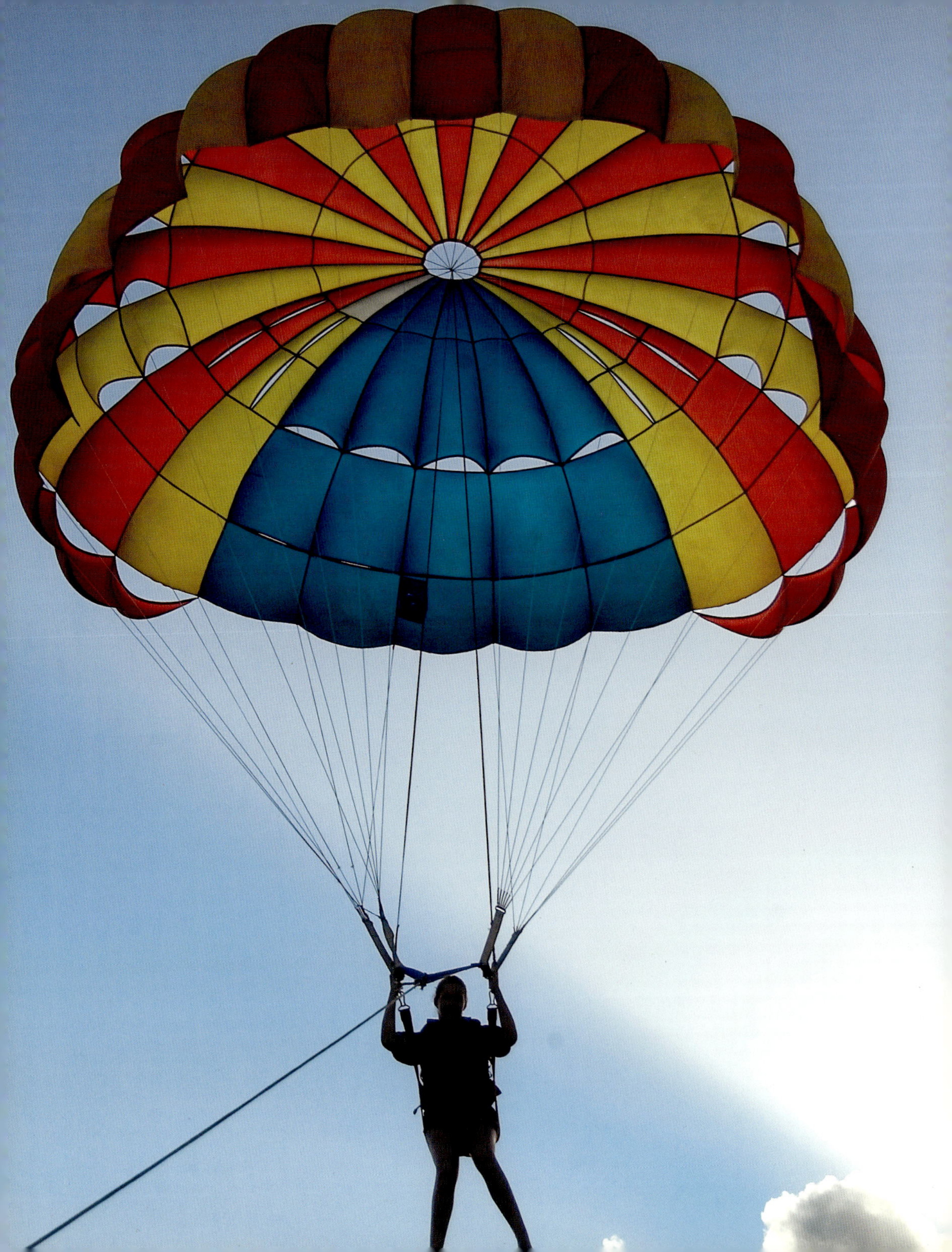

Mauritius is one of the world's most impressive adult playgrounds. Whether you want to get active or relax and indulge in the ultimate pampering package, the island offers exactly what you need.

Of course, the basic ingredients have been provided by Mother Nature but the tourist industry has successfully embellished nature by laying on the toys we need to get out and enjoy the current 'in vogue' activities, whether they be on land, on the water surface, or at the sea bed. Several island spas have been voted in the industry 'Top Ten', gleaming multimillion dollar catamarans and high-speed motor yachts ply the waters, pristinely kept greens beckon, while fleets of gutsy quad-bikes await for cross-country adventures. It doesn't get much better than this!

Left: Parasailing is not only exhilarating but offers great high level views of the lagoon and coastline.

Boats and Blue Marlin

If Ernest Hemingway were alive today he'd certainly be casting his line in Mauritius, universally agreed to be amongst the world's finest sport fishing grounds. Even if you don't want to catch a minnow you can satisfy that fantasy of sunning yourself on your own huge gin palace, forget that it's only rented for the day. The beguiling azure waters of the southern Indian Ocean tempt even the most stalwart landlubber, so get out onto the water and enjoy yourself!

Casting

For sport fishing it's difficult to top Mauritius. More than a few world records have been set here in various International Game Fish Association (IGFA, the sport governing body) sport fish categories.

Pacific blue marlin are the most prized of sport fish. Majestic creatures, female marlin can weigh over 450kg and possess a fearsome spear for a snout. They don't give up without a fight and landing one requires maximum guile, strength and stamina. The best season for mammoth specimens is between November and April but they can be found in Mauritian waters throughout the year, along with the smaller black marlin. The island hosts the prestigious Marlin World Cup every year in December.

Other big strong fish include several species of shark. Mauritius holds the world record for the biggest mako shark (at 505kg) and for the weightiest blue shark caught on a 104kg line (at 181kg). Hammerheads are plentiful in August and September, and tiger sharks can reach over 544kg in weight. The most beautiful if not the biggest sport fish is the sailfish, which sports an iridescent frill for an upper fin. The largest caught in Mauritius waters is 64kg.

Note that boats operate a catch-and-release policy on these impressive sport species so your day of fun doesn't lead to the demise of a prime fish. Your fish will be landed and a tag attached to it before being put back into the water. The tag will allow authorities and boat captains to monitor a range of sport fish populations.

Skipjack tuna make perfect bait for the larger species, but interestingly there's also a healthy sport in catching these super-fast smaller fish. Mauritius holds world records in all skipjack tackle categories and has the current record for dog tooth tuna on a 22kg line. If you just want good eating fish you could cast for wahoo and dorado; however, note that that any catch normally forms part of the remuneration for the crew who sell to local restaurants at the end of the day.

Spotting

One species that's never the object of the sport fishing community is the dolphin. These playful mammals enjoy the warm waters and ocean currents as much as the

Left: *If you want to try sport fishing, boat hire is easy at the hotels or in the major resorts. This shark is just the kind of fish you could get on your line.*

Above: Powerful speedboats are a great way to get around. Hire them by the hour or the day to take you to Île aux Cerfs or other offshore islands.

marlin, and often swim alongside pleasure craft. They are most prolific between May and August but are spotted throughout the year. Dolphin tours head out most mornings but will need pre-booking.

Island Jaunts

Boats aren't just for fishing, however. Charter one to whisk you away to a 'desert' island – there are several just offshore.

The Île aux Cerfs is the stuff of legend. Since Mauritius burst on to the tourist scene, it's become one of the world's most glamorous 'must see' locales. The teardrop-shaped beaches of fine golden sand give way to languid azure shallows backed by a canopy of verdant palms and casuarinas – the essence of a million enticing travel photographs; it's all waiting here to be explored.

The 300-hectare island is a long-time favourite with Mauritian families who take the boat trip from Trou d'Eau Douce on Sundays carrying an ample picnic basket.

Perhaps dad will do some fishing off the rocks on the east coast and an impromptu barbecue will deliver delicious grilled grouper or capitaine fish as an entrée.

If you don't want to rent a fancy yacht to get to Île aux Cerfs, book an organized tour with a company or, if you have your own transport, drive to Trou d'Eau Douce and take one of the small private ferry boats. They'll drop you off and then return at the end of the day to whisk you back to the mainland. But in 2006, Île aux Cerfs is not the virgin island of old; it's been transformed into a 21st-century tourist playground with restaurants, water sports, and, most recently, the Île aux Cerfs golf course operated by One&Only resorts, whose greens flow over expansive grounds on the southern tip of the island.

At low tide, the northern beaches of Île aux Cerfs entwine in a tender embrace with the southern strands of Îlot Mangenie and it is possible to walk through the shallows from one to the other (check tide timetables if you don't want to swim back). The diminutive sibling has many of the alluring characteristics of its bigger sister but no public facilities – though One&Only operate a beach restaurant for their own guests.

Further down the east coast just south of Mahébourg,

Îles des Deux Cocos sits in pristine waters just off Blue Bay. A petite jewel of an island, it was a favourite retreat for British Governor Sir Hesketh Bell who built a splendid little folly, a summerhouse redolent of Morocco or Tunisia, where he held lavish parties for the early 20th-century 'in' crowd. For many years the house was disused but it's been restored with great attention to detail by the Naïade hotel group who run day trips to the island with buffet lunch, drinks and snorkelling or glass-bottom boat trips included. The snorkelling here is excellent because Île des Deux Cocos sits just outside the boundary of the Blue Bay Maritime National Park. It's a fascinating place to watch the coral polyps filter feeding and the numerous tropical fish that call the place home.

Naïade limit the numbers who visit Île des Deux Cocos each day, so it does feel as though you have the place pretty much to yourself and you can spend the afternoon relaxing before being whisked away by boat. Naïade also rent the island out to families or to honeymooners who, after being pampered by staff until late evening, are left alone to enjoy their island getaway.

It's easy to charter a boat for either sport fishing or a pleasure cruise. All the major hotels have staffed craft that you can hire by the day. Sportfisher in Grand Baie is a well-established fishing company, or for boat charters try Terres Oceanes, Croisieres Australes or Gamboro. These are all based in the north of the island around Grand Baie.

Right: *Local fishermen are experts at finding fish in the coastal lagoon. They use simple rods and reels, plus a tremendous amount of patience, to land enough for the evening meal. It's also a great place to hang out with friends.*

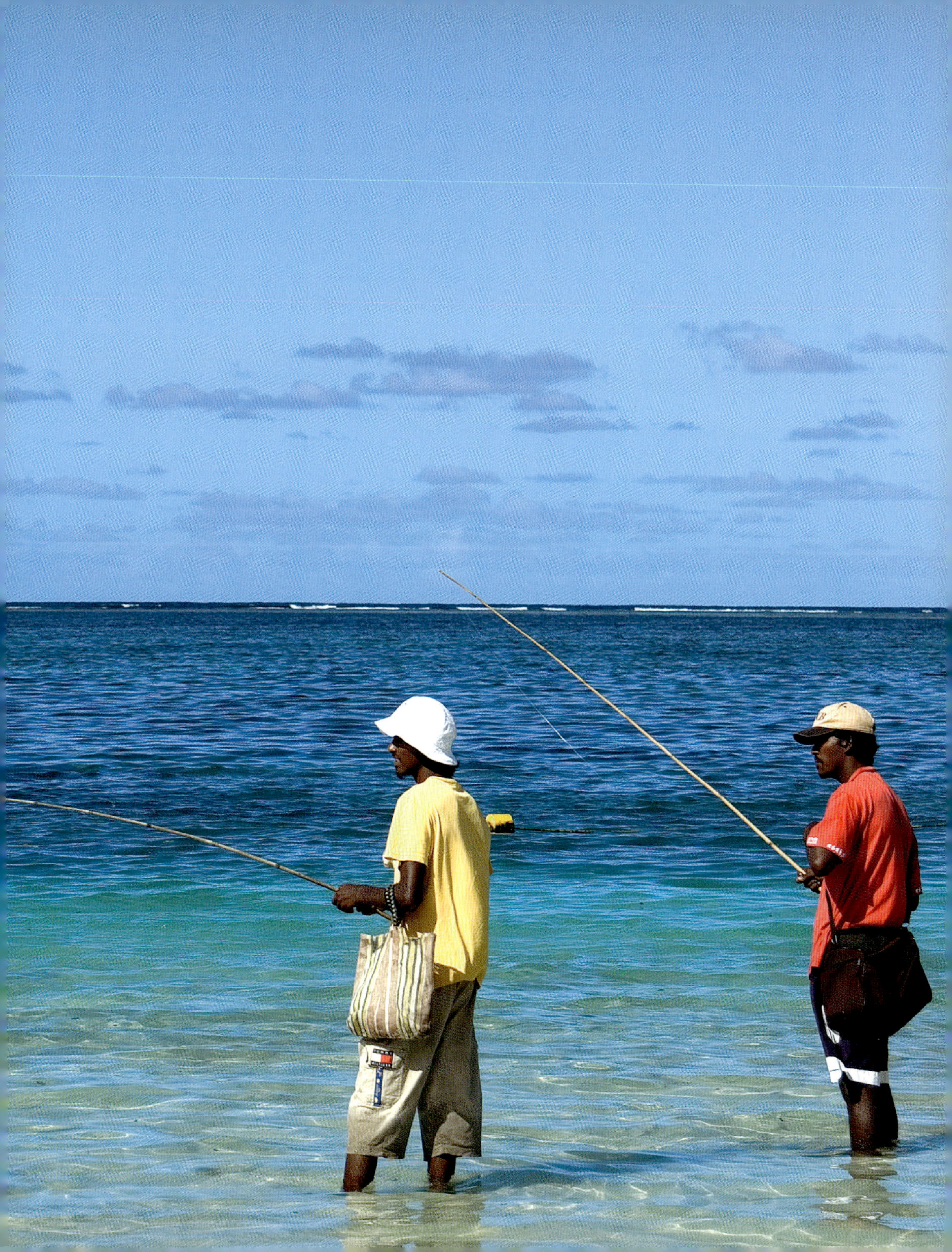

Feet and Wheels

While most travel brochures concentrate on the fantastic beaches and excellent water activities – be they under or on the sea – the hinterland of Mauritius should not be ignored as a source of fun and adventure. Although land activities are only just beginning to get established, there are already high-quality providers waiting to get you started.

Walking and hiking are underdeveloped sports here, but what routes exist lead through some of the last remaining stands of native forest where the rarest Mauritian fauna has taken refuge.

At Black River Gorges National Park, the Pétrin Visitors Centre at the intersection of the Grand Bassin/Curepipe/Chamarel routes makes a good starting point, with information about the plants and animals you may encounter, plus basic maps of the park. From here there's a boardwalk trail set amongst rare marshy heath land and also the Macchabée or Macabe Forest Trail, a 7km looped circuit through some fine tropical upland forest. If you only do one walk make it this one because it could easily be included in a day sightseeing the Route du Thé, Grand Bassin and Chamarel.

Another easy route leads to the summit of the island's highest peak, Piton de la Petite Rivière Noire. The 3km path only becomes difficult in the final short stretch to the summit when even the most exhausted hiker would want to cast fatigue aside for the exhilaration of making it to the top.

More challenging routes include the Parakeet Trail from the Plaine Champagne road that links with the Macchabée Trail or Bel Ombre, a 12km return trail that meanders through semi-humid lower level forest.

Several other smaller Mauritian nature reserves also have trails but you'll need to get the permission of the Conservator of Forests before you can head there.

The sheer curtain of mountains around Port Louis also provide some interesting walking routes plus some climbing sections on *via ferrata* (preset iron ladders and/or rope hooks). Le Pouce is a relatively easy route but the Pieter Both peak with its 'head-like' boulder tip is probably the most challenging and the most rewarding, though it's not for the beginner. You'll certainly need ropes to get to the summit, from where the views are spectacular. Close to Mahébourg, Lion Mountain is another popular route but it again offers challenges before the reward of panoramic south and east coast views.

You'll need to wear strong shoes, preferably proper hiking boots, for the tougher trails. It's advisable to carry a warm layer of clothing as cloud can quickly shroud the mountaintops, and a light folding rain mac or plastic poncho in case you get caught in a tropical shower. If you'd prefer a guided walk or climb you can organize this at Domaine du Chasseur, with Ciel et Nature at Domaine L'Etoile, and with Yemen. Vertical World can run hiking and climbing trips and provide climbing equipment. They also run canyoning trips, where participants swim, jump or abseil down watercourses. Parc Aventure (*see* page 40) offer a fascinating one-hour walk through the forest canopy on a series of elevated rope bridges and *via ferrata* courses at their highland base at Chamarel.

Two wheels may be more to your liking than two feet and many hotels have bikes for rent so you can explore the coastal communities. For something more challenging Yemaya offer guided cycle rides on three circuits around the south of the island including one through the wilds of the La Nicolière Reserve.

Of course you may consider that all this is far too much effort and you really just want a little land sport where you don't have to do all the work. Overland safaris are just coming onto the market as eco-tourism begins to develop. Quad bikes make a fun but somewhat noisy way of exploring. There are quad routes at Domaine Les Pailles, Domaine L'Etoile (Ciel et Nature), Domaine du Chasseur and Yemen, while Mautourco offer 'Espace Adventure', a true eco-safari in the almost indestructible 4WD Land Rover that takes you to rugged corners no other vehicle could reach.

Right: *The Black River Gorges National Park offers wonderful hiking trails through ancient tropical forests to deep valleys and waterfalls.*

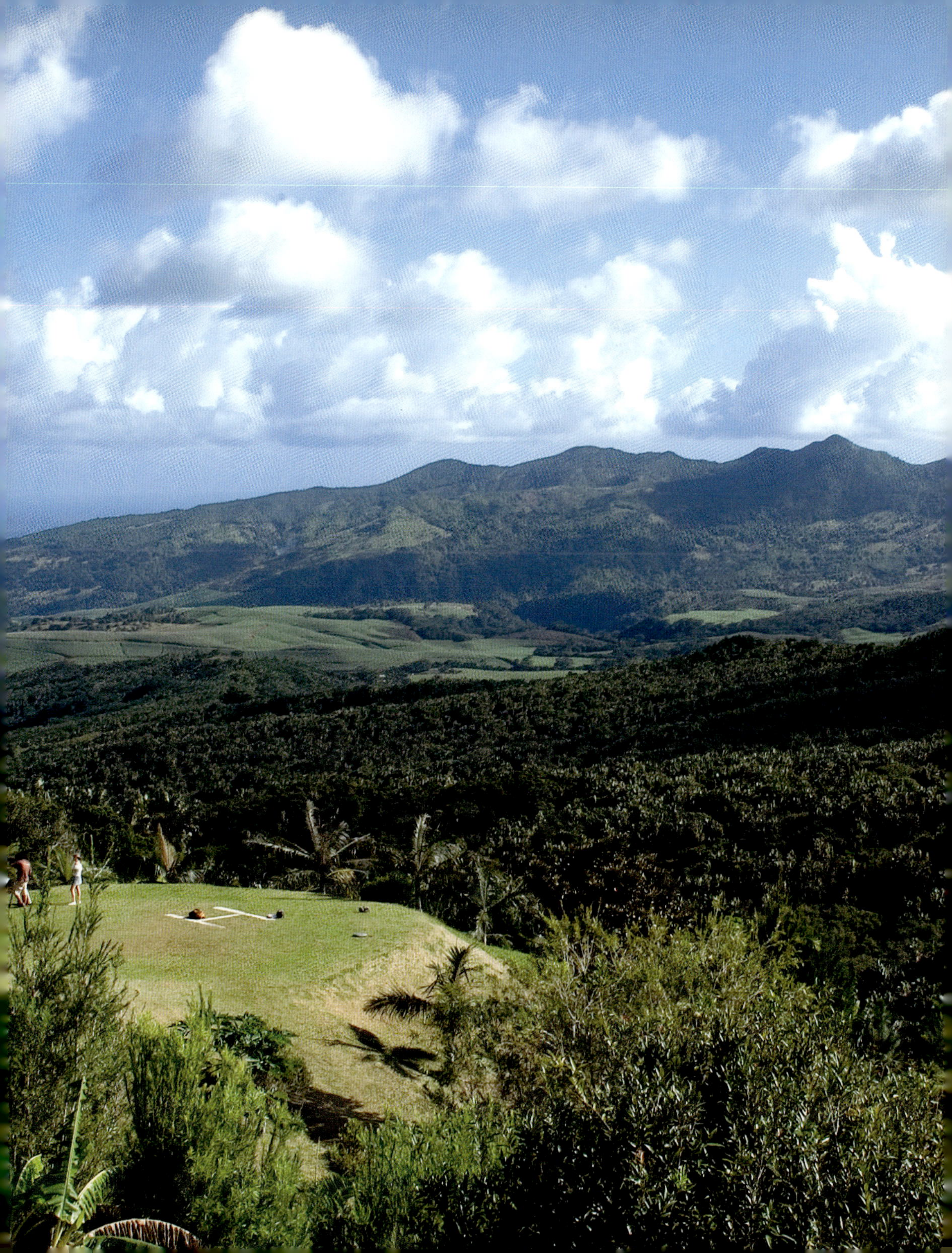

You could also try 'Sport and Nature,' an eco-activity programme run by Beachcomber Hotels (at the Shandrani Hotel) that's also open to non-guests. Each day features a range of activities, from cycling to canyoning, canoeing to hiking and a typical Mauritian lunch is included.

Horsing Around

Get a feel for the Mauritian countryside by exploring it on horseback. Bridle paths meander through cane fields and woodland across the island, and the horses move at a leisurely pace allowing you to enjoy the surroundings.

There are large stable complexes at Domaine Les Pailles where you can trek through the expansive grounds, at Les Écuries de la Vieille Cheminée at Chamarel, from where you can explore the heart of the Plaines Champagne, and at Le Ranch at Rivière Noire. The Sugar Beach Resort and La Pirogue also have stables and guests can book through the concierge service.

A Day at the Races

On winter Saturdays Mauritians are only interested in one thing: it's race day in Port Louis. The Mauritius Turf Club is the second oldest in the world. It was founded by Colonel Edward Draper in 1812 and they've been organizing cards at the Champ du Mars Racecourse almost continuously since then.

At 1298m in circumference it's hardly Ascot or Dubai but the atmosphere is buzzing as thousands come to watch the action. The hoi polloi crowd the tracksides in the central compound where there's a carnival atmosphere. Wealthier race-goers have boxes in the grandstands where they can view the paddock and the course in rather more comfortable surroundings.

If you fancy a flutter, Naïade Hotels has a corporate box available to its guests, while Crown Lodge will book you a day in a box with meals, drinks and transfers included.

Spas and Wellness

Wellness is the mantra of the early third millennium and, with busy lives at home and at work, we look to the quality time our holidays give us to recharge our energy levels and pamper ourselves a little. Massage and other spa treatments have become a popular way of enjoying quality 'me time' and giving tired bodies a much-needed boost.

Mauritius is one of the best locations in the world to immerse yourself in the world of wellness. Massage is an inherent element in Indian life and Hindu Mauritians brought this tradition with them when they arrived on the island, so it's been easy to find and train high-quality therapists. Not only that, but the standard of hotel properties on the island has assured investment in beautifully designed spas with all the necessary state-of-the-art equipment, plus the backing of some of the best cosmetic houses in the industry. Companies including Clarins, Decléor and Givenchy provide ongoing training and carefully researched and tested products, though some locally sourced products are also used.

You're never far from a spa!
Royal Palm Spa
The Royal Palm spa is a little gem. Styled like a scene out of *The Arabian Nights*, the deep terracotta and purple walls are enhanced by Turkish rugs and Moorish lamps. There are two sauna and steam rooms with attached tropical courtyards that can be booked for private sessions, so couples or friends can relax without being disturbed. The main courtyard features an atmospheric three-tier plunge pool and several rattan-sided massage kiosks.

Oberoi
Now listed as one of the 'Leading Spas of the World', this spa brings more than a touch of Bali to Mauritius, with immense busts of Buddha gracing the freshwater pools and vast rattan blinds taking the place of dividing walls, allowing an airy atmosphere but privacy when needed. The pride of the spa has to be the private suites where couples or friends can have treatments together before being left to relax in a luxurious plunge pool. Traditional Mauritian ingredients are used in several treatments.

Left: *The soothing sound of cascading water greets you at the Clarins spa at Royal Palm. Bowls of carefully arranged fragrant flowers add beauty and wafting aroma to the serene atmosphere. These small but delicate touches can be found in spas all across the island.*

One&Only Le Touessrok Spa

Set within the haven of tranquillity that is Frangipani Island, the vast reception atrium where *belle-époque* France and the early days of the House of Givenchy are recreated in sketches and glass mosaics is the signature view of the Touessrok spa. Treatment rooms are designed in a hexagon around a verdant central garden and the quality of the products and Givenchy's high standard of training ensure complete relaxation, and satisfaction.

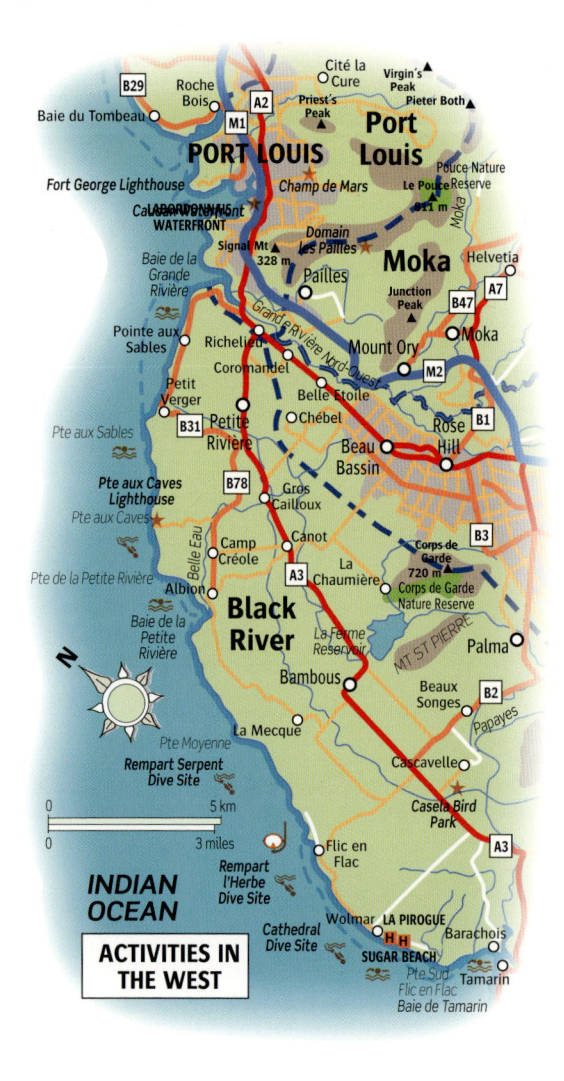

ACTIVITIES IN THE WEST

The Jargon Lexicon

Are you a spa virgin? Then let's try to decipher the standard vocabulary of the industry:

- **Detox or detoxification** – the process of removing toxins (poisons) produced by the body in reaction to things we eat or pollution in the air.
- **Exfoliation** – removal of the upper layers of the epidermis (skin) to eliminate toxins and promote new cell growth. Various ingredients with a slightly rough texture are mixed with an oil or cream and rubbed over the body to remove dead cells.
- **Massage** – a mechanical therapy where pressure is applied to the soft tissues to alleviate strains and relax muscles.
- **Aromatherapy** – the use of essential oils to enhance the mood by scenting the air, or adding to massage oil for use on the skin. A number of minor conditions such as headache and sleeplessness can be improved through the use of aromas.
- **Hydrotherapy** – underwater jets of water are fired at the body either to sooth muscles, boost circulation or release toxins.
- **Reflexology** – the belief that areas of the feet are linked to areas of the body. Massage of these points promotes improvement in problem areas of the body.
- **Thalassotherapy** – the use of sea water for massage.
- **Cathiodermie** – low-voltage electrical stimulation that cleanses the face and stimulates skin regeneration.

One&Only Le Saint Géran

Never missing from the list of the world's favourite spas since its opening, the Saint Géran Givenchy spa offers 696m^2 of treatment space in two 'Louis XVI meets Zen' decorated wings. Between the two and with a backdrop of palm trees is the Roman-style lap pool, which features in so many fashion magazines that it's almost as famous as the supermodels that grace it. As with Le Touessrok, Givenchy is your assurance of quality in both product and customer service.

Nudity or Not?

Many spa treatments require a state of undress but there's no need to be embarrassed as staff are thoroughly professional and discreet. Most spas will offer you disposable pants to wear during your treatment but you can still wear a swimsuit if you prefer. Towels are used to cover the body except for the areas being massaged at any one time so you never feel exposed.

Hammam and sauna sessions are most effective for the skin if you are naked but it's not compulsory and in fact there may be house rules in resorts about the wearing of towels or swimwear.

Right: Surrender to the bliss of warm oil and soothing hands. A massage relieves stress and improves wellbeing; it's also the one place where the phone won't ring and you can let your thoughts wander. This spa at the One&Only Saint Géran has been voted one of the best in the world.

Surya

This private spa just north of Grand Baie is managed by Ayurvedic specialists from Kerala in India, historical homeland of the therapeutic massage. Aromatic oils are used as the basis of treatments, which concentrate on several different styles of massage including Kizhi, massage using a pouch of medicinal herbs, and the Dara forehead 'chakra' massage. Specialist programmes include one- to three-week timetables for weight loss or detoxification.

Le Paradis

One of the largest spas on the island, Le Paradis has treatment rooms set around a central garden soothed by fragrant frangipani and graced with modern stylized statues. Nearby, high plant-draped walls surround a diminutive private plunge pool. Each treatment room is especially designed and equipped for a particular type of therapy, including Shiatsu pressure-point massage or a hydrotherapy jet bath. Training and products are supplied by Clarins, one of the leading French cosmetics houses.

For Feet!

Manicure and pedicure treatments are pretty much standard offerings in beauty salons in all the major hotels but One&Only have got together with Bastien Gonzalez – Hollywood's favourite podiatrist – to offer his unique treatments at both their hotels (also open to non-guests). Clients are given the full pedicure treatment topped off with Bastien's miraculous and very secret non-paint nail polish – the lustrous finish can last for up to four months!

Undersea Adventures

Can't swim? That doesn't mean you have to miss out on the amazing delights that sit just under the surface in the Mauritian lagoon. With some of the healthiest corals in the Indian Ocean, the waters teem with myriad species of fish and other marine life and are a scuba diver's paradise. Still, there are several possibilities that offer a view of the deep and most of the time you don't even need to get wet.

Take a glass-bottom boat for the most sedate glimpse of the shallows. Many hotels offer free trips as part of their non-motorized sports provision and the journey out from the coastline only takes a few minutes on usually placid water, so it's even suitable for seasickness sufferers. One of the best places to explore is the coral reef at the Blue Bay Maritime National Park in the southeast, but there are many secret spots alive with fish and coral that are well known to the boatmen. The only disadvantage of a glass-bottom boat is that you are at the mercy of the whims of the fish, and you are always separate from them in their water realm.

Le Nessee sits a little lower in the water than a glass-bottom boat. This semi-submersible gives you wide sub-surface views but without being totally submerged. For a true impression of the deep you'll need to visit Blue Safari, the only commercial operator of real submarines in the Indian Ocean. Blue Safari operate two craft, BS600 with a capacity of 5 people plus pilot and a length of 6.5 metres, and BS1100 with a capacity of 10 people plus pilot and a length of 10 metres. The larger vessel has portholes for views out from each flank while the smaller vehicle has a large single wrap-around window.

Both craft dive to depth of 35m, offering close-up views of the living corals offshore from Mont Choisy with luminescent marine ecosystems. The wreck of the *Star Hope*, one of the artificial reef ships sunk especially for the purpose, can also be seen. All hazardous materials were stripped from the hulk before it was holed and allowed to fall 58m to the sea bed. It's fascinating to watch new life settling on the metal plate and the fish that seem happy to call the place home.

Underwater time lasts around 40 minutes but transfers and boarding bring the whole operation to around two hours. Past clients have ranged in age from 2 to 92. Blue Safari can also arrange a private lunch or champagne and canapés at a depth of 35m. It makes an unusual location for a birthday or anniversary celebration.

The Undersea Walk is the nearest thing to diving you'll find without the complications of doing a course. You don't need any qualifications and you don't even need to be able to swim – even sufferers of hydrophobia have been happy to don a swimsuit during this adventure. Clients don a specially designed diving helmet that is constantly fed with oxygen from the surface so there's no need to regulate tanks or bite on a mouthpiece. The helmet allows you to breathe normally and your head stays dry. Once the oxygen is flowing you'll climb down into the water and walk along the sea bed, watching the fish swimming around only inches from your head.

In 2005 Blue Safari launched a unique new underwater experience. The 'subscooter' is a two-person submarine scooter that you can drive around up to a depth of 3m below the water's surface. Although riders get wet up to the shoulder, the head sits in a clear canopy that is constantly supplied with air, and also enables you to view the sea-life that's all around. A small engine and rudder controls make your craft manoeuvrable so you can pursue the sea-life. It all feels a little 'James Bond' for those who remember the underwater escapades in *Thunderball* (1965). Curious fish venture to take a look at what is surely the strangest craft in Mauritian waters. Blue Safari provides each 'subscooter' with a qualified diver to accompany the craft so you can be assured of a safe ride. This undersea adventure lasts around 30 minutes.

Water Sports

Any holiday to Mauritius is as much about the water as it is about the land. The long coral reef that circles the island encompasses a languid lagoon that's perfect for a whole range of waterborne activities, having few waves and warm waters.

Right: The 'subscooter' is the newest underwater adventure craft in the world, a revolution in personal sub-surface transport and currently unique to Mauritius. Run by Blue Safari enterprises, it allows you to become your own pilot and sink to a depth of three metres where you can enjoy the local marine life.

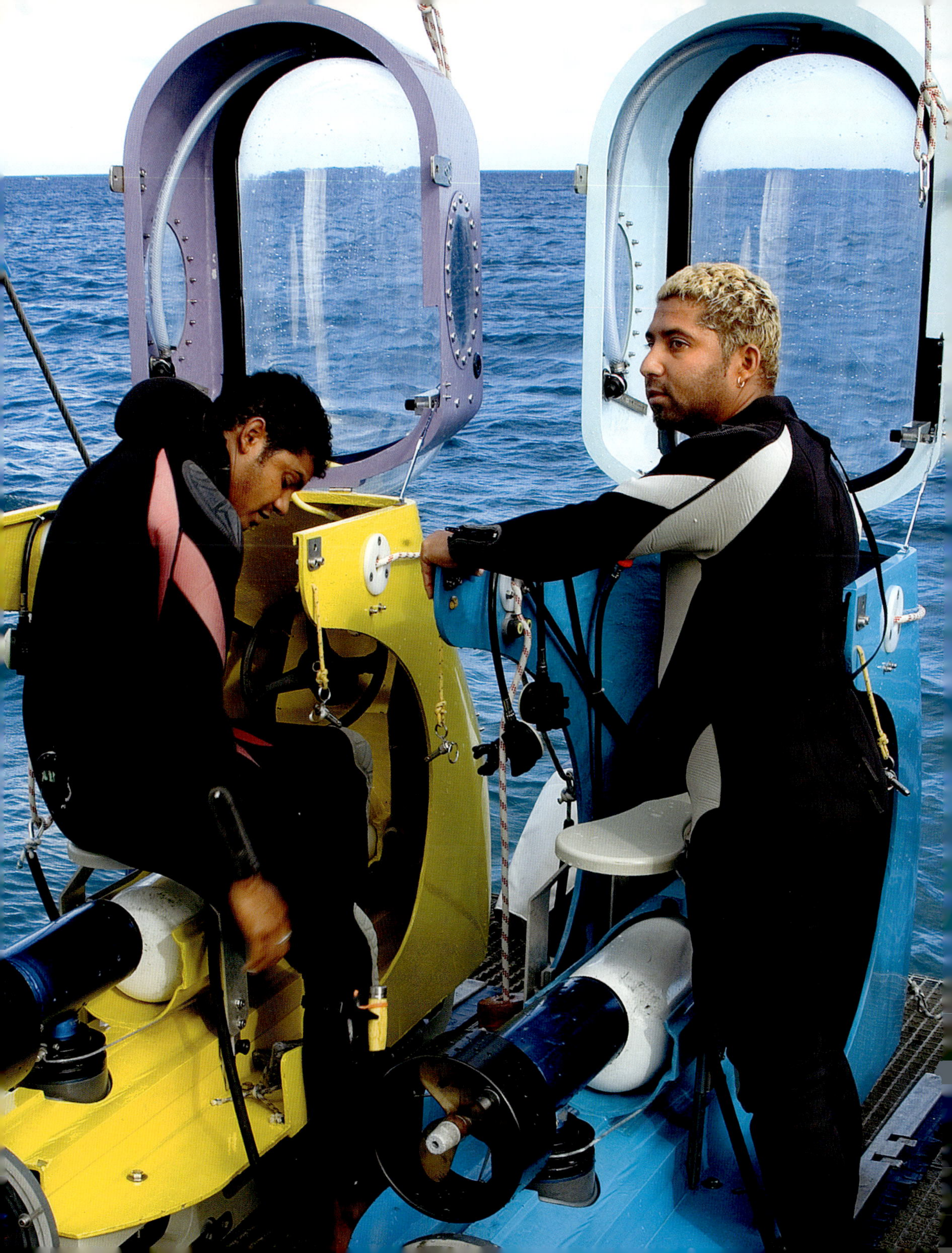

Surf and Turf

All the major hotels keep a stock of craft at the on-site boathouse where you can find well-maintained equipment and good-quality instruction. The water-sport areas are well segregated from the swimming areas and safety is taken very seriously so it's a great place to try something new. If you are already accomplished in any given sport you'll find the professional set-up makes everything really easy and stress free.

Non-motorized water sports are normally provided free of charge and these include pedalos, canoes, kayaks, Hobiecats and windsurfs. Pedalos and kayaks need minimal training and allow you to explore the coastal shallows at your own pace. Hobiecats or Laser sailing dinghies are manoeuvrable little twin-keel craft, perfect for the novice, but they also provide an afternoon of fun for the more experienced sailor, especially on the occasions when the tropical breezes become a little testing. A little air movement also makes windsurfing more fun and it's an exhilarating feeling to zip out across the lagoon and then swing back towards the beaches.

The growing sport of kitesurfing has, quite literally, taken off in Mauritius. Kitesurfing has you strapped to a miniature surfboard while you are pulled along the surface of the water by a flexible parachute wing around 10 or so metres above your head. Expert kitesurfers can leap from the water and perform stunts similar to snowboarders before they land back on the surface.

Below: Kitesurfing is one of the fastest growing sports on the planet and conditions on Mauritius are ideal with calm waters and regular tropical breezes. Here the colourful 'wing' is being prepared for flight.

Water Sports

You'll normally need to pay extra for motorized sports, even at an all-inclusive hotel. Waterskiing is incredibly popular and the boat dock will have someone to take you through the basics before you make your first attempt. Banana boats and tube rides offer a great adrenalin rush – just remember to cling tightly to your hand-hold or you'll shoot off into the water at high speed.

Note that the tide can affect activities like sailing or waterskiing because the water in the lagoon can be too shallow for the keeled craft at certain times of day.

If you are not staying in accommodation with a water-sports centre, then the best places to find a range of companies offering activities are Grand Baie and, to a lesser extent, Flic en Flac. Yemaya can organize one- or two-day sea-kayaking tours if you'd like to explore the island coastline with a guide.

Shadrani Centres of Excellence

The Shandrani Hotel is one of the finest in the Indian Ocean for its professional water-sports training. If you'd like to learn to sail the hotel operates a Mauritius Yachting Association (MYA) affiliated sailing school with experienced instructors trained at the Les Glénans sailing school in France. The programmes cater for students of all ages, with children starting on dingy training while adults can commence on lasers or catamarans. Once you receive your Day Skipper Certificate you can charter yachts anywhere in the world for inshore sailing expeditions. The Shandrani also operates the Shandrani Kitesurf School with qualified and experienced instructors affiliated to the International Kitesurf Organization (IKO), a body set up to promote professional training and safe kitesurfing for beginners and experts.

Right: Mauritius has a fantastic range of water sports with most hotels having craft such as pedalos (pedal boats), kayaks, windsurfs and sailing dinghies lined up around the boat-house or, as here, on the beach. Non-motorized water sports will be included in your 4- and 5-star holiday package; otherwise they can be rented by the hour in the main resorts.

Tee Time

It sounds clichéd to say that Mauritius is a golfer's paradise but year-round warm weather, exceptional facilities, professional tuition and some of the most spectacular settings in the world assure a positive experience whatever a player's level of expertise.

Many hotels on the island now include some form of golf in their programmes even if it's only a driving range as at Legends or the nine holes at the Shandrani Hotel. It's become such a part of the holiday experience that even hotels that have no facilities will happily book you a round at a rival property with a course. But for golf aficionados the combination of staying at a top-class hotel with a championship course on site will be very difficult to resist.

All golf hotels offer group sessions for beginners as well as individual professional tuition to improve technique and iron out bad habits. You will need to be properly attired with spiked shoes and polo shirt but these are readily available in shops at clubhouses. If you don't have your own clubs, these can be hired and some courses stipulate that golf buggies be used. Here is a selection of the best:

Belle Mare Plage

Spoiled for choice at this resort, guests can play two courses. The Legend course is a par 72/6036m course set amongst numerous water features in the heart of an old deer forest. Today it is reserved exclusively for clients of the Belle Mare Plage Hotel who play without green fees. In 2002 the hotel opened The Links course, a par 71 with more undulating fairways and a signature 18th hole played across a small lake. This course is open to non-guests.

Tee Time

Le Golf du Chateau

The island's most recent addition, Le Golf du Chateau is part of Le Telfair Golf & Spa and is at present the only course in the deep south of the island. Designed by Matkovich & Hayes, a South African company, it incorporates two river features in the two nine-hole loops that make up the full par 72 course, all set within the grounds of the 19th-century Belle Ombre Mansion.

Le Paradis Course

This par 72/5899m course sits between the dramatic rock face of the Morne Brabant and 7km of hotel beach with a challenging back nine that includes breathtaking sea views and five water hazards. The course record here is an impressive 7 under par accredited to professional Tony Johnston. Note that a green fee here allows unlimited access throughout the day. On the doorstep of the Paradis and Dinarobin hotels, it's also open to other Beachcomber guests.

Île aux Cerfs

Not without its detractors on environmental grounds, the Île aux Cerfs golf course is spread across the southern tip of the island, surrounded by pristine beaches. A par 72 18-hole course designed by professional Bernhard Langer, it has taken the golf world by storm since it opened in 2003 – being voted in the top 10 in the world by Golf World magazine. Tee shots play across lagoons and beaches at several holes. One&Only guests don't pay green fees.

***Below**: The back nine of the Le Paradis course offer five water hazards and stunning views across the inland lagoon to the Morne Brabant Mountain – keep you mind on your stroke play and don't be distracted by the landscape!*

Diving and Snorkelling

Since Jacques Cousteau invented his 'self-contained underwater breathing apparatus' (SCUBA) in the 1940s, diving has become one of the world's most popular sporting pastimes. Simply to get a personal glimpse of the complicated ecosystem we call the ocean is always incredibly awe-inspiring, but the clear tropical waters and kilometres of coral reef that surround Mauritius offer some of the world's most varied and accessible dive sites. The dramatic geology you see across the island is duplicated beneath the surface. Volcanic peaks, sheer walls and craggy overhangs offer an exciting base topography upon which live a rich diversity of corals that, in turn, attract myriad fish species and other sea-life.

Prime Sites

The islands off the north coast have a good variety of sites. The rock wall off Coin de Mire drops an incredible 100m and isn't for the beginner, but Coral Gardens at 18m would fit the bill nicely for recently qualified divers. More experienced divers head to the 'Shark Pit' beyond Flat Island where black-tailed sharks can be found between November and May. Round Island is known to attract the big fish species at sites such as Banc Rouge.

In the west, the Cathedral (30m) is so named because it is an expansive cavern filled with fish. Equally famous is the Rempart Serpent, with an abundance of moray eels, scorpion fish and lionfish – species to be wary of because each is poisonous to man. The Rempart l'Herbe lies at a depth of 50m and is also known as Shark's Place because these formidable hunters gather in numbers, along with huge manta rays.

In the southwest, Needle Hall and Jim's Place make excellent shallow dives (up to 20m) with good corals and fish species. A little lower at 25m, Japanese Gardens displays a great range of coral within a confined space. A more demanding dive is Michel's Place (40m) where turtles can sometimes be spotted.

The Passe (18m) is considered the best on the east coast, for displays of both coral and fish. Off Mahébourg, sites Roche Zozo and Colorado are the two outstanding locations, plus the wreck of the British ship *Sirius* which sank in the Battle of Grand Port in 1810. Divers can see remains including cannon and cannonballs.

The treacherous waters around the island have resulted in many wrecks that now make dramatic dive sites. The Mauritius authorities have also recently approved several deliberate shipwrecks in the hope that fresh corals can be encouraged to grow on the superstructures; in effect the ships are skeletons for future marine ecosystems.

Dive Training

Mauritius is an excellent place to learn to dive. Each of the many dive schools is certified by either the Professional Association of Diving Instructors (PADI) or the Confédération des Activités Subaquatiques (CMAS); indeed, many major hotels have their own certified dive schools. The basic level of PADI qualification is the 'Open Water Diver' course, which, once successfully completed, allows you to dive in the sea or in lakes without an instructor. The course generally takes around four to five days.

If you are already qualified, all dive schools will offer well-maintained modern equipment for rent, organize guided dives or upgrade training.

With Mask and Flippers

If you are not a qualified diver, you can still enjoy the marine life with a snorkel and flippers. A boat trip will take you out to the reef or you can find the many species in the coastal shallows of the lagoon just a few metres from the beach. If you don't know how to use a snorkel, staff at the hotel boat house will be able to give you instructions.

Right: *Just a peek under the surface only a short distance offshore introduces you to a totally different world, where schools of the most amazing iridescent fish swim by just inches from your nose.*

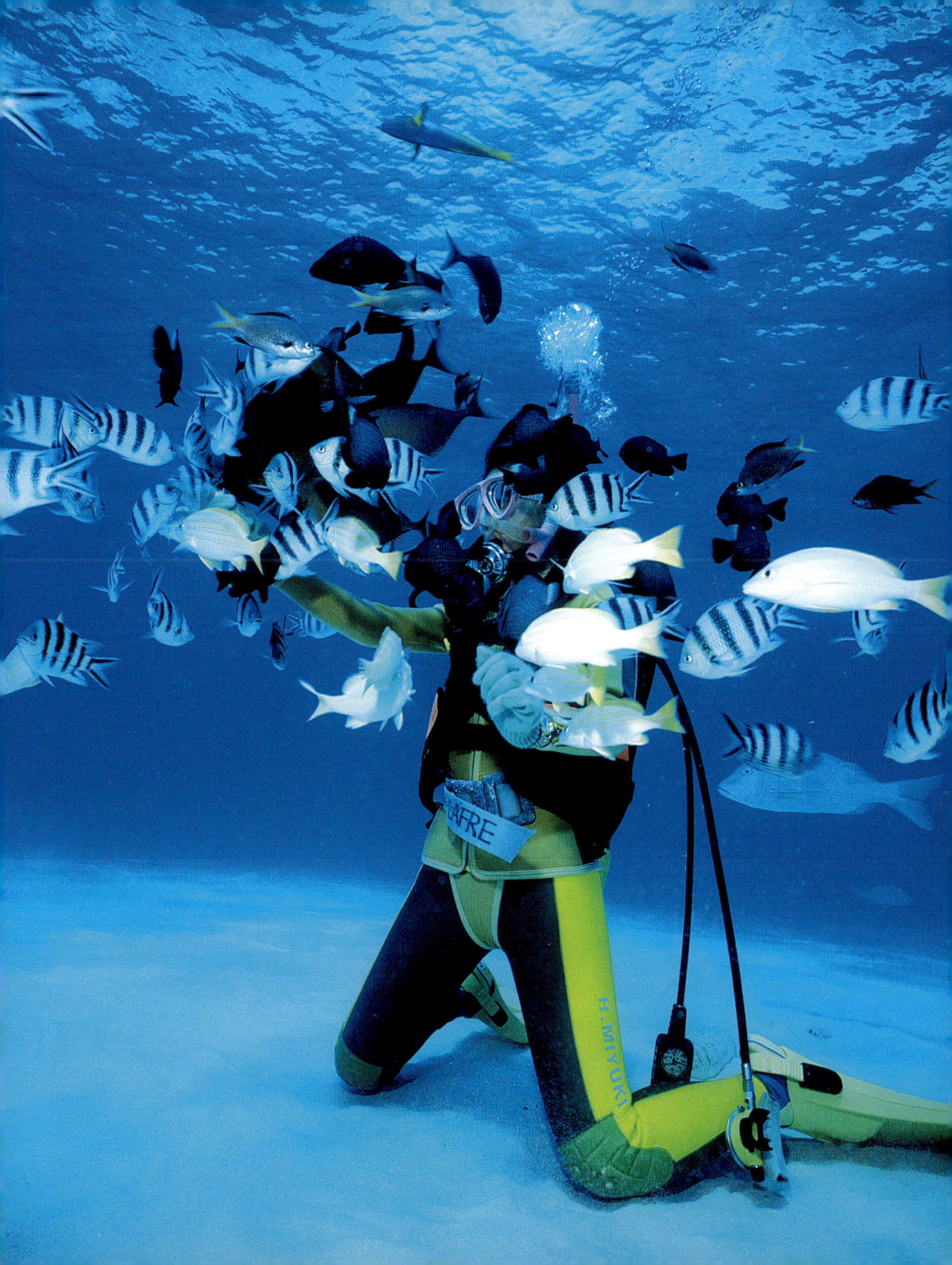
H-MIYUKI

Casinos

Gambling has become big business in Mauritius, where games of chance including the local lottery or a bet or two on a horse race are very much part of daily life.

Casinos are definitely the most glamorous face of the industry but that doesn't mean that one has to be a high roller to enjoy an evening at a casino. Stake money can be as low as 1 rupee on some of the older slot machines, while minimum stakes at the tables vary from around 35 to 50 rupees.

Casinos of Mauritius own five establishments around the island and all offer banks of slot machines, American roulette tables, blackjack tables and poker tables. Increasingly they are also adding electronic betting machines including touch-bet roulette monitors for those who don't want to enjoy the real-life action of the gaming floor.

Their most prestigious property, though not the largest, has to be the Grand Casino du Domaine, at Domaine Les Pailles, which is designed like a classical colonial mansion with verandas and shuttered windows. They have other casinos at Flic en Flac, Trou aux Biches, Curepipe (their largest) and at the Caudan Waterfront, where the clientele includes a mixture of ex-pats and businessmen. The Berjaya Beach Resort, Hotel and Casino on the Morne Peninsula has its own gaming room but also opens its doors to non-residents.

There is an age limit of 18 for all these establishments and ID may be needed. Foreign currency and credit cards are accepted as payment.

Although you don't need to dress formally, it is necessary to be at least 'smart casual', much as it is in the restaurants of many hotels on the island. Men should have full length trousers and shoes, not sandals.

Hunting

Sport hunting has been part of the island's history from the first human settlement; indeed, many animals including Java deer and several species of game bird were introduced specifically for this purpose. Others including pigs and goats escaped their pens and bred very successfully in the wild, causing huge problems for farmers and the indigenous flora and fauna.

With a massively increased human population and pressure on the last remaining tracts of virgin forest, the numbers of deer and feral pigs still need to be controlled so, although sentiments about the killing of wild animals have changed greatly in the last 50 years, Mauritius still welcomes hunters between June and the end of September when shooting is permitted except in designated national parks. Several companies offer expeditions, flushing out major game animals, plus hare and guinea fowl, with dogs.

If you visit Mauritius outside hunting season, Domaine du Chasseur (Estate of the Hunter) is certified to offer hunting throughout the year. The estate has around 1500 animals grazing 1000 hectares and culls a predefined number of animals each year to preserve a viable and healthy population. The experienced guides, who know every inch of the domaine, will pick out suitable animals and give you hints on how to stalk your prey. The carcass remains the property of the estate and the meat is used in the restaurant on site (the principle ingredient in a delicious venison curry). Hunters can take the head, complete with antlers, as a trophy and staff will arrange to have a local taxidermist prepare it and ship it when it's ready. Ironically, these same companies also offer photographic safaris, when these same majestic animals can be 'shot' with digital apparatus for the simple pleasure of looking at them.

Top: At Domaine du Chasseur, a guide helps pinpoint suitable animals to maintain the healthy balance of the deer population. You can taste the venison in the on-site restaurant.

Left: The Casinos of Mauritius property at the Caudan Waterfront complex sits at the heart of the main entertainment complex in the capital.

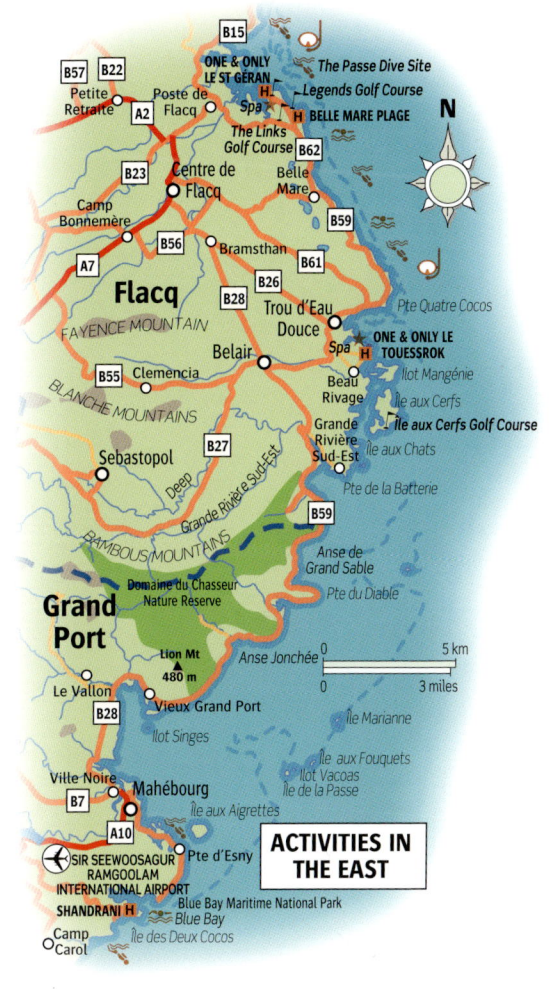

CENTRE DE FLACQ 8 KM
A7
QUARTIER MILITAIRE
A7 8 KM
BLANCHE
B54 4 KM
BEL ETANG
BRIDGE

Travel Directory

Left: *Destinations are well marked on the major highways, but country lanes have few signposts.*

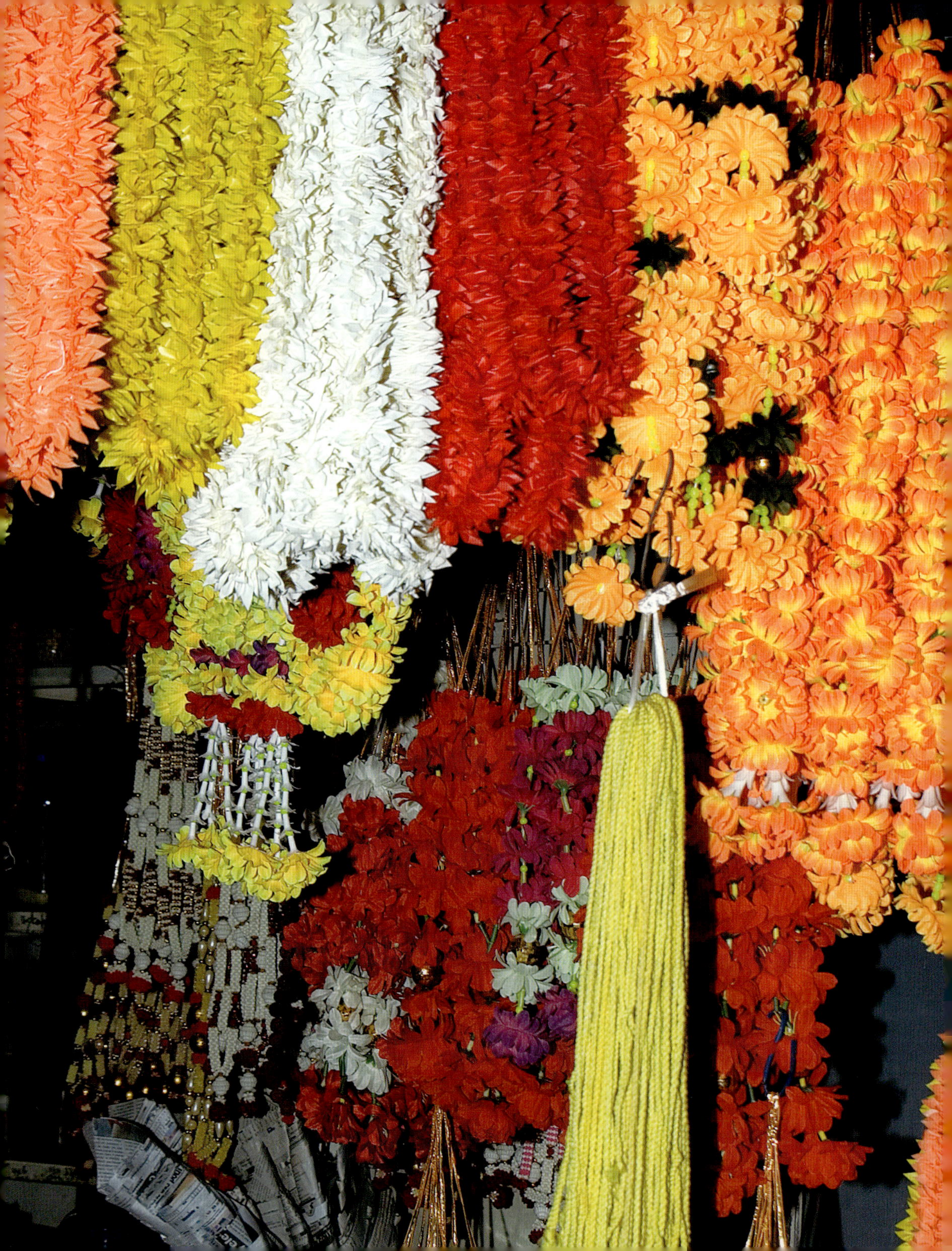

The Travel Directory gives you all the information you need to make the most of your trip to Mauritius.

Practical guidelines are designed to help you plan your visit, with tips on how and when to travel, including contact details of airlines and where to find tourist information. You'll find helpful facts about Mauritian currency, national holidays and climate, along with pointers on what to pack and how to get around. We've included addresses, telephone numbers and websites for all the featured hotels and restaurants, plus a few more for travellers with different budgets. There are also comprehensive details of all the organizations, attractions and museums mentioned in the text. Finally, a few useful phrases will help you get to grips with the language. Have a great time!

Left: *Colourful garlands like these are for sale at markets across the island. They are used in many Hindu festivals and are often draped around the necks of statues of gods and goddesses.*

Travel Directory

Practical Guide
Tourist information
The Mauritius Tourism Promotion Agency is the official body responsible for visitor information. They can be contacted at their head office: 11th Floor, Air Mauritius Centre 5, President Kennedy Street, Port Louis, tel: 210-1545, website www.mauritius.net

The authority also operates agencies in the following countries – UK, France, South Africa, Germany, Italy, Switzerland and India.

Entry Requirements
All visitors must be in possession of a valid passport with at least six months to run at the end of the stay. They must also have a return air ticket and, if asked, be able to prove that they have sufficient funds to finance their stay.

Officials will initially grant entry on a visitor's visa for up to one month. Visas can be extended at the Passport and Immigration Office, Sterling House, 11–19 Lislet Geoffroy Street, Port Louis, tel: 210-9312.

Customs
Passengers over 18 can import the following duty-free:
- 250 grams of tobacco (loose or in the form of cigarettes or cigars – the equivalent of around 200 cigarettes or 50 cigars depending on size).
- 1 litre of spirits
- 2 litres of wine, beer or ale
- One-quarter litre of eau de toilette
- 100ml of perfume

Arriving (Air Travel)
Flights arrive at Sir Seewoosagur Ramgoolam Airport at Plaisance in the south of the island. The terminal is small but modern and air conditioned, with arrival duty-free, banks, ATMs and car rental agency offices.

Mauritius is only served by a small number of airlines and has no charter flights so there is little competition on ticket prices. The national airline Air Mauritius (www.airmauritius.com) operates services to London and several other European cities including a code share on flights to Paris with Air France (www.airfrance.com). Air Mauritius also flies to South Africa, Kenya, India, Singapore, Hong Kong and to three Australian cities: Perth, Melbourne and Sydney. British Airways (www.ba.com) flies from London and Emirates (www.emirates.com) from Dubai with onward travel to both Europe and the Far East.

Unless one of these airlines has a special fare deal at the time of your trip the keenest price competition is to be found with Internet travel shops such as Expedia (www.expedia.com) or Opodo (www.opodo.com).

Roads and Driving
General Guidelines
Driving is on the left-hand side of the highway with overtaking on the right. Most roads are two lane and many are narrow with no pedestrian walkway so you'll see people and dogs walking at the road shoulders. Traffic is controlled by traffic lights and roundabouts (traffic circles) but at peak times may be controlled by police officers. On many routes in towns and villages traffic is controlled by speed bumps. These may or may not be indicated beforehand.

Speed Limits
- Urban/villages: 40kph
- B roads: 60kph
- A roads: 80kph
- Four-lane highways: 90kph

Parking
On-street paid parking is possible in Port Louis and the plateau urban areas (Rose Hill, Quatre Borne, Curepipe, etc.). Parking areas are zoned and you need to pre-buy a parking ticket for your zone (from petrol stations), fill it in and leave it in the windshield of your car. This is a cumbersome procedure for visitors; better to park in a car park where you get a ticket on entry and pay on exit – the closest to the centre of Port Louis is at the Caudan Waterfront. Leaving a car on a street without a ticket can result in the car being towed. In most smaller settlements there is ample free on street parking. Beaches have parking areas that are only busy at weekends.

Fuel
All the main towns have fuel stations, generally open Mon–Sat 09:00–19:00.

Above: Colourful local buses travel to all settlements on the island but journey times can be long.

Car Rental

It's possible to rent a car at the airport on your arrival or to pick up the vehicle in Port Louis or the major resorts. Many rental companies will travel to your hotel to deliver a vehicle. Major companies such as Avis, Europcar and Hertz are well established here but you may get a more competitive rate with a local Mauritian company. The following are reliable: Grand Baie Contract Cars, tel: 263-7845; Holiday Car Hire and Tours, tel: 263-4321; Honey Car Rental, tel: 288-7374.

A full national or an international driving licence will be needed for rental. Minimum age for rental is 21 with a full licence for at least one year (some companies require an age limit of 25 for some vehicles).

Always carry your driver's licence and rental document when you drive the vehicle.

Buses and Taxis

Taxis make an excellent form of transport both for single journeys and for sightseeing. The fleet has been modernized in recent years and offers comfortable and reliable vehicles. Journeys are supposed to be metered but this is rarely done so agree on a price beforehand (ask your hotel reception for a guide price). Taxi drivers are also happy to agree a set price for a morning, day or few days' sightseeing so you don't have the worry of navigating around the island. Again, make sure you agree on a price beforehand.

The bus network on Mauritius is comprehensive but journeys may be long and uncomfortable, with many buses being old and not well maintained, and the timetables may not be ideal for sightseeing. You can find local timetables at all bus depots or stations.

Clothes (What to Pack)

Most of the year, the tropical climate of Mauritius is ideal for light, loose clothing – shorts, T-shirts, short-sleeved shirts and summer dresses. Light long-sleeved shirts and light full-length trousers are advisable cover-ups in case of too much sun exposure. Note that beachwear should not be worn anywhere but at the beach.

In winter (Jun–Oct) temperatures may drop to 20°C up on the plateau and in the mountains and it can feel chilly in the early morning or the evenings, so a light sweater or fleece would be a useful item when hiking.

You'll need to be properly dressed to enter churches and temples. Cover shoulders and knees and leave shoes at the entrance to mosques and Hindu temples. Take hats off when entering Christian churches but women may need to cover their heads when entering mosques.

At most four- and five-star hotels there is a dress code with men needing long trousers and perhaps full shoes (not sandals). Though there are no specific rules for women, smart casual is the guideline and most women make the effort to dress for dinner.

Money Matters
Currency
See panel, page 49.

Currency Exchange
You can exchange foreign currency at banks and most hotels will also offer an exchange service, though they may charge a fee for this.

Traveller's Cheques
These are the safest way to carry holiday cash as they can be replaced if they are lost or stolen. You can change them at hotels, or at bureaux de change and banks.

ATMs
ATMs are becoming more numerous and you will certainly be able to get cash in the major towns with a Cirrus card or credit card as long as you have a PIN.

Credit Cards
Credit cards are widely accepted across Mauritius. The most popular are MasterCard and Visa.

Banking Hours
Mon–Thu 09:15–15:15, Fri 09.15–15:30. Some banks also open Sat 9:15–11:15. Banks at the arrivals hall in Sir Seewoosagur Ramgoolam Airport are always open for flight arrivals and departures.

Taxes
The Mauritius government applies a 15 per cent Value Added Tax on many goods and services. This may or may not appear in the final price. If there is no clear indication as to whether a price includes VAT, always ask.

Tipping
Tipping is not expected but is always welcomed. Some hotels and restaurants automatically add a service charge to the bill. Be sure to clarify whether prices include service. Many hotels operate a tipping pool and suggest that clients not tip individual staff members but contribute to the pool at the end of their stay. This pool is then distributed to all staff members regardless of whether or not they have a customer contact role.

Trading Hours
Shops
Shopping hours are generally Mon–Sat 09:30–19:30 with some shops opening Sun 09:30–12:30. Shops in the main Plaines Wilhems region (Curepipe, Rose-Hill, Vacoas and Quatre Bornes) close on Thu afternoons.

Offices
In the public sector businesses are open Mon–Fri 09:00–16:00, private sector business 08:30–16.15 and Sat 09:00–12:00.

Post Offices
Opening hours are Mon–Fri 08:15–11:15, 12:00–16:00; Sat 08:15–11:45.

Telephones
General Information
Mauritius has a modern telephone system with the main provider being Mauritius Telecom. The island introduced a 3G network during 2006. All hotels have International Direct Dialling for international calls but they will charge a premium for this service. Check the hotel prices before making your call to avoid an unexpected charge.

Public Phones
There are modern public telephones in all the major settlements. Phones accept rupees but also SEZAM phone cards which come in 75Rs, 150Rs and 250Rs, and these can be bought at Mauritius Telecom shops and newsagents.

Mobile Phones

Cellplus and Emtel both have excellent coverage of the island and partnership agreements with major foreign telecom companies. Check with your own mobile provider about continuation of service before departing for Mauritius.

Calling Mauritius

The international calling code for Mauritius is 230. Island numbers have seven digits. Domestic directory enquiries, tel: 150.

Calling Home

To make an international call from Mauritius dial 020 followed by the country code (UK 44, France 33, Aus 61, NZ 64, USA and Canada 1, South Africa 27). International directory enquiries can be contacted on tel: 190.

Crime

Mauritius is not a destination that is known for its major crime; however, so-called petty crime is a growing problem, especially in tourist resorts and major attractions.

Pickpockets operate in crowded areas such as markets so keep cash and passports in a secure place. Bags should be held close to the body with straps across the chest.

Do not leave valuables in a car and leave nothing at all on show.

Don't carry large amounts of cash or valuables with you. Deposit valuables in the hotel safes.

Take extra care at cash point machines – don't allow bystanders to see your PIN or grab your cash.

Put all money away before you leave banks or bureaux de change kiosks.

Don't leave valuables unattended in cafés or restaurants, or on the beach.

Electricity

220 volt with a mixture of British-style three-pin and European-style two-pin plugs. Most large hotels will have the three-pin variety.

Embassies

UK High Commission
Les Cascades Building
Edith Cavell Street
Port Louis
tel: 202-9400.

US Embassy
4th Floor, Rogers House
John Kennedy Street
P.O. Box 544, Port Louis
tel: 202-4400.

Australian High Commission
2nd Floor
Rogers House
President Kennedy Street
Port Louis
tel: 202-0160.

Canadian Embassy
Nearest representation is in South Africa.

Republic of Ireland
Diplomatic problems are handled by the New York office.

New Zealand
Nearest representation is in South Africa.

South Africa
Nearest representation is in South Africa.

Emergencies

The emergency numbers are:
Police 999
Fire brigade 995
Ambulance (SAMU) 114.

Health
Vaccinations

No vaccinations are required to enter Mauritius; however, a yellow fever vaccination certificate will need to be shown by those travelling from an infected area.

Water

Water is treated and tap water is safe to drink (though after a cyclone the supply may be temporarily contaminated). However, you may prefer the taste of bottled water, which is produced on the island or imported from abroad.

Health Hazards

Mauritius suffered an outbreak of chikungunya during late 2005 and early 2006. This mosquito-borne virus produces severe flu-like symptoms with joint pain and rashes 3–12 days after infection. The initial episode lasts from three to seven days but can cause debilitation for two to three months in severe cases. Since there is no vaccine the only way to be sure to prevent infection is to deter mosquito bites by using lotions, creams or by covering the body.

Most other holiday 'nasties' are preventable and are generally the result of the hot climate. Limit your time in the sun, particularly in the early phase of your trip, to avoid sunburn. Drink plenty of fluids (but limit alcohol intake) to avoid dehydration. Make sure that street food is properly cooked.

Although there are no poisonous animals on the island be aware that there are dangers in the water. Avoid stepping on or touching sea urchins as the spines can break off and become embedded in your skin. It's recommended that you wear rubber shoes when swimming to avoid accidental penetration. Both stonefish and lionfish have venomous barbs and should never be touched.

Mauritius has many dogs, which although generally docile, should never be petted as they may have ticks and other parasites, and any bites may become infected. There is no rabies on the island.

Medical Services

There are five public hospitals on the island and public clinics in all the major towns. There are private clinics where staff will charge a fee for treatment. Your hotel will have the telephone number of a doctor on call. Carry adequate insurance to cover injury or illness whilst on your trip.

Language

Most Mauritians are bi- or trilingual, speaking French and English and perhaps Hindi or a Chinese language. In restaurants and hotels both languages will be spoken fluently though out in the countryside French may be preferred to English. The street language, however, is Creole, a unique blending of simplified French with English and Hindi vocabulary that developed in colonial times. It is understood by all islanders – and almost no outsiders.

The general principle of Creole is that it simplifies formal French rules of grammar. It has no gender assignment to articles and it softens the pronunciation of French words, in many instances combining the article found in authentic French with the noun.

Public Holidays

Mauritius has 15 public holidays a year – the major religious celebrations along with key historical dates. Because many festivals are held in accordance with the lunar calendar, not all public holidays happen on the same dates every year so consult the Mauritius Tourism Promotion Agency for the dates during the year of your visit.

Fixed Dates

1 and 2 January – New Year celebrations
1 February – Abolition of Slavery Day
12 March – Independence Day
1 May – Labour Day
21 October – Arrival of Indentured Labourers Day
2 November – All Saints' Day (Christian)
25 December – Christmas Day (Christian)

Moveable Dates

Jan/Feb – Thaipoosam Cavadee (Hindu)
Feb/Mar – Maha Shivaratree (Hindu)
Feb/Mar – Holi (Hindu)
Mar/Apr – Ougadi (Telegu)
Aug/Sep – Ganesh Chaturthi (Hindu)
Eid-El-Fitr (Muslim)
Eid-El-Adha (Muslim)

Time

Mauritius is 4 hours ahead of Greenwich Mean Time.

Contact Details

Hotels

Beau Rivage (*see* page 120)
Belle Mare
tel: 402-2000, fax: 415-2020
www.naiade.com

Dinarobin (*see* page 112)
Le Morne Peninsula
tel: 401-1900, fax: 401-4910
www.beachcomber-hotels.com

La Pirogue
Wolmar, Flic en Flac
tel: 453-8441, fax: 453-8449
www.lapirogue.com
Four-star hotel with Mauritian-style cabanas set in lovely verdant gardens.

Labourdonnais Waterfront Hotel
(*see* page 109)
Caudan Waterfront
tel: 202-4000, fax: 202-4040
www.labourdonnais.com

Legends (*see* page 107)
Grand Gaube
tel: 204-9191, fax: 288-2828
www.naiade.com

Le Paradis (*see* page 116)
Le Morne Peninsula
tel: 401-5050, fax: 450-5140
www.paradis-hotel.com

Le Telfair Golf and Spa Resort
Bel Ombre Estate, Bel Ombre
tel: 601-5500, fax: 601-5555
www.letelfair.com
New 5-star resort with golf course set on an old sugar estate. Rooms have sea or river views.

Le Tropical
La Pelouse, Trou d'Eau Douce
tel: 480-1300, fax: 480-2302
www.naiade.com
Cosy, friendly 3-star all-inclusive beachfront property comprising two-storey cottages. Facilities include a pool restaurant and bar.

Merville Beach
Royal Road, Grand Baie
tel: 209-2200, fax: 263-8146
www.naiade.com
A 3-star 169-room hotel situated just minutes north of central Grand Baie.

Oberoi Mauritius (*see* page 108)
Turtle Bay, Pointe aux Piments
tel: 204-3600, fax: 204-3625
www.oberoi.com

One&Only Le Saint Géran
(*see* page 118)
Pointe de Flacq
tel: 401-1688, fax: 401-1668
www.oneandonlylesaintgeran.com

One&Only Le Touessrok
(*see* page 117)
Trou d'Eau Douce
tel: 402-7400, fax: 402-7500
www.touessrok.com

Royal Palm (*see* page 104)
Grand Baie
tel: 209-8300, fax: 263-8455
www.royalpalm-hotel.com

Shandrani
Blue Bay
tel: 603-4343, fax: 637-4313
www.beachcomber-hotels.com
All-inclusive 5-star with diving centre and new kitesurfing school.

Sugar Beach Resort
(*see* page 111)
Wolmar, Flic en Flac
tel: 453-9090, fax: 453-9100
www.sugarbeachresort.com

Restaurants

Café des Arts (*see* page 147)
Victoria, Trou d'Eau Douce
tel: 480-0220
Open daily lunch and dinner, booking advised.

Chez Manuel (*see* page 147)
St Julians
tel: 418-3599
Open Mon–Sat lunch and dinner.

Citronella's Café (*see* page 142)
Sugar Beach Resort, Wolmar, Flic en Flac
tel: 453-9090, fax: 453-9100
www.sugarbeachresort.com
Open daily lunch and dinner.

Domaine du Chasseur
Anse Jonchée
Vieux Grand Port
tel: 634-5011, fax: 634-5261
www.domaineduchasseur.mu
Typical Mauritian curries and daubes with venison from the land. Open daily lunch only.

Karma House Restaurant
(*see* page 143)
Legends, Grand Gaube
tel: 204-9191, fax: 288-2828
www.naiade.com
Open Mon–Sat dinner only.

La Bonne Marmite
18 Sir William Newton Street
Port Louis, tel: 212-2403
Formal restaurant serving French and Creole dishes. Open Mon–Sat lunch only.

La Dolce Vita (see page 145)
Domaine Les Pailles, Les Guibies, Pailles
tel: 286-4225, fax: 286-4226
www.domainelespailles.net
Open daily for lunch, Wed, Fri and Sat for dinner.

La Pescatore (see page 145)
Trou aux Biches
tel: 265-6337
Open daily lunch and dinner.

La Ravanne (see page 143)
Le Paradis, Le Morne Peninsula
tel: 401-5050, fax: 450-5140
www.paradis-hotel.com
Open daily dinner.

Le Barachois (see page 147)
Le Prince Maurice Hotel, Choisy Road, Poste de Flacq
tel: 413-9100, fax: 413-9129
www.leprincemaurice.com
Open daily dinner only.

Le Capitaine
Royal Road, Grand Baie
tel: 263-6867
Mauritian and Indian dishes overlooking the beach. Open daily lunch and dinner.

Le Chateau de Bel Ombre
(see page 147)
Le Telfair Golf and Spa Resort,
Bel Ombre
tel: 601-5500, fax: 601-5555
www.letelfair.com
Open daily lunch and dinner.

Le Fangourin
L'Aventure du Sucre, Beau Plan, Pamplemousses
tel: 243-0660, fax: 243-9699
www.ladventuredusucre.com
Modern Creole cuisine and a tempting range of snacks. Open daily brunch, lunch and dinner.

Le Mouillage
Pointe aux Canonniers
tel: 263-8766
Popular for Creole and French-style seafood. Open daily lunch and dinner.

Le St Aubin
St Aubin
tel: 626-1513
Table d'hôte serving typical island dishes. Open Mon–Sat lunch only.

Namaste (see page 144)
Caudan Waterfront, Port Louis
tel: 211-6710
Open daily lunch and dinner.

Niu (see page 144)
Ruisseau Creole Complex,
La Mivoie, Rivière Noire
tel: 483-7118, fax: 483-6837
Open daily lunch and dinner.

Safran
One&Only Le Touessrok,
Trou d'Eau Douce
tel: 402-7400, fax: 402-7500
www.touessrok.com
With the first Michelin-rated chef producing Indian cuisine, this restaurant offers diners excellent modern regional cuisine in an elegant setting. Open Thu–Tue dinner only.

Spoon des Îles (see page 142)
One&Only Le St Géran,
Pointe de Flacq
tel: 401-1551, fax: 401-1552
www.spoondesiles.com
Open Tue–Sun dinner only.

Symons
Belle Mare
tel: 415-1135
Creole food and seafood is served here in wonderful farmland surroundings. Open daily lunch and dinner.

Varangue sur Morne
(see page 144)
110 Plaine Champagne Road, Chamarel
tel: 483-6610, fax: 483-5410
www.leschaletsenchampagne.com
Open daily lunch only.

Attractions

Blue Penny Museum
(see page 70)
Le Caudan Waterfront, Port Louis
tel: 210-8176
Open Mon–Sat 10:00–17:00

Blue Safari and 'subscooter'
(see page 164)
Royal Road, Mont Choisy
tel: 263-3333, fax: 263-3334
www.blue-safari.com
Open daily, booking essential.

Contact Details

Casela Nature and Leisure Park
(see page 93)
Royal Road, Cascavelle
tel: 452-0695, fax: 452-0694
www.caselayemen.mu
Open daily 09:00–17:00

Chamarel Terre de Sept Couleurs
(see page 40)
Chamarel, tel/fax: 483-8298
Open daily 07:00–17:00

Curepipe Botanical Gardens
(see page 32)
Botanical Garden Street, Curepipe
tel: 674-0003
Open 06:00–18:00

Domaine de L'Ylang Ylang
(see page 39)
Anse Jonchée, Vieux Grand Port
tel: 263-5518
Open daily 09:00–17.00.

Domaine du Chasseur
(see page 38)
Anse Jonchée, Vieux Grand Port
tel: 634-5011, fax: 634-5261
www.domaineduchasseur.mu
Open daily 09:00–16:00

Domaine Les Pailles
(see page 95)
Les Guibies, Pailles
tel: 286-4225, fax: 286-4226
www.domainelespailles.net
Open daily 09:00–18:00

Eureka (see page 66)
Moka, tel: 433-2584, fax: 433-4951, www.maisoneureka.com
Open Mon–Sat 09:00–17:00, Sun 09:00–15:30

Frederik Hendrik Museum
(see page 58)
Royal Road, Vieux Grand Port
tel: 634-4319
Open Mon–Sat 09:00–16:00

Grand Rivière Noire National Park (see page 27)
Pétrin Information Centre
Open daily 09:00–16:00

Île des Deux Cocos
(see page 156)
Blue Bay, tel: 423-1752, fax: 720-4047, www.naiade.com
Open daily by pre-booked tour.

L'Aventure du Sucre
(see page 87)
Beau Plan, Pamplemousses
tel: 243-0660, fax: 243-9699
www.aventuredusucre.com
Open daily 09:00–17:00

La Vanille Réserve des Mascareignes (see page 91)
Rivière des Anguilles
tel: 626-2503, fax: 626-1442
www.lavanille-reserve.com
Open daily 09:30–17:00

Le Nessee (see page 164)
Gustave Collin Street, Forest Side
tel: 674-3695, fax: 674-3720
Open daily, booking essential.

Mauritius Aquarium
Pointe aux Piments
tel: 261-4561, fax: 261-5080
www.mauritiusaquarium.com
Open Mon–Sat 09:30–17:00, Sun 10:00–16:00. Fish feeding 11:00 daily.

National History Museum
(see page 88)
Main Road, Mahébourg, tel: 631-9329. Open Wed–Mon 09:00–17:00

Natural History Museum
(see page 85)
The Mauritius Institute, La Chaussée Street, Port Louis
tel: 212-0639, fax: 212-5717
Open Mon–Fri 09:00–16:00, Sat–Sun 09:00–12:00

Parc Aventure (see page 40)
Chamarel
tel: 234-4533, fax: 234-5866
www.parc-aventure-chamarel.com
Open Thu–Tue 09:15–16:00

Robert Edward Hart Memorial Museum (see page 84)
Autard Street, Souillac, tel: 634-4319. Open Mon and Wed–Sat 09:00–16:00, Sun 09:00–12:00

Route du Thé (see page 91)
Bois Cheri, tel: 626-1513, fax: 626-1535. The Tea Museum is open Mon–Fri 08:30–15.30, Sat 08:30–11.30; Le St Aubin is open Mon–Sat 09:00–17:00

Sir Seewoosagur Ramgoolam Botanical Gardens (see page 32)
Pamplemousses, tel: 243-3531, fax: 243-9402. Open 08:30–17:30

Undersea Walk (see page 164)
Royal Road, Grand Baie
tel: 263-7819, fax: 263-3101
www.captainemo-underseawalk.com
Open daily, booking essential.

Shopping

Adamas Jewellers
(see page 126)
Richmond Hill, Grand Baie
tel: 269-1609, fax: 269-1607;
Palm Beach Boutique, Belle Mare
tel: 415-5356, fax: 415-5398;
Mangalkhan, Floréal
tel: 686-5246, fax: 686-6243

Café Coton (see page 128)
Caudan Waterfront, Port Louis
tel: 211-6954;
Pasadena Centre, Flic en Flac
tel: 453-5490;
Sunset Boulevard, Grand Baie
tel: 263-4601;
Centre l'Harmonie, Le Morne
tel: 540-5414;
Sunsheel Centre, Curepipe
tel: 675-1953

Caudan Waterfront
(see page 132)
Port Louis harbour
tel: 211-9500, fax: 211-6612
Visitor information centre
tel: 211-6612

Cledor (see page 126)
Mangalkhan, Floréal
tel: 698-8959;
London Complex, Rivière Noire
tel: 483-8446

Comajora (see page 131)
Brasserie Road, Forest Side
tel: 670-1472

Comptoir des Mascareignes
(see page 132)
Pamplemousses
tel: 243-9900, fax: 243-4862

Etoile d'Orient (see page 130)
Caudan Waterfront, Port Louis
tel: 210-4660;
John F Kennedy Ave, Floréal
tel: 696-6110

Floréal Square Shopping Centre
(see page 133)
1 John F Kennedy Ave, Floréal
tel/fax: 698-8007

**Galerie Françoise Vrot
'Chane-Cane'** (see page 130)
Reservoir Road, Grand Baie
tel: 263-5118

Galerie Helene de Senneville
(see page 130)
Royal Road Pointe aux
Canonniers
tel: 263-7426

Galerie Raphael (see page 130)
Pointe aux Canonniers
tel: 263-6470

Harpers (see page 128)
Caudan Waterfront, Port Louis
tel: 211-6960;
Sunset Boulevard, Grande Baie
tel: 263-55340

Historic Marine (see page 131)
St Antoine Industrial Estate,
Goodlands, tel: 283-9304

Karl Kaiser (see page 128)
Sunset Boulevard, Grand Baie
tel: 263-8864;
Le Caudan Waterfront, Port Louis
tel: 211-7262;
Arsenal
tel: 249-2296

La Flotte (see page 131)
53 Sir John Pope Hennessy Street,
Curepipe
tel: 670-2674

**La Pirogue Maquettes de
Bateaux** (see page 131)
32 Gustave Colin Street, Curepipe
tel: 674-0161

Macumba (see page 130)
Caudan Waterfront, Port Louis
tel: 210-2286;
Sunset Boulevard, Grand Baie
tel: 263-6404

Maille Street/In'Am
(see page 128)
Sunset Boulevard, Grand Baie
tel: 263-6444;
Palm Beach Boutiques, Belle Mare
tel: 415-5704

NHPA Shops (see page 130)
Craft Market at the Caudan
Waterfront
tel: 210-0139;
Astrolab Complex Port Louis
tel: 211-9972;
Mahébourg National Museum
complex
tel: 631-8671;
SILWF Complex, Royal Road
tel: 263-5423

Parure (see page 126)
Corner Lord Kitchener Street
and Caudan Street,
Port Louis, tel: 208-1309;
Le Mauricia Complex,
Grand Baie, tel: 263-5200;
Le Paradis, Le Morne
tel: 450-5050

Contact Details

Poncini (*see* page 126)
Caudan Waterfront, Port Louis
tel: 211-6921;
Sunset Boulevard, Grand Baie
tel: 263-8607

Port Louis Market (*see* page 132)
Block of Farquhar and Sir William
Newton Street, Port Louis

Pushkaar (*see* page 130)
Curepipe Road, Curepipe
tel: 670-9897;
Fond de la Baie, Grand Baie
tel: 263-8253
www.pushkaar.com

Ruisseau Creole
(*see* page 133)
La Mivioe, Rivière Noire
tel: 483-8000, fax: 483-6642
www.ruisseaucreole.com

Silk & Persian (*see* page 130)
Palm Beach Boutiques
Belle Mare
tel: 415-5226

The Mauritius Glass Gallery
(*see* page 131)
Pont Fer, Phoenix
tel: 696-3360, fax: 696-8116
Open Mon–Sat 08:00–17:00

Vaco Baissac Gallery
(*see* page 129)
Royal Road, Grand Baie
tel: 263-3106

Vendome Jewellers
(*see* page 126)
Caudan Waterfront, Port Louis
tel: 211-3863, fax: 211-4462

Spas and Wellness

Givenchy Spa (*see* page 162)
One&Only Le Saint Géran,
Pointe de Flacq
tel: 401-1688, fax: 401-1668
www.oneandonlylesaintgeran.com;
One&Only Le Touessrok,
Trou d'Eau Douce
tel: 402-7400, fax 402-7500
www.touessrok.com

Oberoi (*see* page 161)
Turtle Bay, Pointe aux Piments
tel: 204-3600, fax: 204-3625
www.oberoi.com

Révérence de Bastien
(*See* page 163)
One&Only Le Touessrok,
Trou d'Eau Douce
tel: 402-7400, fax: 402-7500
www.oneandonlylesaintgeran.com;
One&Only Le Saint Géran,
Pointe de Flacq
tel: 401-1688, fax: 401-1668
www.bastiengonzalez.com

Royal Palm Spa by Clarins
(*see* page 161)
Royal Palm Hotel, Grand Baie
tel: 209-8300, fax: 263-8455
www.royalpalm-hotel.com

Spa by Clarins (*see* page 163)
Paradis Hotel & Golf Club, Le
Morne Peninsula
tel: 401-5050, fax: 450-5140
www.paradis-hotel.com

Surya Ayurvedic Spa
(*see* page 163)
Royal Road, Pereybère
tel: 263-1637, fax: 263-1637

Sports and Recreation

Sport Fishing (*see* page 154)
Beachcomber Fishing Club
Le Morne
tel: 450-5142, fax: 450-5162

Domaine du Pecheur (part of Domaine du Chasseur)
tel: 634-5097
www.domaineduchasseur.com

La Pirogue Hotel (*see* page 111)
Wolmar, Flic en Flac
tel: 453-8441, fax: 453-8449
www.lapirogue.com

Morne Anglers Club
Rivière Noire, tel: 483-5801

Organisation du Pêche Nord (Corsaire Club)
Trou aux Biches, tel: 263-8358

Sportfisher
Sunset Boulevard, Grand Baie
tel: 263-8358, www.sportfisher.com

Sailing/Boat Rental
(*see* page 155)
Croisières Australes
Royal Road, Grand Baie, tel: 670-4301, www.c-australes.com

Gamboros
Cap Malheureaux, tel: 263-7809

Grand Bay Yacht Club
Royal Road, Grand Baie
tel: 263-8568

Terres Oceanes
Cap Malheureaux,
tel: 262-7188

Travel Directory

Diving (see page 170)

Blue Water Dive Centre
Le Corsaire, Trou aux Biches
tel: 265-7186
www.bluewaterdivingcentre.com

Blues Diving Centre
Belle Mare Plage Resort, Poste de Flacq, tel: 402-2600, fax: 402-2616
www.bellemareplagehotel.com

Diving Style Centre Ltd
Royal Road, Flic en Flac
tel/fax: 452-2235

East Coast Diving Centre
One&Only Le Saint Géran,
Pointe de Flacq
tel: 401-1688, fax: 401-1668
www.oneandonlylesaintgeran.com

Klondike Diving
Klondike Hotel, Flic en Flac
tel: 453-8333

La Pirogue Diving Centre
Wolmar, Flic en Flac
tel: 453-8441, fax: 453-8449
www.lapirogue.com

Mascareignes Plongée
Royal Road, Grand Baie
tel: 269-1265

Merville Diving Centre
Merville Hotel, Grand Baie
tel: 263-8621

Nautilus
Trou aux Biches Hotel, Royal Road, Trou aux Biches
tel: 265-5495
www.nautilusdivers.com

Pierre Sport Diving
One&Only Le Touessrok, Trou d'Eau Douce, tel: 402-7400, fax 402-7500
www.touessrok.com

Prodive
Casuarina Hotel, Royal Road, Trou aux Biches, tel: 265-6213

Shandrani Diving Centre
Blue Bay
tel: 603-4343, fax: 637-4313
www.beachcomber-hotels.com

Sinbad
Kuxville, Cap Malheureaux
tel: 262-8863

Racing (see page 160)
Crown Lodge, tel: 670-3303

Mauritius Turf Club
Champ du Mars, Port Louis
tel: 211-2147, fax: 208-3211
www.mauritiusturfclub.com

Stables
Domaine Les Pailles
see Attractions page 184

Le Ranch
Rivière Noire, tel: 483-5478

Les Ecuries de la Vieille Cheminée
Chamarel
tel: 686-5027, fax: 686-1250
www.ecuriecheminee.com

Golf (see page 168)
Île aux Cerfs
One&Only Le Touessrok,
Trou d'Eau Douce

tel: 402-7400, fax: 402-7500
www.touessrok.com

Le Golf du Chateau Le Telfair Golf and Spa Resort
Bel Ombre, tel: 601-5500, fax: 601-5555, www.letelfair.com

Le Paradis Course
Le Morne Peninsula, tel: 401-5050, www.paradis-hotel.com

The Links Belle Mare Plage Hotel
Poste de Flacq
tel: 402-2999, fax: 402-2616
www.bellemareplagehotel.com

Windsurfing (see page 166)
Centre Nautique
Grand Baie, tel: 263-8017

Kitesurfing (see page 166)
Kite2fly
Colombière Tourists Residence, Bras d'Eau, tel: 755-8343, fax: 410-5015, www.kite2fly.com

Shandrani Kitesurf School
Blue Bay
tel: 603-4343, fax: 637-4313
www.beachcomber-hotels.com

Adventure Sports
Beachcomber Sport and Nature Package
Shandrani Hotel, Blue Bay
tel: 603-4343, fax: 637-4313
www.beachcomber-hotels.com

Ciel et Nature
Royal Road, Moka
tel: 433-1010, fax: 433-1070
www.cieletnature.com

Contact Details

Conservator of Forests
Botanical Garden, Curepipe
tel: 674-0003

Vertical World
P.O. Box 289, Curepipe
tel: 254-6607, fax: 395-3207
www.verticalworldltd.com

Yemaya Adventures
Calodyne, Grand Gaube
tel: 752-0046
www.yemayaadventures.com

Casinos (see page 172)
www.casinosofmauritius.com

Berjaya Le Morne Beach Resort and Casino
Le Morne
tel: 450-5800

Casino de Maurice
Teste de Buch Street, Curepipe
tel: 602-1300

Flic en Flac
Pasadena Building, tel: 453-8022

Grand Casino du Domaine
Domaine Les Pailles, Pailles
tel: 286-0405

Le Caudan Waterfront
tel: 675-5012

Trou aux Biches
Royal Road, tel: 265-6619

Wildlife
Durrell Wildlife Conservation Trust
Les Augres Manor, La Profonde Rue, Trinity, Jersey, Channel Islands, British Isles
tel: +44 1534 860000
www.durrellwildlife.org

Mauritian Wildlife Foundation
Grannum Road, Vacoas
tel: 697-6097
www.mauritian-wildlife.org

Tour Operators
Mauritours
tel: 467-9700, www.mauritours.net

MTTB Mautourco
tel: 670-4301, fax: 675-6425
www.mautourco.com

White Sand Tours
tel: 213-3712, fax: 212-0265
www.dmltourism.com

Helpful Phrases

English	French	Creole	Creole Pronunciation
Hello	Bonjour	Bonzour	Bon-zoor
What is your name?	Comment vous appéléz-vous?	Como ou appélé?	Ko-mah oo a-pey-ley?
I don't understand	Je ne comprends pas	Mo pas comprend	Moh-pa compren
I would like ...	Je voudrais ...	Mo oulé ...	Mo oulay ...
Where will I find ...?	Où se trouve ...?	Cotte ...?	Cot ...?
I'd like to reserve a table	Je voudrais réserver une table	Mo lé résérve aine la table	Moh lay rey-zerv hen lah tab
Drive me to the hotel	Conduisez-moi à l'hôtel	Amène moi lotel	A-men mwa loh-tel
Can I hire a car?	Puis-je louer une voiture?	Mo capave louè aine loto?	Moh kapav loo-ay en loh-toh?
How much is it?	C'est combine?	Comié couté?	Komee-eah koot-ay?
Do you have ...?	Avez-vous ...?	Ou éna ...?	Oo eynah ...?
Can you help me?	Pouvez-vous m'aider?	Ou capave aide moi?	Oo kah-pav aid moi?
What time to do you open/close?	Vous ouvrir/fermé a quelle heure?	Qui lère ouvert/fermé?	Kee lair oo-ver/fair-may?
What time is it?	Quelle heure est-il?	Qui lère?	Kee-lair?

Index

Page numbers given in **bold** type indicate pictures.

accommodation 104–120
agriculture **48**
artists 83
arts and crafts 82, 130
Asian cuisine **144**

Balaclava 23
beaches **8**, **12**, **16**, 33, **34–35**, **46–47**, 105
Beau Plan sugar refinery **86**
Beau Rivage Hotel 120, **121**
beer **142**
Belle Mare **42–43**, 59
birds 20–21, **93**, **94**
Blue Bay 23
boating 154, **155**
British, the 52, 61, 66

Café des Arts 147
Cap Malheureux **70**
Casela Nature and Leisure Park **93**, **94**
Casinos of Mauritius **172**
Caudan Waterfront, Port Louis **68–69**, 71, **109**, **172**
Chamarel **40**
Chamarel Falls **36**
Chateau Gheude **89**
Chez Manuel 147
Chinatown, Port Louis 62, **64–65**
Chinese, the 63
Citronella's Café 142, **143**
Clarins Spa **161**
climate 24
clothing **128**
cocktails **140**
communications 180
conservation 31
contact details 183–189
coral reefs *see* reefs
Creole spices **139**
crime 181

crocodiles **92**
cuisine 63, 138–148
culture 58–71
Curepipe Botanical Gardens **30**, 31, 32
customs 178
Customs House 66

dance 78–82
diamonds 126
Dinarobin Hotel Golf & Spa **8**, 112, **113**
diving **22**, 170, **171**
Domaine du Chasseur **173**
Domaine de l'Ylang Ylang **39**
Domaine Les Pailles 95, **96–97**
domaines 37–39
Dutch, the 46–49, 59
duty-free shopping 128

electricity 181
emancipation 52, 66
embassies 181
entry requirements 178
essential oils 38
Eureka 66

fauna 19, **20**, 21, **92**, **93**, **94**, **95**
festivals 74–77
fishing 154, **157**
flora 16, **17**, 18, 19, **30**, **33**
Fort Adelaide 66
French, the 50–52, 59

gambling 172
Ganga Talab *see* lakes, Grand Bassin
geography and geology 12–16
giant tortoise **94**
golf **168–169**
Government House, Port Louis **56–57**, 66
Grand Baie **132**

haggling 133
health 181–182

hiking 158
Hindu festivals **74**, **75**, **176**
Hindu gods 62
Hindu saris **44**
Hindu sites **60**
Hinduism 61
history 46–57
horse racing and horse riding 160
hunting **173**

independence 55
industry 66
islands
    Coin de Mire 12
    Flat Island 12
    Île aux Aigrettes 21, **26**, **41**
    Île aux Cerfs **10**
    Île aux Serpents 12
    Ilot Mangenie **28–29**
itineraries 98

Java deer **20**
jewellery **126**

Karma House **143**
kitesurfing **166**

L'Aventure du Sucre 71, **86**, 87, **129**
La Dolce Vita 145
La Pescatore 145
La Ravanne 143
La Vanille Reserve des Mascareignes 23, 91, **92**
Labourdonnais Waterfront Hotel **109**
Labourdonnais *see* Mahé de Labourdonnais, Bertrand François
lakes 35
    Bassin Blanc 15, 37
    Grand Bassin 12, 15, 35, **60**
language 182, 189
Laval, Père 54, 66, 73
Le Barachois 147
Le Château de Bel Ombre 147
Le Paradis golf course **168–169**

INDEX

Le Paradis Hotel and Golf Club **100–101**, **114–115**, 116, 163
Legends Hotel **106**, 107

macaws **94**
Mahatma Ghandi Institute 84
Mahé de Labourdonnais, Bertrand François 32, **50**, 59, 72
Mahébourg 15, 26, 60
mammals 21
markets 132, 147–148, **149**
Mauritian curry **145**
Mauritius districts 24
Mauritius Institute **85**
Michelin star guide 141
Mon Plaisir 32
money matters 180
monuments 30, 72, **73**
Morne Peninsula **8**
mountains 15
    Coin de Mire **15**
    Morne Brabant **114–115**, **168–169**
    Pic du Lion **14**
museums
    Blue Penny Museum **68–69**
    National History Museum 88, **89**
    Natural History Museum 21, 66, **85**
music 78–82

Namaste 144
national flag **55**
national parks and reserves
    Black River Gorges National Park 17, **18–19**, 23, 27, 31, 158, **159**
    Coin de Mire 27
    Flat Island 27
    Gabriel Island 27
    Île aux Aigrettes National Reserve 30
    Île d'Ambre National Park 27
    Île de la Passe 30
    Îlot Mariannes National Reserve 30
    Îlot Vacoas National Park 30
    Pigeon Rock National Park 27

national parks and reserves (continued)
    Rivulet Terre Rouge Estuary Sanctuary 31
    Round Island 27
    Serpent Island 27
Niu 144

Oberoi Mauritius Hotel **108**, 161
One&Only Le Saint Géran **12**, 118, **119**, **134–135**, **136**, 162, **163**
One&Only Le Touessrok **117**, 162

Pamplemousses Gardens *see* Sir Seewoosagur Ramgoolam Botanical Gardens
parasailing **152**
Parc Aventure 40, 158
Paul et Virginie 73, **84**
Paul et Virginie Restaurant **134–135**, **136**
philately 67
pink pigeon **93**
places of worhip
    Chinese temple **76**
    Friday Mosque 62
    Hindu and Tamil temples 62
    Hindu temple, Belle Mare **42–43**
    Hindu shrine, Riambel **63**
    Notre Dame Auxiliatrice, Cap Malheureux **70**
Pointe Lafayette **25**
Poivre, Pierre 32, **51**
Port Louis 15, 26, **56–57**, 60, **64–65**, **68–69**, **71**, 82, **109**
public holidays 182

Ramgoolam, Sir Seewoosagur **54**, 72
Ravaton, Jean Alphonse 73, 79
reefs **12**, 23
restaurants 142–148
Riambel **63**
Route du Thé 91
Royal Palm Hotel **84**, 104, **105**, 161
rum **129**

sabrage 120
Saint-Pierre, Bernardin de 73
seafood **134–135**, **146**
sega 61, 78–82
    dance **80–81**
    music **78**
shopping **99**, **122–133**, **176**
Sir Seewoosagur Ramgoolam Botanical Gardens 32, **33**
snorkelling 170
spas 161–163
Spoon des Îles 142
sport fishing **154**
St Aubin 66
statistics 49
statues 72
subscooters **165**
sugar 54
Sugar Beach Resort **110**, 111, **143**
sugar cane **53**
Sunset Boulevard Shopping Centre, Grand Baie **132**

tea 63
tea-picking **90**
textiles 126, **127**
theatre **82**
tourist information 178
trading hours 180
transport 178–**179**
Trou aux Biches **34–35**
Trou aux Cerfs 12

underwater activities 163–164

Varangue sur Morne 144
volcanoes 12

water sports 164–**167**
waterfalls 35, **36**, 37
wetlands 31
windsurfing **150–151**
writers 84

Imprint Page

First edition published in 2007
by New Holland Publishers (UK) Ltd
London • Cape Town • Sydney • Auckland

10 9 8 7 6 5 4 3 2 1

website: www.newhollandpublishers.com

Garfield House, 86 Edgware Road
London W2 2EA
United Kingdom

80 McKenzie Street
Cape Town 8001
South Africa

14 Aquatic Drive
Frenchs Forest, NSW 2086
Australia

218 Lake Road
Northcote, Auckland
New Zealand

Distributed in the USA by
The Globe Pequot Press
Connecticut

Copyright © 2007 in text: Lindsay Bennett
Copyright © 2007 in maps: Globetrotter Travel Maps
Copyright © 2007 in photographs:
Individual photographers as credited (right).
Copyright © 2007 New Holland Publishers (UK) Ltd

All rights reserved. No part of this publication may be reproduced, stored in a retrieval system or transmitted, in any form or by any means, electronic, mechanical, photocopying, recording or otherwise, without the prior written permission of the publishers and copyright holders.

ISBN 978 1 84537 553 9

Although every effort has been made to ensure that this guide is up to date and current at time of going to print, the Publisher accepts no responsibility or liability for any loss, injury or inconvenience incurred by readers or travellers using this guide.

Publishing Manager: Thea Grobbelaar
DTP Cartographic Manager: Genené Hart
Editor: Thea Grobbelaar
Design and DTP: Nicole Bannister
Cartographer: Nicole Bannister
Picture Research: Shavonne Govender
Proofreader: Alicha van Reenen
Reproduction by Resolution, Cape Town
Printed and bound in China by C & C Offset Printing Co., Ltd.

Photographic Credits:
Pete Bennett: pages 6, 8–9, 10, 16, 17, 18–19, 28–29, 42–43, 44, 46–47, 48, 50, 51, 53, 54, 55, 56–57, 59, 60, 63, 64–65, 68–69, 71, 76, 80–81, 82, 84, 85, 86, 89, 90, 92, 94 (top and bottom), 99, 100–101, 102, 105, 106, 108, 109, 110, 113, 114–115, 117, 119, 121, 124, 126, 128, 129, 130, 132, 134–135, 136, 140, 142, 143, 144, 145, 146, 149, 152, 154, 155, 157, 159, 161, 163, 165, 166, 172, 173, 174–175, 176, 179;
Shaen Adey/Images of Africa: title page, pages 14, 26, 30, 36, 38–39, 40, 41, 70, 74, 75, 78, 93, 96–97, 122–123, 127, 148, 167, 168–169;
Juan Espi/Images of Africa: page 139;
Alain Proust/Images of Africa: cover, half title, contents page, pages 12, 15, 20, 25, 33, 34–35, 72–73, 150–151;
Pictures Colour Library: pages 22, 171.

Keep us Current
Information in travel guides is apt to change, which is why we regularly update our guides. We'd be grateful to receive feedback if you've noted something we should include in our updates. If you have new information, please share it with us by writing to the Publishing Manager, Globetrotter, at the office nearest to you (addresses on this page). The most significant contribution to each new edition will receive a free copy of the updated guide.

Cover: *Aerial view of Le Morne Brabant.*
Half title: *View of the beach at Trou aux Biches.*
Title page: *Fishermen on pirogues heading out to a reef.*
Contents page: *Resort on the beach, Le Touessrok.*